# THE USE OF FORCE IN
# HUMANITARIAN INTERVENTION

# The Use of Force in Humanitarian Intervention
## Morality and Practicalities

JOHN JANZEKOVIC

*University of the Sunshine Coast, Australia*
*and Vaxjo University, Sweden*

Routledge
Taylor & Francis Group

LONDON AND NEW YORK

First published 2006 by Ashgate Publishing

Reissued 2018 by Routledge
2 Park Square, Milton Park, Abingdon, Oxon OX14 4RN
605 Third Avenue, New York, NY 10017

First issued in paperback 2021

*Routledge is an imprint of the Taylor & Francis Group, an informa business*

A Library of Congress record exists under LC control number: 2006928101

Notice:
Product or corporate names may be trademarks or registered trademarks, and are used only for identification and explanation without intent to infringe.

Publisher's Note
The publisher has gone to great lengths to ensure the quality of this reprint but points out that some imperfections in the original copies may be apparent.

Disclaimer
The publisher has made every effort to trace copyright holders and welcomes correspondence from those they have been unable to contact.

ISBN 13: 978-0-815-39834-9 (hbk)
ISBN 13: 978-1-351-12680-9 (ebk)
ISBN 13: 978-1-138-35766-2 (pbk)

# Contents

# List of Maps and Figure

# List of Abbreviations

| | |
|---|---|
| AFRC | Armed Forces Revolutionary Council |
| AIDS | Acquired Immune Deficiency Syndrome |
| AIMAV | International Association for Cross-Cultural Communication |
| B.C.E.T.S | Board Certified Expert in Trauma |
| BSA | Bosnian Serb Army |
| CDR | Coalition Pour la Defense de la Republique. Coalition for the Defence of the Republic. |
| CIC | Commonwealth of Independent States |
| CSCE | Conference on Security and Cooperation in Europe |
| DCJC | Delaware Criminal Justice Council |
| EU | European Union |
| EU/WEU | European Union/Western European Union |
| FMLN | Farabundo Marti National Liberation Front |
| HIV | Human Immunodeficiency Virus |
| HRW | Human Rights Watch |
| ICG | International Crisis Group |
| ICJ | International Court of Justice |
| ICRC | International Committee of the Red Cross |
| ICTY | International Criminal Tribunal for the former Yugoslavia |
| ILC | International Law Commission |
| IFOR | International Peacekeeping Force |
| KFOR | NATO-led Kosovo Force |
| KLA | Kosovar Liberation Army |
| KPS | Kosovo Police Service |
| KVM | Kosovo Verification Mission |
| MRND | Mouvement Republicain National Pour la Democratie et le Development. The Republican National Movement for Democracy and Development. |
| MSF | Medecines sans Frontières |
| NATO | North Atlantic Treaty Organization |
| NGO | Non-government organizations |
| ONUCA | United Nations Observer Group in Central America |
| ONUSAL | United Nations Observer Mission in El Salvador |
| OSCE | The Organization for Security and Cooperation in Europe |
| PFP | Partnership for Peace |
| POW | Prisoners of War |
| PTSD | Post Traumatic Stress Disorder |

| RMAWCHR | Regional Meeting for Asia of the World Conference on Human Rights |
|---|---|
| ROE | Rules of Engagement |
| RPF | Rwandese Patriotic Front |
| RUF | Revolutionary United Front |
| SAE | Services Assisted Evacuation |
| SFOR | UN Stabilisation Force |
| UDHR | Universal Declaration of Human Rights |
| UN | United Nations |
| UN SCR | UN Security Council Resolutions |
| UNAID | The Joint United Nations Programme on HIV/AIDS |
| UNAMIR | United Nations Assistance Mission for Rwanda |
| UNEF I | First United Nations Emergency Force |
| UNMIK | U.N. Interim Administration Mission to Kosovo |
| UNMOT | United Nations Mission to Tajikistan |
| UNOSOM | United Nations Operation Somalia |
| UNPROFOR | United Nations Protection Force |
| UNSC | UN Security Council |
| US | United States |
| WCHR | World Conference on Human Rights |
| WMD | Weapons of Mass Destruction |
| WPC | World Peace Council |
| WW II | World War II |

# Preface

If the broad concept of a moral and civil society has any meaning then the international community has a moral obligation to protect the oppressed and the exploited. When non-forcible intervention fails to stop deliberate and persistent acts of genocide, torture, rape, mutilation and murder then the option of using force to stop determined belligerents must be seriously considered.

Many realists challenge the fundamental idea that morality itself has a place in international affairs yet this ignores the reality that ethical behaviour actually does matter to the international community. The whole notion of ethical behaviour may be perceived and applied very differently, and indeed very selectively, but one could not reasonably argue that it does not exist or that it has no relevance. If a moral and civilised society exists then one cannot ignore the concept of ethical behaviour.

Pacifists on the other hand are affronted by the notion that sometimes lethal force may be the only way to stop terrible things from happening. Many will argue that there is always an alternative to the use of direct force and that violence will only result in more violence. It is true that there are alternatives to the use of force that are specifically intended to stop extreme human behaviour but the hard reality is that such alternatives are often ineffectual with disastrous outcomes for the abused. The persistence in the application of ineffective non-violent strategies to confront belligerents who are clearly intent on widespread, repeated and deliberate crimes against humanity is not only a disaster for the victims and their families but it reflects a level of moral ineptitude that should not be acceptable in a civil and just society.

Consequentialism, in particular welfare-utilitarianism, is an ethical theory that supports the view that a moral obligation exists for the international community to respond effectively to extreme human rights abuse. My aim is not to defend the various shades of utilitarianism as such, but to show the practical consequences of taking this position seriously. My methodology is similar to that employed by Peter Singer in a now classic treatment of the obligations of people living in affluent countries to those suffering the impact of famine. Singer believes that if one has the power to do good, to relieve suffering and to alleviate pain, then other things being equal one is morally obliged to act.

Human beings must not be allowed to suffer or die simply because the use of force itself affronts the ethical sensibilities of those who could help or because some people see no obligations where in fact very plausible ethical theories imply obligations. It is also true that the use of force is sometimes not an option because it will cause an even worse humanitarian disaster than it tries to avert. This follows from welfare utilitarianism. However, where the overall benefits of such intervention can be reasonably judged to outweigh the human costs and suffering *of not intervening* then it is morally wrong to dismiss the use of military force as an international response option.

International and humanitarian law are important adjuncts to the use of directed force to stop human rights abuse. A moral and just society needs the support of law and social convention for guidance in dealing with extreme acts of unprovoked aggression. In this book, I present an analysis of such laws and conventions as applicable to the use of direct force during humanitarian intervention.

I do not suggest that using military force for humanitarian purposes will alone resolve complex international issues because ultimately it is up to the conflicting parties to resolve or reconcile their own differences. Negotiators, diplomats and international tribunals all provide a valuable contribution to this process but a peaceful outcome is simply not possible if the killing and serious abuse just continues on. The primary objective of using military force must be to immediately stop the killing and atrocities. Peacekeepers, negotiators and diplomats must then move in to mediate some sort of peace between parties who consistently have demonstrated that they are unable or unwilling to achieve such a condition by themselves.

My approach is a pragmatic one where I explore the application of certain ethical positions to the fundamental idea of humanitarian obligation. Some readers will be affronted by the notion that sometimes deliberate and directed violence may be the only effective response possible against a ruthless belligerent. I ask these readers to equally consider the desperate plight of tens of thousands of helpless people who are subjected daily to the most appalling atrocities.

Readers looking for cast iron guarantees that military intervention for humanitarian purposes 'will work' will not find such assurances here. However, there are no guarantees that embargos, protests, diplomatic shuffling, peace conferences or anything else will work either. We do not dismiss such efforts to resolve international conflicts, and neither should we dismiss the idea that sometimes direct force may be the only way to stop those who deliberately set out to injure and kill others. The notion of using force under these terrible circumstances only as a 'last resort' must be challenged. If the threat is real and imminent the response must be real and imminent.

Interventionist casualties must be expected when operating in a dangerous, perhaps lethal, conflict environment. To place peacemakers and peacekeepers in harm's way, but then not accept that some of them will be injured or killed is illogical. Extreme casualty aversion strategies result in humanitarian 'intervention' by remote control or, more likely, non-intervention. Both are totally inadequate responses for those doing the dying and suffering.

This book challenges the fundamental way the international community responds to gross violations of human rights. The current response to such appalling human behaviour is a brief outpouring of concern over a couple of particularly gruesome events that manage to somehow come to our attention. The media in its various forms will selectively show us some truly awful examples of extreme human behaviour but only enough not to violate our sensitivities too much. This uncomfortable moment passes very quickly as national issues once again dominate.

The problem is not only what to do about unacceptable human behaviour but also in defining what unacceptable human behaviour actually means. Measuring the effectiveness of humanitarian intervention is not about how many peace initiatives are implemented, how concerned the international community is, how much humanitarian aid is delivered, or how many cease fires have been instigated. Effectiveness is measured by how many people are not killed, not subjected to atrocities and not abused.

John Janzekovic

# Acknowledgements

This book is dedicated to the many millions of people around the world who are, at this very moment, suffering deliberate and persistent abuse at the hands of fellow human beings. My fervent hope is that the reader finds some resonance of humanity in this modest work and that the views expressed here have some meaning in the overall discourse of humanitarian intervention. For people of good intent and good heart I ask only that you are prepared to at least seriously consider the options put forward in this book because those who are being subjected to the most appalling cruelty and violence have no say and no hope without you.

Thank you to Professor Robert Elliot, formerly Dean of Arts and Social Sciences at the University of the Sunshine Coast in Queensland Australia, who helped guide me through the bewildering maze of normative and not so normative ethical arguments regarding humanitarian intervention. Thank you also to my many other colleagues and my students who listened to my views with forbearance and understanding. Some of these that I must mention are Professor Jim Waite of Utah University in the United States, Professor Manuela Aguilar Dean of the School of Diplomacy and International Relations at Universidad Americana in Managua, Nicaragua, and Professor John Dalton of Bond University in Queensland, Australia. Their very kind reviews and advice on parts of this book gave me the strength to finish the thing.

My parents Walter and Maria Janzekovic instilled in me my moral values and they showed me that in the end semantics are quite irrelevant. There are no excuses for human abuse, and there can be no excuses for not acting and speaking out against them. They arrived in Australia as refugees from a war torn Europe after World War II with one suitcase, and a wedding dress that was traded for 3 bananas for my young sister, Barbara. Their quiet and gentle determination to make a new life in a new land for our family has always been an inspiration to me.

A final but most important thank you to my wife, Marie. Her constant support and unshakable good heartedness helped me through the many years of research for this book. She has a sense of right and wrong, and a fundamental personal decency, that is a guiding light for me.

# Introduction

## Overview

I propose that short term, military intervention by external parties against those who conduct serious and ongoing violations of human rights is morally justifiable. Such a response should be considered when non-coercive intervention (meaning *not* using physical force) fails or it is doomed to failure by the intransigence of determined belligerents. My fundamental approach in this book is with the here and now. I frequently use the term 'immediate' throughout this work. This in no way implies that longer term strategies to severe and deliberate human abuses are not necessary; indeed they are critical, if humanity can ever hope to coexist in a more peaceful world – but first things first.

Forcible humanitarian intervention, if applied robustly with speed and determination, can make a difference to the multitudes suffering from extreme humanitarian abuse. But such intervention still needs to be judiciously applied. If forcible intervention is deemed by any reasonable measure to make things worse for the victims of abuse then effective alternatives must be found. This is one of the most difficult decisions we must make if we claim to be part of a moral society. This book outlines a range of possible approaches and strategies to deal with this very complex issue.

My focus is directly on the needs and wants of the victims, and then on the difficulties faced by potential interventionists. The monumental challenge for all of us is the balance between these two, often competing, interests. Currently the 'balance' clearly favours the needs and wants of interventionists and potential interventionists. I argue that this is, morally at least, untenable in a civil society.

This book is not about the imposition of democracy or some particular political ideology. It is also not about the views of any particular religious faith regarding whether or not intervention on humanitarian grounds (forcible or otherwise) has merit. I propose that notions of simple human decency and empathy with those who are suffering under the most appalling conditions transcends religion and religious beliefs. Many religious or faith based organisations are attempting to alleviate human misery wherever it is found, and this excellent humanitarian work is often undertaking under the most extreme conditions where poverty and abuse is commonplace.

These individuals and organisations of good heart and intent get little recognition by the wider human community for the essential work that they do but they are the frontline troops (often the only troops) who dig the latrines, clean the filth from the bodies of the neglected or the abused, build the hospitals, deliver the food and other aid, and they are the ones who try to provide at least some level of comfort for those whose life is all about trying to survive for just another day.

For people who are unable or unwilling to be these frontline troops there are a number of possible options that should resonate with the requirements of a civil and moral society. In this book I argue that fundamental to such a society is some empathy to what is happening with the majority of humanity who live in poverty and filth, and who must deal with deliberate gross abuses every day. The trouble is that empathy, feeling bad and a lot of hand winging about the plight of the suffering millions is just not enough. Empathy must be associated with effective action if we really hope to make a difference.

The use of military force for humanitarian reasons is sometimes required because many determined belligerents cannot be dissuaded to cease their appalling practices in any other way. This is very difficult, perhaps impossible, for many people who are fortunate to live in a society that has a healthy measure of law, order and justice to accept. It is not difficult at all for those being subject to deliberate and ongoing extreme abuses to accept. The fortunate ones will say that surely all other strategies must be tried first, or they must be tried again and again, or what has all this got to do with us anyway? The mantra of 'the national interest first' is in competition with the claim that a wider notion of collective humanity actually does have some relevance outside state borders aside from economic and secular security issues.

The effective application of the use of force for humanitarian reasons has been highly selective and very infrequent but this does not mean that it should not be seriously considered when other options, again by any reasonable measure of effectiveness, are deemed to be not working. Reasonable measures of success, effectiveness and 'not working' are of course highly subjective to all except for those on the receiving end of gross human rights violations. In the end questions about the immediacy and direct effectiveness of humanitarian intervention are of direct relevance to the victims but not only to the victims. If we collectively claim to be part of a civil and moral human community then such considerations should be important to all of us.

Chapter One, *Ethical Reasoning and Moral Principles* is an analysis of the practicalities and ethics of humanitarian intervention. My aim is to present an ethical dimension on the practicalities of humanitarian intervention. The international community requires laws and formal procedures for dealing with extreme human rights abuses but all the legislation and all the laws and all the rhetoric are mostly ineffectual unless they are supported by a robust moral position and the will to act.

A range of ethical considerations are presented in this chapter with the intent of trying to address the question of morality itself when talking about humanitarian intervention. I ague throughout this book that a civil and moral society has an obligation to directly and effectively act where and when intentional and persistent abuse occurs. But what does all this talk about morals and ethics relative to the use of forcible humanitarian intervention really mean? Are there some universal humanitarian claims that apply to most of humanity or could it be argued that different societies and cultures should be able to pursue their own notions of moral right and moral wrong?

Supporters in both camps passionately claim their own moral validity in this area but if the idea of separateness can be put aside for the moment, and consideration be given to the wider human collective as a whole, then there are some commonalities that can be identified for all of human society. Some readers will be challenged by some of the philosophical positions presented in this chapter but my intention is to attempt to present some balance to the various ethical arguments for and against the use of force in humanitarian intervention. In order to do this some possibly contentious views are investigated and analysed. It is for the reader to decide which if any of these views have some resonance to their own experience and understanding of humanitarian intervention – forcible or otherwise.

In Chapter Two, *Plausible Interventionist Strategies* I discuss plausible scenarios for military intervention, constraints on intervention, outcomes of intervention, costs and likelihood of success. This section of the book looks closely at the whole idea of peacekeeping, peacemaking and peace enforcement. These are very different approaches with specific requirements for successful outcomes. The idea that humanitarian intervention is just about peacekeepers trying to keep the peace is challenged because this simplistic approach has led to the deaths and suffering of millions. I question the rationale of even sending 'peacekeepers' into potentially lethal conflict zones where belligerents are engaged in high levels of ongoing violence and abuse. In these situations there is no peace to keep and a more robust response in the form of peacemaking and peace enforcement (direct intervention) must prevail before the peacekeepers are sent in.

Chapter Three, *Humanitarian Law and Military Intervention* investigates humanitarian law as applicable to the use of force in international affairs, and it outlines the development of international law, humanitarian law, and the laws of armed conflict from early concepts of natural justice and natural law. Without law there is anarchy. This is true at the national or domestic level and at an international level. But just having a law or perhaps a social convention is not nearly enough. Anthony Hartle makes the important observation that some legal scholars consider 'International Law' not to be law at all, in any strict sense, because all law is ultimately based on moral authority.[1] Without such moral authority any law is subject to challenge. Therefore, justice, empathy, connectiveness and a sense of moral value are all important adjuncts to laws and conventions.

In *Objections to the Ethical Principles and Applications* (Chapter Four) the major objections to military intervention for humanitarian reasons are investigated. The objections vary widely from the ethical to the practical. Most objections are centred on the needs, fears and concerns of potential or actual interventionists. I argue that objections to humanitarian intervention must also seriously consider the plight of those doing the suffering and the dying.

---

1    Anthony Hartle, *Moral Issues in Military Decision Making* (Lawrence: University of Kansas Press, 1989), p. 56.

Chapter Five, *Ethnic Conflict in the Balkans 1992–1999* considers the strategic realities and constraints in international relations when dealing with humanitarian crises. The case study of conflict in the Balkans is an example of how military intervention was, and is, being managed. There are serious inadequacies in both international law and moral fortitude when dealing with humanitarian crises, and the Balkans conflict demonstrates the international community's total ineptness at managing such humanitarian crises.

Throughout this book (particularly in Chapter One) I assert that it is unacceptable for a moral and civilised society – I argue that such a society actually exists – to permit serious and deliberate violations of human rights to occur without implementing effective strategies to halt such practices. One such strategy is the direct use of coercive force to immediately stop belligerents from illegally killing, torturing and deliberately abusing other human beings.

The term 'moral society' is used a number of times in this book but this is mainly to suggest that a civil and caring society is more than just the sum of its institutions or the effectiveness of its administration. Such a society is one that responds to the welfare of its citizens in a material sense but it is also a society that demonstrates tolerance, compassion, and understanding. If these terms are to have any real meaning then the international community has a moral obligation to address deliberate breaches of humanitarian law wherever and whenever they occur, despite the many difficulties faced by potential interventionists.

Where it is just not physically possible to address some serious breaches of human rights; for example, the opposing military forces are too strong, then all other effective means of halting the abuse must be vigorously and relentlessly pursued. Such alternatives are discussed and presented to the reader for consideration. To do very little that is really effective as in Rwanda, Sierra Leone and Angola, or to react in a half-hearted way, as in Bosnia Herzegovina, Somalia and Kurdistan, in order to protect the national or domestic concerns of possible interventionists is morally wrong. The view that helpless human beings should be allowed to suffer or to die simply because the use of force itself affronts the ethical sensibilities of those who could help is morally defective.

The international community must confront the moral irrationality of proclaiming concern over serious human rights issues, yet not acting effectively to stop the abuses. 'Immediately' means right now, 'effectively' means doing something that works even if that something means forcibly stopping belligerents from deliberately abusing the weak and the innocent.

The traditional view of the sanctity of state sovereignty is changing from an absolutist position to a more qualified view where considerations of how humans treat each other impacts not only on state relations but also on the wider human community. The concept of state sovereignty in its most basic sense is being redefined.[2] States are increasingly conceptualised as instruments in the service of their peoples, not vice versa. This is a significant departure from traditional views

---

2    Kofi Annan, 'Two Concepts of Sovereignty. Paper Presented at the Heads of State and Governments at the Annual Session of the United Nations General Assembly,' *The Economist*, 18 September 1999: pp. 49–50.

of the sanctity of sovereignty. Kurt Mills argues that the sovereignty of states is legitimate only to the extent that they protect the human rights of individuals.[3] This is an important point that is contested by many but it has direct relevance to the notion of a civil and moral society.

Despite its many failings the United Nation's enforcement power is its deterrent power – providing enforcement is forthcoming. For the sake of all of humanity the international community must be able to assert itself collectively where the cause is just, the means available and the consequences anticipated to be positive. If states, quasi states, organisations, groups and individuals bent on criminal behaviour know that borders are not an absolute and final defence, then they should also understand that their actions are not beyond the reach of international and moral justice.[4]

I place equal weight on interventionist ethics and international humanitarian law for the following reason. It is highly unlikely that humanitarian conflicts can ever be successfully resolved if the international community simply focuses its response options on strategic issues, rationalism, or self interest dressed up in the all encompassing term 'the national interest'. We must have a robust moral perspective when attempting to deal with humanitarian disasters of all types. Yet, a simple moral imperative to help the desperate and abused is not enough in this cynical and pragmatic world. International humanitarian law and justice are critical if we are to progress from proclamations of outrage from some lofty moral position to actually doing something to stop such human behaviour.

Most people verbally reject unprovoked violence and aggression as being morally wrong, but this is not the same as doing something effective to redress such activity. The world is full of 'concerned citizens' and we have many hand wringers but this means very little in the torture and rape chambers. Chapter One, *Ethical Reasoning and Moral Principles* discusses the fundamental moral arguments in support of the use of force to redress grievous human rights violations. The combination of a robust moral position to support conventions of social justice with international law facilitates turning words into action.

## Humanitarian Intervention Ethics and the Meaning of Success

I favour the utilitarian position of combining consequentialism with welfarism. Consequentialism holds that an act is morally right and obligatory if it leads to what may be considered to be the 'best consequences'. Welfarism holds that the goodness of an outcome is ultimately directly linked to the greatest total amount of wellbeing.

---

3  Kurt Mills, *Human Rights in the Emerging Global Order: A New Sovereignty?* (New York: St Martins Press, 1998), pp. 42–43.

4  Law Key Centre for Ethics, Justice and Governance (KCELJAG), 'Globalising the Rule of Law' (paper presented at the Griffith University's Vice Chancellor's Symposium, Parliament House, Brisbane Australia, 2000).

Welfarism aligns more closely to the notion that the welfare of the community is of primary importance rather than the more generalised 'best outcomes' simply having precedence. Best could mean more expedient, more efficient, greater participation or higher rates of achievement with little reference to actual wellbeing. Wellbeing is enhanced if the welfare of the human community as a whole is increased. UN Secretary-General Kofi Annan stated in 1998 that preventing the savagery of modern ethnic and tribal conflicts (particularly in Africa) was, '...no longer a matter of defending states or protecting allies but a matter of defending humanity itself.'[5]

The most desirable outcomes include a significant improvement in the welfare of those being abused. The wellbeing and welfare of interveners is also important, but in order to achieve the greatest utility for the greatest number of people some interventionists' welfare may need to be sacrificed for a greater good. We must accept that there is a cost, sometimes a cost in human lives, of interveners taking on the role of human rights enforcer. It is a fantasy to assume that taking on a determined, well armed and prepared belligerent under these circumstances will not result in casualties, perhaps many casualties, on all sides.

A right to life, freedom from persecution, and adequate food and shelter are essential for human existence. These are what many people claim are 'essential rights' that should apply to all of humanity regardless of ethnicity, culture or ideology. The Universal Declaration of Human Rights proclaims a number of rights to be important ideals in a humane civil society. For example, the right to free association, to marry whom one wishes, to have freedom of movement and residence within one's state's borders, and to form or join trade unions. These are all important rights but they are not crucial life or death matters.

My focus is on rights that are essential to human life. Human welfare and wellbeing are seriously compromised if these essential rights are ignored or threatened. One could dispute the validity or intent of many so-called 'rights', but those rights that directly affect human life or death surely must have priority over all others.

There is a fundamental flaw in how the international community responds to critical humanitarian need. That is, international response options are primarily focused on the concerns and needs of potential interventionists rather than on those suffering serious deprivations and abuse. Much is made about possible interventionist casualties, the financial costs involved – who's going to pay for it all? – and possible economic ramifications to intervening states. This approach places potential interventionist's concerns well before those who are doing the dying and suffering on a scale that is truly monstrous and should be unacceptable to all reasonable thinking people.

This does not mean that interventionists' concerns should be ignored but if the humanitarian situation is extremely desperate for large numbers of abused people then their needs should have priority over the less urgent needs of fewer numbers of

---

5    John Stremlau, 'Ending Africa's Wars,' *Foreign Affairs* 79, no. 4 (2000): pp. 117–19.

potential interventionists. This is particularly relevant when failure to address such a situation may have wider ramifications for the defence of human rights generally.

There are a number of plausible interventionist strategies involving peacekeeping, peacemaking and peace enforcement. The plausibility or otherwise of direct intervention for humanitarian reasons is subject to many constraints – real and perceived. There is moral repugnance at the use of force, there are domestic concerns over the national interest, concern over possible interventionist casualties, likely damage to relations between conflicting powers, and possible economic penalties for antagonising potential trading partners. The staggering financial cost of directly undertaking full-scale humanitarian relief is of concern to many.

The problem with these and similar types of challenges to the plausibility of intervention, at least from a humanitarian perspective, is that they are primarily centred on the domestic concerns of interventionists rather than being focused on the plight of millions of desperate people around the globe needing immediate humanitarian relief. Interventionists are rightly concerned about possible casualties to their own forces, but it is not realistic to aim for zero casualties in a dangerous and often lethal conflict environment. The United States (U.S.) and the North Atlantic Treaty Organization's (NATO) refusal to commit ground troops in Yugoslavia in 1998/99 to directly address severe human rights concerns was primarily linked to concerns over own force casualties.

The notion of 'success' in humanitarian intervention is an important one. It is important because when the international community is confronted by a humanitarian disaster the questions that should constantly be asked are: is what we are doing now effective in stopping the killing and abuse, and what needs to be done to ensure that once the international community's back is turned protagonists do not simply continue on with their violent ways? Unless these important questions are seriously addressed the cycle of violence will continue.

The implementation of a particular interventionist strategy cannot be considered to be a success unless there is immediate relief to those suffering extreme violations of human rights. Such a measurement of effectiveness is equally relevant in the medium and longer terms. In these cases, conceptualisation and measurement of effectiveness is even more difficult.

Regardless over what time period people try to measure success, simply implementing an interventionist strategy is by itself a poor measure of effectiveness. During the first eight weeks of NATO action in Kosovo in February and March of 1999, the nightly NATO news briefings continually praised the ongoing NATO air campaign as being '...very successful'. NATO repeatedly stated that they were 'winning' and Slobodan Milosevic was 'losing'.

During this period, over 850,000 Kosovar refugees were forced at gunpoint out of Kosovo and were reportedly subjected to widespread abuse by Serb forces. These Kosovars would have an entirely different notion of the so-called success of humanitarian intervention in the Balkans.

My aim in outlining the development of international law, humanitarian law, and the laws of armed conflict from early concepts of natural justice and natural law is to analyse the legal impediments and challenges of conducting an interventionist military strategy. A moral and just human community requires the support of law and social convention to guide it in the management of aberrant human behaviour. Those who conduct crimes against humanity are criminals who must be held accountable for their actions.

Military intervention for humanitarian reasons is usually subject to very specific Rules of Engagement (ROE) and conduct. These are not just rules for the military because political and ideological approaches to man-made humanitarian disasters also follow a number of carefully constructed conventions. Some of these conventions are appropriate. UN forces should represent the military forces of the international community, for example, rather than individual countries acting on their own to address human rights abuses. Others are highly questionable. UN forces were not permitted to directly attack the Serb heavy artillery and mortars around Srebrenica in the Balkans in order to protect tens of thousands of people herded together in killing zones erroneously named 'protected areas'.

The UN ROE only allowed for self-protection of its own forces and UN forces were only allowed to respond if directly attacked. Rigid adherence to convention dictated that the international community kept trying to maintain its neutral mandate in Bosnia Herzegovina when there was clearly no peace to keep and many innocents were slaughtered.

A significant problem facing the international community is that many of the traditional conventions and so called ROE (including Just-war theory) applied during non-conventional warfare – civil conflict, guerrilla war, insurrection and the like – do little to relieve the plight of those being seriously abused. They are ineffective because belligerents in these conflicts will not play by the rules. Vicious ethnic or cultural conflicts appear to be conducted with very few rules at all.

This does not mean that the international community should throw out the rulebook or the conventions on how it tries to manage conflict. On the contrary, it means that if international law is deficient in bringing to justice war criminals and others who commit crimes against humanity (as it surely is in many cases) then new legal processes, perhaps requiring military or police enforcement, must be found to address unrestrained aggression.

Humanitarian and international law defines certain human behaviour, such as genocide and torture, as being 'crimes against humanity'. These crimes are subject to severe punishment – if the perpetrators can be apprehended, if they can be extradited to an appropriate court of law, and if complicity can be proven. Sanctity of statehood, and the individual human rights of those determined to be complicit in severe and deliberate violations of human rights, should be suspended or removed entirely in order to stop serious criminal activities.

An important trend in the application of international law has been the attempt to prosecute state leaders before international tribunals (with widely varying levels of success) for the violent crimes they have committed against their own and foreign nationals. In 1998, General Augusto Pinochet was indicted by a Spanish lawyer for crimes against humanity and in May of 1999, Slobodan Milosevic, the President of

Yugoslavia, became the first sitting head of state to be indicted for war crimes and crimes against humanity by an international tribunal. Milosevic was arrested at his home in Belgrade on 9 April 2001 by Yugoslav security forces, and Saddam Hussein is currently in the dock of the International Criminal Court for his involvement in many Iraqi atrocities.

Critics will point out the ponderous machinations of getting someone suspected of crimes against humanity to an international court of law, never mind actually achieving a conviction. This does need to be addressed but the fact that such legal constructs of international justice exist in the first place is a crucial step in the development of a moral and civil human society. International courts of law are a step in the right direction.

A civil society needs rules and conventions to guide its domestic and international affairs. However fervently such a society claims some sort of moral imperative as being the primary impetus for action, it will always need the force of law to support this activity. Increasingly there is a requirement for the application of international and humanitarian laws to counter humanitarian abuse in today's violent world.

If I can show an ethical imperative to respond to fellow human beings in extreme need then objections to the use of coercive force may take on a new perspective. Objections become objectives to be overcome in order to alleviate the misery of millions of desperate people. This will only occur if humanitarian assistance is viewed from the perspective of those most in need and not only from the perspective of those who may or may not be willing to assist.

Those who object to the use of military force outright and those who demand cast-iron guarantees of success and other impossible conditions to be satisfied before they are prepared to act are primarily focused on their own welfare and comfort. In a more moral world the focus would be on those who need immediate relief from abuse.

# Chapter 1

# Ethical Reasoning and Moral Principles

## Introduction

Each day human beings are deliberately and systematically being abused by fellow human beings. Extreme abuse such as mental and physical torture, summary killings, and cruel, inhuman and degrading punishments are commonplace in many parts of the world. They continue to occur despite these abhorrent acts violating most of the norms of what is often called moral or 'civilised' behaviour. The concept of a moral and/or civilised society is discussed later in this chapter.

There are many ethnic, religious and ideological groups who use brutal force by jailing, murdering, torturing, raping, starving and otherwise abusing their opponents. When we become aware of cases of this sort, we are likely to describe them as violations of human rights, instead of simply saying that they are immoral, unjust or barbaric. This provides us with a formal framework to specify conduct deemed to be unacceptable (at least by some people) human behaviour.

In an effort to be more specific, we may add that such actions violate rights to freedom from arbitrary arrest, to freedom from torture, to due process and to life. Geoffrey Robertson argues that these are regarded by many as fundamental human rights that are internationally recognised in the Universal Declaration of Human Rights (UDHR) and by other conventions and treaties.[1] We may individually, in small groups, in non-government or government organisations, or in the collective of variable membership sometimes known as the international community, voice our protest at extreme violations of fundamental human rights. Our responses vary between '...it's terrible, we should do something about it', to '...its not our problem.', depending on what our individual moral predilections dictate and on how long we are able to maintain our focus on a particular incident.

Despite the frequent disinclination for direct action to address these appalling human behaviours, few would disagree that the scale and brutality of some atrocities shocks and affronts many of us. Most people would find it difficult not to be morally appalled by the ongoing atrocities in Africa, in the Balkans and in Afghanistan. The following are some examples of these and other recent human rights abuses that I class as serious human rights abuse. My intention in presenting these examples is to clearly identify what types of human rights abuses should warrant direct intervention by the international community.

---

1    Geoffrey Robertson, *Crimes against Humanity. The Struggle for Global Justice* (London: The Penguin Press, 1999), pp. 26–31.

Human Rights Watch (HRW) reported in mid 1998 on the continuing atrocities being committed in Sierra Leone. The Armed Forces Revolutionary Council (AFRC) and the Revolutionary United Front (RUF) are in constant tribal conflict against opposing power factions within the country. They specifically target civilians in a terror campaign intended to oust President Alhaji Dr. Ahmad Tejan Kabbah and the ruling elites.

The atrocities listed and investigated by HRW involved the physical mutilation, torture and murder of Sierra Leonean civilians and those whom the AFRC/RUF suspected of Kabbah or Kamajor sympathies. Atrocities include: amputations by machete of one or both hands, arms, feet, legs, ears and buttocks; lacerations to the head, neck, arms, legs, feet and torso; the gouging out of one or both eyes; rape; gunshot wounds to the head, torso and limbs; burns from explosives and other devices; injections with battery acid; beatings; and sexual mutilation such as the cutting off of breasts and genitalia.[2]

This is a war waged through attacks on an unarmed and helpless civilian population. AFRC/RUF militias typically capture civilians and commit atrocities against them in an effort to instil terror. The soldiers force their victims to participate in their own mutilation by making them choose which finger, hand, arm or leg to cut off. The AFRC/RUF uses the civilians it abuses to send a message to its opponents in government. Victims of amputations or other mutilations are frequently told that they should take their amputated limb or limbs and a verbal or written message to the Kabbah government. The messages typically demand that Kabbah should '… leave the country to Sierra Leoneans' or that Kabbah should replace the limbs of amputees.

The imperatives for forceful intervention that are defended in this book are focused on these types of severe human rights abuses. The moral arguments for or against military intervention were and are of little immediate interest to the victims of torture. They just want the pain and the killing to stop. But these arguments are very important in a civil and humane society because they have direct relevance on whether or not this society is willing to act to address such abuses.

The conflict in Sierra Leone is not new nor is it particularly unusual for some of the more dangerous states in Africa and elsewhere. Eyewitness reports of massacres and other atrocities have emanated from this tiny state for decades. There is little, if any, accountability for these abuses and perpetrators often act with complete impunity.

Mass killings are widespread and the human rights situation is dire in the Great Lakes Region of Africa. The government of the Democratic Republic of Congo treats the United Nations (UN) with contempt and refuses to allow yet another investigation on massacres. In Liberia, Amnesty International stressed the necessity of accountability and of rebuilding institutions to uphold the most basic rule of law and international human rights standards. Torture, lack of medical care, deliberate

---

2   'Sierra Leone: Sowing Terror. Atrocities against Civilians in Sierra Leone, Part 3,' *HRW Report* 10, no. 3a (1998).

starvation, and cruel and inhuman or degrading prison conditions has led to many hundreds of thousands of deaths in over fourteen African countries.

There are many examples of extreme human rights violations elsewhere. In Afghanistan, at about 9:30 a.m. on 8 August 1998, Taliban troops entered the western outskirts of Mazar-i Sharif. Witnesses described the next 24 hours as a killing frenzy by occupying troops against unarmed civilians.[3] The central jail in Mazar-i Sharif was used as a collection point and holding pen for thousands of people. The jail has one well for drinking water and two toilets.

The jail and surrounding compound quickly filled to capacity with Hazaras and Shi'as until there was no room to sit or lie down, so the Taliban used large metal containers between twenty and forty feet in length to hold and to transport prisoners. Up to 300 people were forced into each of these metal containers. There was no water for the already thirsty prisoners, and the blistering heat and very little ventilation inside most of the containers meant that few people could survive longer than ten minutes. Transportation time between jails often took three hours. Even in containers with less than 300 people the death rates were very high.

In Shiberghan, they brought three containers to Bandare-i Ankhoï, close to the jail. When they opened the door of one truck, only three persons were alive. About 300 were dead. The three were taken to the jail.[4]

On 29 July 1999, Amnesty International warned of the ongoing humanitarian disaster in Afghanistan. Tens of thousands of civilians in northern Afghanistan, particularly in the Panjshir region, were being systematically killed and abused by Taliban forces.

Once again, civilians are the likely targets of human right abuses in the context of a conflict they have no active part in...caught in a game of war between armed groups, they have only the international community to turn to for protection. Civilians who are unable to flee immediately after a new area is captured are often subjected to systematic abuses by the victorious forces...thousands have been massacred, beaten or ill-treated. Will the world again stand by and watch as more civilians die?[5]

The Balkan's conflict was another example of ongoing, extreme human rights abuse. The Nobel laureate, Elie Wiesel had said to President Bill Clinton during the 1993 opening of the Holocaust Memorial Museum,

> Mr President, I must tell you something. I have been in the former Yugoslavia last fall. I cannot sleep since what I have seen . . . We must do something to stop the bloodshed in that country. People fight each other and children die. Why? Something, anything, must be done.[6]

---

3    'The Massacre at Mazar-I Sharif,' *HRW Report* 10, no. 7c (1998).

4    Ibid.

5    Amnesty International, 'Thousands at Imminent Risk of Human Rights Abuses,144/99, Ai Index: Asa 11/08/99,' (Amnesty International: The International Secretariat News Service, 1999).

6    Richard Cohen, 'Something Must Be Done in Bosnia,' *St. Louis Post-Dispatch, Washington Post Writers Group* 1995.

The central prison in Foca, called the Kazneno-Popravni Dom (KP Dom-Home for Criminal Rehabilitation) was, prior to the Balkan's war of 1991–96, the central prison for the entire south eastern region of Bosnia and Herzegovina. It was one of the largest prisons in the former Yugoslavia.[7]

Bosnian Serb civilian, police, and military officials, in collaboration with paramilitary troops and former Yugoslav Army reservists called in from Serbia and Montenegro, took over Foca in April 1992. They established a wartime government called the 'Crisis Committee', much like those established in many towns in Bosnian Serb-controlled territory, to plan and carry out the expulsion of the non-Serb population.

Using a thorough propaganda campaign to convince the local Bosnian Serb population that they were under threat of a Muslim fundamentalist coup, the Crisis Committee established a network of detention centres, where non-Serb civilians were detained, tortured, raped, and either expelled, killed, or 'disappeared', leaving the town almost completely ethnically Serb. Businesses and properties of non-Serbs were expropriated or destroyed.

The KP Dom detention centre was used during the Balkan's war as a detention and interrogation compound for non-Serbs. It contained on average approximately 800 detainees at any one time. At various times up to 600 people were 'disappeared' to make way for a new influx of detainees.[8]

Survivors of this camp told gruesome tales of starvation, torture, intimidation and threats, beatings, disappearances and systematic rape. E.D., a survivor of KP Dom, reported to HRW.

> They took people and beat them, we heard them scream. For more than one hour they beat them. They were beating people always in the basement, so you could hear them screaming. We were sitting in the corner afraid in our room. After more than one hour everything stopped and was quiet. We never slept at night because we were so scared. One morning they took us room by room out to the bridge and those people who had been taken that night all had their heads cut off. There were nine bodies and the heads were separated from the bodies....I recognised some of them as Munib Vejz, Salem Bico, and Ekrem Dzelilovic.[9]

Another detention centre called the Partizan Sports Hall was a rape and torture centre. It was originally used as a staging area for women and children who were to be deported from Foca. Located next to the police station in the centre of town, residents of Foca realised that the detention centre was being used as a site for torture, killings and rape by Bosnian Serb guards.[10]

---

7　　Human Rights Watch, 'Bosnia and Herzegovina. A Closed Dark Place. Past and Present Human Rights Abuses in Foca,' *HRW Report* 10, no. 6d (1998).

8　　Ibid.

9　　Ibid.

10　　Gordana Igric, 'Kosovo Rape Victims Suffer Twice,' (Institute of War & Peace Reporting, 1999): p. 1.

Residents reported to the local police what was happening in the building next door but the police, rather than intervening, continued to send citizens to the sports hall for 'detention'. 'Women who were kept there were taken to be raped every evening.' One survivor who spent two months in Partizan reported. 'What they went through can simply not be described.'[11]

Survivors of Partizan were interviewed in refugee camps. They described experiencing rape as a systematic ritual. Several women reported that they had been raped over one hundred times during the period of their imprisonment. One woman told Newsday journalist Roy Gutman that she had been raped approximately one hundred and fifty times during her detention in Partizan.[12] Another reported having been raped up to six times a night. Women were sometimes raped in front of other prisoners in the hall. They were routinely taken to locations outside the hall in houses and apartments to be gang-raped by groups of soldiers.

A woman who hid in an apartment close to the hall witnessed the same soldiers removing women from the hall every day. She estimated that there were over fifty soldiers involved in the daily raping of prisoners. Another woman tells of being taken to an outdoor stadium where she was gang-raped by uniformed soldiers. '…I counted 29 of them. Then I lost consciousness.' When she regained consciousness, she was taken back to the camp.

The practice of rape as ethnic cleansing was widespread and widely known throughout Bosnia Herzegovina. The rape camp at Patrizan was only one of many throughout Yugoslavia. One woman interviewed in a refugee camp noted that the group of men who raped her and thirteen other women with whom she was imprisoned, '…were a kind of military police [that] did nothing but rape. It was all organised. They had a group for raping and a group for killing.'[13]

Serious human rights abuse is motivated by more than ethnic hatred. In the Sudan, human atrocities are directly linked to the exploitation of natural resources. Amnesty International reported in May 2000 about the many human rights abuses committed by Sudanese security forces and various government allied militia groups against Sudanese civilians. Very little has changed in 2006, six years on.

The civilian population living in oil fields and surrounding areas has been deliberately targeted for massive human rights abuses – forced displacement, aerial bombardments, strafing villages from helicopter gunships, unlawful killings, torture including rape and abduction.[14]

Sudanese government troops cleared the area around the town of Bentiu using helicopter gunships allegedly piloted by Iraqi soldiers. The troops used aerial cluster

---

11 Filip Svarm, 'Bosnian Thunder: Refugee Days,' *Vreme News Digest Agency*, no. 79 (1993): pp. 1–2.

12 Human Rights Watch, 'Bosnia and Herzegovina. A Closed Dark Place. Past and Present Human Rights Abuses in Foca.'

13 Ibid.

14 Amnesty International, 'Sudan: The Human Price of Oil, 079/00, Ai Index: Afr 54/04/00,' (Amnesty International: The International Secretariat News Service, 2000).

bombs dropped by Antonov aircraft flying at high altitude. Amnesty International reported that government troops on the ground drove people out of their homes by committing gross human rights violations. Male villagers were killed in mass executions, and women and children were nailed to trees with iron spikes. Reports from other villages claim that soldiers slit the throats of children and killed male civilians by hammering nails into their foreheads.[15]

Such horrific examples are not especially unusual or particularly isolated in many parts of the globe where law and order is at the point of a gun. Even the presence of legal regimes in many states is absolutely no guarantee that its citizens will be treated with respect or dignity. I make no distinction between the cultural, ethnic, religious or ideological backgrounds of those perpetrating atrocities and serious human rights abuses.

Many of the examples of atrocities and human rights abuses presented in this book are derived from incidents occurring in 'third world' or developing countries because this is where the majority of them happen. This in no way implies that the 'developed world' does not engage in similar criminal acts. For example, Lieutenant William Calley led the massacre, accompanied by sadism and sexual violence, of about 500 unarmed civilians in the Vietnamese hamlet of My Lai in March 1968.[16]

In September 1969, Calley was charged with premeditated murder for the death of 109 Vietnamese near the village of My Lai. 500 villagers, mostly women, children, infants and elderly, were assembled and then shot by soldiers of Charlie Company. In March, 1971, Calley was sentenced to life in prison. Only Calley was convicted out of the 26 officers and soldiers who were initially charged for their participation in the My Lai massacre or the subsequent cover-up.

Joanna Burke claims that there was widespread endorsement of certain atrocities within the armed forces, and that the conviction of Calley outraged many Americans, especially the military. Senior Officers bombarded him [Calley] with supportive letters and the night after the conviction one hundred GIs paraded outside Fort Benning, chanting, 'War is hell! Free Calley'.[17] Herbert Rainwater, the National Commander of the Veterans of Foreign Wars was appalled at the trial and subsequent conviction of Calley. He informed journalists that there have been My Lais in every war and that for the first time in American history a soldier is tried for performing his duty.[18]

One day after Calley was sentenced, President Richard Nixon ordered him to be released from prison. In August 1971 his term was reduced to 20 years and, in 1974 a Federal Judge released Calley after 3 ½ years of house arrest.

---

15  Ibid.

16  Douglass Rossman, *On Killing: The Psychological Cost of Learning to Kill in War and Society* (Boston: Little Brown and Company, Back Bay Books, 1996), p. 190.

17  Joanna Bourke, *An Intimate History of Killing : Face-to-Face Killing in Twentieth-Century Warfare* ([New York]: Basic Books, 1999), p. 180.

18  Herbert Rainwater, 'Judgement at Fort Benning,' *Newsweek* (1971): pp. 27–28.

Calley was not the only one who protested over his indictment and eventual conviction for premeditated murder. Eight out of ten Americans disapproved of the conviction or sentencing of William Calley according to one US opinion poll.[19] Some even insisted that the massacre could never have happened. The governor of Alabama hotly proclaimed that, 'Any atrocities in this war were committed by the communists.'[20]

## *Wrong...and Right*

It is difficult not to be shocked and appalled by such human rights abuses, yet clearly there are people and groups who not only condone these activities but actively support them. They would not occur otherwise, particularly on such a large scale. Although one cannot say that absolutely everyone is shocked and appalled by these types of acts, it is not unreasonable to say that most people have feelings of revulsion and horror about how humans often treat each other.

One could come up with all sorts of reasons why these abuses occur. Historical precedent, acts of revenge and retaliation, ethnic or religious differences and ideological conflict are commonly cited as excuses for extreme human behaviour. Some will argue that if a particular incident of gross human rights abuse occurred during the heat of battle then it is sometimes 'understandable' for atrocity and counter-atrocity to follow. Hard-core Realists will shrug their shoulders and say that morality itself is suspended during times of warfare, or that warfare and conflict is not about morality in the first place.

One could also argue about the precise definition of morality and whether a particular act could be considered to be wrong in this or that situation; and whether or not the perpetrators of extreme human rights abuses were somehow forced or coerced to take part in the acts, were confused about what they were doing, or even that some cultures and societies accepted the traditional outcomes of their bloodthirsty activities. Gouging out one or both eyes and rape are traditional Serb and Muslim weapons of war.

Yet, few people would say that such extreme human rights abuse is acceptable in a civilised and humane society. I argue that it is not acceptable, but more to the point, that something effective must be done to stop this abuse. Large scale, carefully planned and systematic extreme human rights violations raises the question of what the rest of us are doing to stop these atrocities. After the shock value has worn off and we have stopped simply saying that these are terrible acts, what then? A range of responses is possible. We could protest in the streets and make banners that say 'Stop the killing and torture in Africa...Afghanistan...Bosnia Herzegovina...'. We could shout at our elected officials and tell them to demand that the torturers and the abusers stop their immoral activities.

---

19 'The Morality of Warfare: Is Closer Necessarily Worse,' *The Economist*, 17 July 1999: p. 1.

20 Ibid.

What else could we do? We could donate spare cash to a humanitarian organisation in the hope that money for food and water will somehow reach the women being raped in Bosnia Herzegovina. We could make up food parcels, knit socks, bake cakes and make toys, and send them directly to a friend of a friend in Afghanistan who will try to get the items to the adults and children of the Hazaras and Shi'as.

We could support Medecines sans Frontières (MSF) for the delivery and administration of medical supplies and to help medical personnel in the field. We could write articles to newspapers, write a book, send e-mails and set up local support groups. We could buy a one way ticket to a conflict zone and set up tents for shelter, dig latrines, bury the dead, comfort the abused and volunteer to transport aid supplies to where they are most needed.

Many people choose to let their elected officials, governments or humanitarian organisations, such as the United Nations, address issues of humanitarian concern without any further direct action by themselves. They expect their officials and governments – particularly where these are elected persons and democratic entities – to represent their interests in humanitarian organisations such as the United Nations, the International Committee of the Red Cross (ICRC) and so on. They may sometimes be called upon to endorse UN peacekeeping efforts, and to support their politicians diplomatic and mediation endeavours for a better and more peaceful world.

*Are We Making a Difference?*

Protesting and banner waving, giving money to needy causes and so on are all worthy humanitarian support actions but, despite all these efforts, the world is a far more lethal place today than at any other time in recorded history. The international community has not been successful in addressing many of the desperate humanitarian crises occurring around the globe and compassion fatigue is a significant contributing factor.

The difficulty with being compassionate is that compassion is not limitless. A great deal of research has been done in this area but the problem remains about what the actual symptoms and outcomes in the complex area of trauma management are and how to deal with them. One commonality in much of the literature is the acknowledgement that human empathy is both a help and a hindrance to clinicians and other interventionists. Helpful because without human empathy intervention would probably only occur for pragmatic reasons, and a hindrance because a desire to help can result in compassion fatigue and even compassion confusion resulting in little effective intervention in the conflict area.

Danica Borkovich Anderson is a forensic psychotherapist and a Board Certified Expert in Trauma (B.C.E.T.S.). She explains her personal account of dealing with compassion fatigue and 'burn-out' as she reviewed her clinical work in war ravaged Bosnia Herzegovina in March 1999.[21]    The warning signs of critical incident/compassion fatigue, she says, include using work or working excessively to avoid looking at issues or emotions.  She says that this is a 'numbing' process. Other indicators are; sharing a common history or traumatic events (this blurs the difference between self and other/s) and being unable to share or express first person story – lacking a vocabulary or feeling that 'no one would understand', or that 'no one cares enough to actually listen'.

Mooli Lahad  suggests the symptoms of compassion fatigue that resemble the physiological, emotional, and cognitive symptoms of victims appear among those who administer help to them.[22]    In 3 percent to 7 percent of cases, these may be so severe that the professional helpers themselves develop Post Traumatic Stress Disorder (PTSD).  He argues that most of those involved in intervention have experienced traumatic events in their lives.

Those who administer help after trauma cope with a variety of events and at some time they inevitably encounter some that are similar to the trauma in their own life experience.  Larry Minear proposes that the interconnectedness between peace-making, peacekeeping, and peace-enforcement and other central concerns such as humanitarian action, development, and human rights sheds a new and different light on what is widely viewed as 'compassion fatigue'.[23]  A more apt description, he claims, might be 'compassion confusion'.  That is, rather than weariness in assisting those in need, there is widespread anguish and confusion about how best to do so.

Saying that we should be compassionate is very different to actually being compassionate in an effective and material way.  Effective compassion must be actually doing something constructive that would relieve the plight of those who need our help.  There are all sorts of constraints as to how far we as a society are willing to care for others.  By caring for others we must by necessity be prepared to sacrifice something of our own.  This may be materiel, personal comfort, money, position, or a whole raft of similar constraints.  Limits to compassion may just be time or even the inclination to become involved in other people's suffering, or sometimes the suffering of others is just too overwhelming to bear.  How can we be compassionate about everything and everyone all the time without compassion fatigue invariably setting in?  The harsh truth is that we cannot.  Most of us are selectively compassionate.  We pick and choose what we are compassionate about.

The logistics and technicalities of trying to help the suffering millions around the world today are daunting and to many people overwhelming.  How does one get the material aid and other help needed by those who are suffering to them?  How do we

---

21   Danica Borkovich Anderson, *Bosnia's Death Highway: My Personal Story of Trauma Work, Compassion Fatigue and Hope* (2000 [cited 1 June 2005); available from http://www. giftfromwithin.org/html/bosnia.html.

22   Mooli Lahad, 'Darkness over the Abyss: Supervising Crisis Intervention Teams Following Disaster,' *Traumatology* VI, no. 4 (2000): pp. 1–2.

23   Larry Minear, 'The International Relief System: A Critical Review' (paper presented at the Parallel National Intelligence Estimate on Global Humanitarian Emergencies, Meridian International Center, Washington, D.C., September 22, 1994 1994).

deal with the HIV/Aids crises in Africa where even the most optimistic predictions by The Joint United Nations Programme on HIV/AIDS (UNAID) claim that the disease will still result in at least 53 million adult deaths with a possible 43 million new HIV infections.[24]

Keith Epstein outlines some of the 'silent tsunamis' that afflict humanity. Each month, he says, more than 106,000 people, mostly children, die of malaria although inexpensive remedies exist. Some 150,000 people, again mostly children, die of infectious diarrhoea often linked to unsafe water, sanitation and hygiene. At least 150,000 people die of famine while health experts speak of an obesity epidemic in the world's wealthiest nations. An estimated 231,000 people die of AIDS, which has overwhelmed Africa and causes the fourth-most deaths worldwide. Epstein claims that about 31,000 die in one nation alone, the Democratic Republic of Congo, of disease, malnutrition and other effects of a war. The Congo's grinding conflict has claimed 3.8 million lives since 1998.[25]

Our response to these sorts of questions must be to firstly recognise that we have a problem of such proportions but then we must move beyond the concern stage to do something constructive and effective to address these humanitarian disasters. The problem is not that there are not enough resources to go around. The problem is that resources are inequitably distributed and inappropriately used. Humanitarians will argue that it is not acceptable to condemn tens of millions of people to death in Africa because we cannot decide what to do or how to do it.

The international community cannot be said to be effectively addressing these issues by any reasonable measure of success. In the sphere of man-made disasters, more and more people are being subjected to deliberate atrocity. For example, the UN and dozens of humanitarian organisations, supported by thousands of caring individuals, have been operating in Africa for over 60 years yet the humanitarian situation there is as appalling, if not worse, than it has ever been.[26][27]

It is true that there have been some selective improvements on the human social front. Since the 1960s the quality of life in some parts of the world has unquestionably improved. As a measurement of life expectancy, world health has made gratifying gains, especially in some of the less developed countries.

Yet, despite some successes in health and some social issues, the world is not a more peaceful place. This is the most productive yet the most destructive century since recorded time. This century outstrips by far any other in civil violence, the number of conflicts waged, numbers of refugees created, millions of people killed

---

24   The Joint United Nations Programme on HIV/AIDS, 'Aids in Africa: Three Scenarios to 2025,' (United Nations, 2005): p. 193.

25   Keith Epstein, *A World of Troubles* (MEDIA GENERAL NEWS SERVICE, 2005 [cited 29 April 2005]); available from http://washdateline.mgnetwork.com/index.cfm?SiteID =wsh&PackageID=46&fuseaction=article.main&ArticleID=6501&GroupID=214.

26   Thalif Deen, 'Politics: Un Laments World's Two Forgotten Emergencies,' *World News, Inter Press Service*, 23 April 1998.

27   Kofi Annan, 'The Humanitarian Challenge Today' (paper presented at the Los Angeles World Affairs Council, Los Angeles, April 21 1998).

in conflict and vast military expenditures.[28]   In only 5 years, between 1990 and 1995, 70 states were involved in 93 wars that killed nearly 6 million people.[29]   This modern century has been responsible for more than 250 wars and 109,746,000 conflict related deaths. This number is larger than the current populations of France, Belgium, the Netherlands, Denmark, Sweden, Finland and Norway combined.

Those who have the highest casualty rates today are civilians. At the beginning of this century, 50 percent civilians and 50 percent military personnel were casualties. In the 1960s, approximately 63 percent of conflict related deaths were civilian; in the 1980s 74 percent of deaths were civilian; and today over three quarters of conflict related deaths are civilian.[30]

So, for all our increasingly sophisticated mediation schemes, diplomacy, pleas for non-violent resolution to disputes and complex negotiations the world is overall a more dangerous and dreadful place. Despite all the pleas to elected officials, all the banner waving and shouting, all the support for the UN and all the cakes made and socks knitted, we are worse off than before. Very few statistics are available which even attempt to quantify the misery and suffering involved in re-building blasted infrastructure and shattered societies.

There are essentially two ways of looking at our efforts and progress to reduce severe humanitarian abuse so far.   Firstly, many people will say that individually and collectively we are just not doing enough of what we are already doing to make a meaningful difference. They will call for more of the same. More support, more mediation, more negotiation, more money, more food, more medicines and more shelter.

I present another, more confronting, view. That is, our individual and collective efforts to improve things for humanity is not effective in decreasing violent conflict, therefore we must seriously consider other options and alternatives.   One such alternative is the direct use of coercive military force to at least immediately stop severe human rights abuses.

The use of force in this way is not always technically feasible and it may not always be a viable option.  It is possible that the opposing forces are too strong or tactically that they are unreachable.  The terms 'too strong' and 'tactically unreachable' must be used with great caution because even a well-armed and highly trained force could not withstand for long a determined military coalition such as NATO operating under the auspices of the United Nations.

Western military superpowers have quick reaction forces of battalion size and firepower that can reach most areas of the globe within seventy-two hours. With supporting air and sea power, such a force would very quickly overwhelm most belligerent states or factions within states today. A significant challenge for such

---

28   Ruth Sivard, *World Military and Social Expenditures*, 16 ed. (Washington: World Priorities, 1996), pp. 6–13.

29   Dan Smith, *The State of War and Peace Atlas: International Peace Research Institute, Oslo*, 3 ed. (London: Penguin Books Limited, 1997), pp. 1–13.

30   Sivard, *World Military and Social Expenditures*.

a force would be to deal with atrocities where entire populations are involved but this does not mean that all such intervention should automatically be rejected. The combination of military power with strong coercive diplomacy and a concerted and unified strategic approach to the problem is required. Many military strategic response options are available in a world armed to the teeth with sophisticated military hardware but they require the political will to become effective and they require the moral fortitude to deal with extreme and deliberate abuse of state or group against citizen.

Coalition action during the recent Gulf Wars is an example of what is, initially at least, militarily possible if interventionist forces are determined and prepared for action. The 1991 Gulf War was a war about restoration of Kuwaiti sovereign territory and continuing western access to oil reserves. It was not a humanitarian war: Nonetheless it demonstrated what is militarily possible against a well-armed and ruthless opponent. The second Gulf War in 2003 was also not a war intended to liberate the Iraqis from severe human rights abuses although, after failing to discover Weapons of Mass Destruction (WMDs) or finding that Iraq had links with 'terrorist organisations', the mantra of 'regime change' and an apparent sudden need for some democracy in Iraq (as perceived by the Coalition of the Willing governments) began to dominate the discourse.

Today Iraq is an ongoing disaster area. Poor, if not non-existent, post-invasion or post-liberation (depending on which side of the fence you are on) planning, a lack of any real understanding of the politics and power dynamics within Iraq, the appalling treatment of those incarcerated in prisons such as Abu Ghraib and elsewhere, the practice of 'Rendition' where coalition forces send suspects to other states for interrogation …the list goes on. The conflict in Iraq is a specific example of how not to use military force, never mind the use of force for humanitarian purposes.

Examples where the concentrated use of military force has been more effective include the UN sponsored NATO air attack against the Serbs in Bosnia Herzegovina, NATO action in Kosovo and UN action in East Timor. It took six years for the international community to respond directly and with effective force against the ongoing Serb brutalities in the Balkan conflict of 1992–96, but in a matter of weeks NATO airpower, combined with a Bosnian government and Croat offensive, was successful in halting the widespread slaughter of non-Serb civilians in Bosnia Herzegovina.

In Kosovo, it took NATO air power seventy-eight days to force a full-blown Serb retreat from the region; and in East Timor, the International Peacekeeping Force (IFOR) led by Australia imposed the international rule of law within days of arriving on the tiny island. UN action in East Timor was assisted by the lack of any serious opposition but this could have been very different if some sort of multilateral coalition had tried to intervene for whatever reason without a UN mandate. The UN still has a unique moral authority that unilateral or limited multilateral action has great difficulty in procuring. Of course, the UN has its own serious problems with mandates, not the least of which is gaining unanimity about what to do in the first place.

The frequency and ferocity of conflict is increasing not decreasing overall despite the amount of non-coercive humanitarian assistance over the past fifty years. Things would be a whole lot worse without our current efforts, but this does not address the fact that international conflicts are increasing, more and more people are dying and being grossly abused. The world is a more violent place, despite all our efforts.

Some people will insist that violence only breeds violence and that the use of force will just cause further bloodshed. They will be genuinely morally appalled by the use of force, but the reality is that violence does not always breed further violence and the use of force will not always cause a worse human catastrophe than that which exists in the first place. To reject the use of directed force based on the assumption that it only ever has negative outcomes means that law enforcement agencies must never apply force to uphold the law. It means that our corrective institutions should open their doors and not constrain violent offenders.

The total rejection of all force is unrealistic in today's violent world. Child sex offenders, rapists, serial killers and other extremely violent individuals must be apprehended and constrained by force. The use of force in these instances is surely morally justifiable. Being prepared to use force is not the same as having no moral conscience about violence. When other options are not available or they have not worked then force may be the only way to stop unrestrained aggression. We may be morally dismayed at NATO's use of force to stop the atrocities in Bosnia Herzegovina, but if there simply is no other effective way of stopping such atrocities then the use of force must be considered as a plausible moral option.

Directed force is needed to immediately stop atrocities and as a warning to belligerents that they are accountable for their actions to the wider human community. Using force in this way is not about punishment, revenge or even justice. This is not the job of interventionists. International courts are available (assuming that we support the idea of international law and international courts of law) to decide punishment, retribution and justice. The interventionists' task is stop belligerents illegally killing and torturing helpless people.

In order to stop extreme human rights abuses peacemakers are required. Peacemakers must not be confused with peacekeepers. The peacekeepers role should be one of enforcing, policing and upholding international law. The peacemaker's role must be to impose minimum international standards of behaviour where anarchy reigns or where national legal regimes deliberately and persistently brutalise citizens.

I do not present arguments for or against the delivery of international humanitarian aid, which organisations should be involved in humanitarian relief, or what we individually should be doing to address serious human rights abuses. I also do not rationalise important medium to long-term strategies that try to address complicated ethnic or religious conflicts. These are all vital tools in the humanitarian relief arsenal and they are essential for the betterment of humankind but my focus is not with these matters.

My aim is to discuss plausible immediate and short-term strategies to halt the brutality and killing to give mediation, discussion, diplomacy and all the other humanitarian tools a chance to work. Human rights abuse occurs because those doing the abusing are rarely, if ever, held accountable for their actions. Accountability is not just a question of punishment or the delivery of justice on society's part. Some violent individuals will kill and keep on killing until they are physically stopped. They are not concerned about societal punishments or ill defined notions of justice. Accountability for them means being forced to stop their abuse of human rights.

The international community mistakenly believes that it just needs to rationally appeal to the abusers to stop. We hope that the use of reasoned argument or an appeal to some moral value will make a difference or, if we are a little firmer, we may threaten some sort of trade or diplomatic sanctions which, in the end, will usually harm those already suffering deprivations the most. A characteristic of economic sanctions is that they are specifically intended to cause economic harm to another state. The basic idea is that the burden of economic hardship imposed by sanctions will become intolerable to the citizens of the target state, who in turn will pressure their leaders to change undesirable policies. This has rarely, if ever, actually worked to reduce the severe deprivations of the abused. In fact, it usually just makes things worse.

We may send in lightly armed peacekeepers (usually on invitation only) to 'monitor and observe'. Such approaches to some of the world's most depraved and ruthless individuals or organisations have repeatedly proven to be naïve and dangerous. It is lethal to the victims on the receiving end of severe human rights abuse and it sows the seeds for future revenge based hate conflicts. The perpetrators of crimes against humanity have little, if any, empathy with their victims. They do not care what the international community threatens unless punitive action delays or stops them from their objectives.

Most of the current efforts of international humanitarian action that are intended to stop serious human rights abuses are ineffectual. They are ineffectual because we are far more concerned about our own national interest issues or possible casualties to our own people than the suffering and slaughter of tens or hundreds of thousands of helpless victims of brutal regimes in far away places.

My arguments are initially based on a simple premise. The premise is that deliberate human rights abuse is morally wrong, even according to common sense moral thinking, and that it must be stopped. Some of us arrive at such a conclusion in different ways. We will contest the meaning of 'extreme', we will endeavour to determine what the precise definition of a human right actually is and we will debate endlessly about how human rights abuse can be stopped. But the bottom line is morally irrefutable. Human rights abuse is wrong and it must be stopped.

The '…and it must be stopped.' part of the premise is not intended just to complement the observation that human rights abuse is wrong. All too often this is simply a tag attached after the first part of the statement. It actually means that human rights abuses must be stopped if we claim to have moral values that have any relevance at all to those being abused on a daily basis. What is relevant to those being abused is that the abuse stops, not just that we are concerned or appalled.

The examples of horrific human rights abuses that I present are what I consider to be extreme. I develop the idea of 'degree of abuse' later in this chapter. The reason I deal with this as a separate issue is that I am arguing that the international community's response to abuse is strongly dependent on whether or not we are sufficiently shocked for a sufficient length of time to actually do something about the problem. Extreme levels of abuse sometimes provide the impetus for us to focus our attention a little longer on a particular humanitarian crisis.

It is very difficult to see how one could say that extreme, deliberate and ongoing human rights abuse is wrong, and then not go on to say that it should be stopped. Being morally outraged by such atrocities is important, proclaiming that they must be stopped is important, threatening all sorts of retribution if abusers do not stop is important, but most important of all is actually doing something effective to stop atrocities. The term effective means doing something that works. If those who deliberately conduct such violations cannot be persuaded to halt their murderous activities by non-violent means then they must be physically stopped.

So far, I have presented my most basic moral reasoning behind the use of force for humanitarian purposes. I will now further develop this theme by addressing some important ethical principles behind such reasoning, and I will argue that a moral and civil society (and an international community) actually does exist.

*Acknowledgment of a Moral and Civil Society*

Fundamental to the idea that a civil and caring society has some sort of moral obligation to intervene in severe humanitarian crises is an assumption that such a community actually exists in the first place. A further assumption is that this community has a moral conscience and that the wider concept of humanitarianism is valid and relevant in today's world. The idea of a moral and civil society is important because it implies a wider moral and social conscience outside individual endeavour or mere group interest.

A 'civil society' is more than just the sum of its institutions or the effectiveness of its administration. A civil and moral society is one that responds to the welfare of its citizens in a material sense but it is also a society that demonstrates tolerance, compassion, and understanding. Humanitarians transpose this idea to the wider human community, and they say that tolerance, compassion and understanding should not simply be limited to statism and the all pervasive 'national interest' arguments.

Ethnicity, ideology and statehood are not ignored by such a concept of civil society, rather they are subsumed by a wider consideration for the human condition. There are at least two major challenges to the idea of a civil and humanitarian society – sometimes also referred to as the 'international community'.

Firstly, does it actually exist as a moral entity? I argue that it does. Secondly, if it does exist, is the use of force appropriate to impose upon others the ideals and values of such a society or community? The second issue is dealt with later in this chapter in a discussion of moral obligation and the ethical principles underpinning the use of military force for humanitarian purposes. The following section will deal with the notion that a moral society actually exists in the first place.

The idea that a moral society exists revolves around the notion that there is some sort of connectivity between human aspiration, the physical world and in the sharing of at least some human values. It is not necessary for there to be a direct physical link between individuals or groups for such connectivity. For example, most people are morally affronted by the ongoing human rights abuses in the Balkans, in Africa, in Afghanistan, and elsewhere. This is regardless of whether one lives in Iceland, Africa, Sweden or Australia. Simple human empathy is able to transcend state boundaries, ideologies, religion or ethnicity.

Our response to some natural disasters is often very different to crises that humankind deliberately inflicts upon the weak and the helpless. The global response to the December 26, 2005 Tsunami disaster where an undersea earthquake led to the deaths of at least 157,000 people from Indonesia to Africa resulted in pledges of over $US4 billion being raised in a matter of weeks.[31] George Rupp, President of the International Rescue Committee observed that,

> The world's overwhelming and totally appropriate response to the Asian tsunami nonetheless illustrates how little we are doing to assist with humanitarian crises of equal or greater proportions.[32]

Connectivity in the physical world may mean shared human aspirations and endeavour through worldwide telecommunications, economic trading, defence arrangements or cultural exchange. For example; global warming, overfishing of the oceans, pollution and many other environmental concerns are increasingly seen as being important to all of humanity. They are not just local or regional issues.

When a state or group of states engages in conflict with others then there is a likelihood that such conflict will spread the circle of death, suffering and destruction. Regional trading partnerships and economic arrangements set up to benefit all parties may be jeopardised. No state of armed conflict and insurrection could be said to mutually benefit all parties, and a long and difficult period of rebuilding usually follows such upheaval.

Respect and admiration for other human beings, the desire to help natural disaster victims no matter where the disaster occurs, and concerns over human rights issues (whatever these so-called rights are determined to be) all point to human interests above and beyond those merely of self or state. Realists who insist that interests of state must always come first ignore the reality that people share common aspirations and values with others outside arbitrary state borders. If the realists were right then the national interest would always dominate and only self-interest would rule. The simple fact is that humans do not, and cannot, live in isolation with only self-interest as the primary motivator.

---

31 The China Daily, 'Leaders Put $4b to Work at Tsunami Summit,' *The China Daily* 2005.

32 Epstein, *A World of Troubles* ([cited).

Sharing human aspirations and claiming a common human empathy between people on different parts of the globe does not mean that such perceived values are boundless; indeed they are frequently very selectively applied depending on convenience or circumstance. Despite these limitations, one could not logically argue that all individuals or all groups are only interested in their own welfare and that a wider concept of human connectivity does not or cannot exist at all.

Providing one is able to accept the idea of the existence of some sort of connectivity between human endeavour, human aspiration and human value then it is not unreasonable to suggest that whenever and wherever humans deliberately inflict pain and suffering on each other all of humanity is affected in some way. Long-term relationships between peoples and the development of a wider human society depend on such connectivity.

All people of a caring disposition who are aware of human rights abuses need to search their consciences as to the level of moral concern they feel about such matters. More importantly a moral society needs to seriously consider taking direct and effective action to stop such atrocities from continuing. I do not suggest that the use of military force will not cause pain, suffering and death to others. The use of military force, for whatever reason, is a brutal business where human beings attempt to maim and kill each other in large numbers. To morally justify military intervention the cause must be just, but there must also be constraint on how this force is used. This is because the use of excessive force exceeds the moral boundary associated with unnecessary death and suffering. The idea of 'proportionality' in military conduct is discussed later in this chapter.

Even if we accept the fundamental notion of moral right and wrong we may still argue that the deliberate use of violence is itself morally wrong regardless of its intent or conduct. My response is that there is an important moral difference between the deliberate use of force specifically aimed at limiting further unnecessary violence compared to the use of force for its own sake, or force being used to further some ideological or cultural end at the expense of others who are not like-minded. The moral difference between these two forms of force and violence is directly related to their intent.

The intent of the use of force, where it specifically aims to bring about a greater good, is an important consideration. Those who abhor violence under any and all circumstances should not just dismiss the use of force when it may be the only way to defend a moral good. Violence is itself not intrinsically good or bad but, like most human activity, it is a means to an end. The use of force is morally justifiable when it is required for a greater good that is weighted against the inherent harm of violence.

Some people perpetuate violence simply for violence's sake but even then it could be argued that the end is self-gratification. The notion that the use of military force for humanitarian purposes is somehow inherently bad simply because it involves the use of force conforms to a very narrow view of human values. Unless physical force is used to stop some of the world's most determined belligerents and their followers then human suffering, pain and rates of death will be much worse.

To allow this state of affairs to exist is morally abhorrent in a civil society. There is a clear moral case for the use of directed force in order to limit the pain and suffering of those unable to relieve their own pain and suffering if that is the only way that such suffering can be addressed. However, if military intervention causes or is likely to cause even more suffering and misery to the majority of people being abused then it must not be used. Ethical means and outcomes are important during humanitarian intervention.

Violence and force may be necessary to stop atrocities from occurring but this does not mean that any level of violence is acceptable. For example, the use of biological or nerve agents against human rights abusers would not usually be morally acceptable because of the severe suffering such weapons cause, but also because the future ramifications of using such dreadful weapons is unknown. The use of atomic weapons against Japan during WW II in order to bring the war to a quick end introduced human society to a headlong race for WMDs with the result that there are enough of these weapons to wipe out all life on this planet many times over.

There is an important moral difference between killing someone with a bullet or deliberately allowing someone to suffer a horrible death through the use of an nerve agent. The difference is not in the dying – both weapons will kill – the difference is also in how one dies. Important ethical principles are at stake in relation to why and how people die, not just that they die, and we ignore such principles at our peril.

This line of thought will not convince everyone. One could argue that it is irrelevant how death has occurred if violence is involved. That is, death has occurred by the deliberate use of force, therefore it is morally wrong to use force in this way. I will not persuade these people that the use of military force, even if it is specifically intended to stop mass atrocities against large numbers of innocent and helpless people, is morally acceptable.

They will simply say that the use of force is always wrong and that it must not be used anytime, under any circumstances, or for any reason. However, if they say that there may be just one case (real or imagined) where the use of force could be morally justifiable, then they cannot logically dismiss outright the use of coercive force to address extreme human rights abuses. When such a case morally justifies the use of force, then the application of force should at least be effective in carrying out its objectives.

The following section deals with some of the fundamental ethical arguments that relate to the issues raised so far. As previously stated, a civil and caring society needs law and order but these two imperatives are by themselves not enough because they can be diverted and manipulated for the benefit of the few and to the detriment of the many. What must complement law is justice (not all law is just) and a willingness to support the notion of a free and fair society, and an ethical perspective is an important cornerstone of a civil and moral society.

Consequentialism and its cousin Utilitarianism are not exclusive or definitive moral arguments but they do provide a useful reference point when attempting to analyse particular aspects of human behaviour. The reason that I discuss such normative ethical concepts is for the reader who would like to investigate a little further some of the underlying philosophical rationale behind arguments that condemn the international community for not acting against severe human rights abuses when it clearly could and should do so.

## The Utility of Consequentialism

Consequentialism in its purest form is a moral doctrine that says that the right act in a given situation is the one that will produce the best outcome.[33][34] Utilitarianism is a form of consequentialism. It is a form of consequentialism that explains the moral 'rightness' of actions in terms of outcomes. This differs from nonconsequentialist or deontological (duty based) thinking which contends that factors besides an action's consequences determine whether it is right or wrong.

Richard Haass proposes that consequentialist theory is grounded upon the belief that the sole criterion for decision-making is that actions have the intended effect of producing a greater balance of good consequences over bad ones than any other policy option.[35]  Haas claims that what distinguishes deontological theories from consequentialist ones is not necessarily a lack of belief on the part of the utilitarians that a standard of ethical obligation exists. What may distinguish the two types of theories is instead the political relevance of such a standard. Even if consequentialists believe that humans are capable of discerning principles of obligation that are formed independently of the ends they bring about, these individuals hold that these principles are, for whatever reasons, simply not applicable to the pragmatic world of politics.

Consequentialism and utilitarianism have room for both 'common sense morality' and a more rational moral response to difficult ethical dilemmas.  Common sense morality should not be confused with intuitionism that judges a particular activity to be intrinsically wrong without any further complex rationalisation. This is discussed more fully later in an analysis of R. M. Hare's Two-Tiered Model of Utilitarianism. Hare sometimes uses the term 'intuitionism' to refer to the outputs of commonsense morality.  Intuitionists say moral principles, rules or judgements appeal to a sense of reasonableness, and that there are apparent truths that may be thought of as being self-evident.[36]

Critics of intuitionism say the alleged self-evident nature of such judgements is questionable.  They argue that intuitionism has no underlying rationale, that intuitionism has nothing helpful to say about resolving moral conflict and that it is

---

33  Samual Scheffler, *Consequentialism and Its Critics* (Oxford: Oxford University Press, 1988), p. 2.

34  For a thorough analysis of the nonconsequentialist position see F Kamm, 'Responsibility and Collaboration,' *Philosophy and Public Affairs* 28, no. 3 (1999): pp. 169–206.

35  Richard Haas, 'Reinhold Niebuhr's Christian Pragmatism: A Principled Alternative to Consequentialism,' *The Review of Politics* 61, no. 4 (1999): p. 609.   See also William K. Frankena, *Ethics* (New Jersey: En&wood Cliffs, Prentice-Hall, 1973), p. 14.

36  D McNaughton, 'Intuitionism,' in *The Blackwell Guide to Ethical Theory*, ed. Hugh LaFollette (Oxford: Blackwell Publishers, 2000), pp. 268–71.

unable to contribute much to general moral knowledge. Intuitionism, for example, cannot explain why it is wrong to torture somebody. Intuitionism is a kind of non-consequentialist or deontological moral thinking. A utilitarian view that torture is morally wrong has nothing to do with some form of intuition; rather, so-called 'common sense' morality condemns torture or child abuse as being wrong because of the negative outcomes of such acts.

Such terrible acts will have significant consequences for the individuals suffering the abuse. Any society that knows this activity is happening and does nothing to stop it must be condemned as being morally deficient. Not addressing human rights abuse does not increase utility; therefore, common sense morality dictates that we must stop human rights abuse.

Noel Preston proposes that a consequentialist theory is one that identifies some state of affairs to be the best state of affairs and then identifies the right action to be the action that best promotes the attainment of such a state of affairs. This ethical position is based primarily on a calculation of the moral good relative to the consequences of an act.[37]

By contrast, he says, non-consequentialist thinking refers to a sense of duty, the idea of obligation or principle to prescribe the ethical decision. Non-consequentialists encourage us to do the right thing simply because it is intuitively the right thing to do.[38] That is, do not torture people because torturing is morally wrong. Consequentialism is concerned about the outcomes or consequences of acts, which in turn will determine the moral rightness of the acts. Marcia Baron suggests a more complicated view. That is, acts are neither intrinsically nor inherently right or wrong. It depends on what the outcomes of acts are.[39]

Many consequentialists would argue that it is morally acceptable to apply the death penalty to convicted murderers. Firstly, putting murderers to death guarantees that they will never murder again; therefore, innocent lives will be saved. Secondly, capital punishment must deter at least some people from becoming murderers in the first place. According to consequentialist thinking, the benefits of capital punishment (the saving of innocent lives) outweigh the costs (the life of the murderer). Applying the above rationale to genocide and other types of mass killings means that putting murderers to death will save many lives.

Of course, it could be argued that because there is no absolute guarantee that a convicted murderer will murder again then one cannot assume that killing the murderer will save other innocent lives. There is also little empirical evidence to suggest that the death penalty actually lowers the overall murder rate. Approximately 2 percent

---

37  Noel Preston, *Understanding Ethics* (Sydney: The Federation Press, 1996), p. 40.

38  Ibid., p. 45.

39  Marcia Baron, 'Kanatian Ethics,' in *Three Methods of Ethics*, ed. M. Baron, P. Pettit, and M Slote (Oxford: Blackwell Publishers, 1997), pp. 7–10. Baron provides a comprehensive discussion of the differences and similarities between act and rule consequentialism. See also, Piers Benn, *Ethics. Fundamentals of Philosophy* (London: Mcgill-Queen's Universtity Press, 1998), p. 72. and Joseph DeMarco, *Moral Theory: A Contemporary Approach* (London: Jones and Bartlett Publishers, 1996), p. 132.

of the human population have a predisposition to be aggressive psychopaths – the modern term is sociopath – who will kill without regret or remorse.[40]   Incarcerating such individuals in jail does not guarantee that they will never be released or that they will not escape custody to murder again.

Questions of scale and levels of risk are important.  Whilst one could argue that we should try to rehabilitate then release convicted one-time killers back into society, the risk that these people will kill again is far less compared to releasing those who have killed many times.  When mass murders occur and large numbers of victims are the result then premeditated killing is the primary goal of the killer/s.  Many lives will be saved if these people are permanently stopped from carrying out their genocidal activities.  The deterrent value of removing killers from society in this way is difficult to absolutely quantify, but it cannot be argued that eliminating habitual killers will not save at least their potential victims.

An important feature of consequentialism is its fundamental denial of what is known as the act-omission distinction.  For the consequentialist, the ultimate criterion of moral requirement turns on the consequences of the courses of action we adopt. Doing nothing or doing very little when much more could be done entails a moral penalty because in the words of Peter Singer, 'Doing nothing...is itself a deliberate choice'.[41]   Where one is capable of doing good deeds then one should do good deeds to the best of one's capacity and capability.  There is a significant moral requirement to act, and to act quickly, in order to stop arbitrary killing, if we decide that such acts are morally unacceptable in the first place.  Not acting decisively or effectively in such circumstances is an omission of action for which we are individually and collectively morally responsible.

Consequentialism and utilitarianism are distinct, in that one may be a consequentialist without being a utilitarian.  The issue of utility and the greater good is a vital one for consequentialists, yet there is a practical problem in applying such theories.  For example, what is this greater good regarding military intervention on humanitarian grounds?

Does the greater good refer to those being directly persecuted, are we talking about our own state's greater good, or are we talking about humanity in general? And what is this vague notion of 'humanity' anyway?  Utilitarians will say that we are talking about the greatest good for the most people, but which people are we talking about?

Suppose that the number of people who will benefit from military intervention is estimated to be more than the number of people who may become conflict casualties or is more than those who will suffer generally as a result of military action.  It is not unreasonable to suggest that such estimations have some validity – at least some of the time.  According to utilitarian thinking, military intervention in this situation would be warranted because, as a consequence of direct action, utility is

40   Dave Grossman, *On Killing* (New York: little Brown and Company, 1996), p. 180.

41   Peter Singer, *Practical Ethics*, 2 ed. (Cambridge: University Press, 1993), pp. 208–09.

maximised. Military intervention would not be warranted if more rescuers would be killed or wounded than the number of people being rescued...unless overall utility is enhanced.

This is a very difficult measure of effectiveness because it relies on anticipated negative humanitarian outcomes should intervention not be undertaken. For example, there may be heavy loss of life to interventionists, to belligerents and to the belligerent's victims during a particular conflict. The problem is that non-intervention may cause an even greater humanitarian disaster with even more casualties and deliberate abuse.

Other belligerents may be encouraged by the international community not acting effectively and by the lack of all round accountability. The international community and belligerents are both morally accountable for the existence of severe human rights abuse: the international community for failing to act to stop atrocities, and belligerents for carrying out atrocities in the first place. It is not enough to simply blame belligerents for atrocities. We are all to blame for not responding directly and effectively to stop such activities.

When discussing own-side casualty risks there is the problem of coming to grips with the potential scale of interventionist's losses compared to the number of people such intervention aims to save. Military intervention may result in interventionists suffering many casualties in order to alleviate the plight of those suffering extreme abuse, yet the principle of utility is again useful as a moral guide. The question of whether military intervention is really the only effective option remaining to address humanitarian outrage is a difficult one. Would it not be better for the intervening forces not to intervene and to allow other non-violent humanitarian action to be instigated or sustained? There is no clear utilitarian answer to this question.

Yes, it may be best to give all other reasonable attempts to halt humanitarian abuse a chance to work. When other strategies have been tried and they just do not work then utilitarians will say that there is a moral justification, and therefore a requirement, for military intervention to take place. We need to be careful in relegating the use of force as an absolute last option because it may actually be better to respond forcibly immediately if it can be reasonably anticipated that this would immediately stop the majority of the killing and the abuse.

Despite some utilitarians talking about overall cost/benefit style analysis in these situations the unpredictability of these variables makes it very difficult to accurately predict outcomes. Whatever means are used to calculate the greater good, a response decision should be primarily based on providing immediate relief to those being seriously abused and it must consider the enhancement of overall utility. Shelly Kagan argues that a valid objection to utilitarianism and its consequentialist component is that it is impossible to know the future.[42] She says that all the talk about the consequences of military action or other international action intended to help those in dire need is really just estimation and projection. Often it's outright guesswork.

---

42   Shelly Kagan, *Normative Ethics* (Oxford: WestviewPress, 1998), p. 64.

To try to place an 'objective' spin on consequentialism is at odds with the reality that consequentialism is based on guesswork derived from assuming various outcomes will happen.[43] Most consequentialists accept that their outcome projections are nothing more than dedicated guesswork – to do otherwise would be to ignore the literal meaning of forecasting. There may be bad effects in the short or long term from a particular act totally at odds to what any counting of consequence may seem to suggest. One specific objection is that consequentialism may therefore be unusable as a moral guide to action. This argument is as follows.

At best, consequence projections are based on historical or regional trends, and other on-the-ground assessments. Humanitarian disasters each have their own special difficulties and complexities that make such assessments and projections of consequences difficult. This means that the international community can never be absolutely certain as to what the consequences of its acts will be. For example, NATO's air campaign against the Serbs and Slobodan Milosevic in the early months of 1999 was intended to quickly halt ethnic cleansing activities in Kosovo. It took seventy-eight days of the concentrated use of massive air power to stop Serb activity. During this time the Serbs forcibly expelled over 850,000 ethnic Albanian Kosovars from Kosovo. [44][45]

The difficulty noted in such objections is real, but this does not mean that this, or any other normative ethical theory, is unusable as a moral guide. It means that the expected utility of an action cannot be assumed to be totally accurate. Virtually all ethical theories give the consequences of an act considerable weight with the goodness of consequence being a major factor relevant to the moral status of acts. To reject utilitarianism on the basis that consequence is unpredictable means to reject most other ethical theories as well.

One may still apply consequentialism and other ethical theories to morally challenge human activity because human response is reactive to what could happen as well as to what actually happens. Much about military intervention for humanitarian purposes is uncertain, but such uncertainty must not lead to paralysis. We can still make rational estimates of the probability of actions having particular consequences. Those who are subject to atrocity depend utterly on the application of such rationale processes.

Consequentialism is important when considering military intervention on humanitarian grounds. It is important because the consequences of action or non-action are of direct relevance to both the intervening forces and to those being abused. If military force is used, the intervening forces may suffer casualties as a result of

43   Peter Railton, 'Alienation, Consequentialism, and the Demands of Morality,' in *Ethics: The Big Questions*, ed. James P Sterba (Malden, Massachusetts: Blackwell Publishers Ltd, 1998), pp. 164–67.

44   Australian Broadcasting Commission News Report, 'Albanian Kosovar Ethnic Cleansing,' (1999).

45   (ICG) International Crisis Group, 'Annual Report 2000: Review of 1999, Plans for 2000,' (2000): p. 10.

intervention. If military force is not used, the abuse will most likely continue for those seeking relief from persecution.

Fundamental to how utilitarians see the moral rightness or wrongness of human behaviour is the question of whether the ends justify the means. For example, could it be morally defensible to support the use of nuclear, chemical or biological warfare to stop a despot and his or her supporters from carrying out severe human rights abuse? Why not use any means of stopping dictators and psychopaths from their activities?

Utilitarians, consequentialists, and Just-war theorists would generally reject the use of such weapons on the basis that they cause 'unnecessary suffering' to their victims. They may also reject such weapons because their use would be deemed a disproportionate response even against extreme levels of humanitarian abuse. There are other reasons why such weapons would most likely not be used. The longer term ramifications of using nuclear, biological or chemical weapons on a mass scale are simply incalculable. Despite these uncertainties it does not mean that there are absolutely no circumstances under which WMDs might be used.

These types of weapons may used if circumstances dictate that they were part of a proportionate response to unprovoked aggression, or where overall utility is deemed to be significantly enhanced. It is not impossible to imagine a scenario where this could happen. The Israelis declared that they would not rule out using nuclear weapons against the Iraqis if Saddam Hussein used his chemical weapons during the Gulf war of 1991. Britain, France, the US and others in the nuclear club retain such weapons in case they are subjected to massive military aggression.

Those on the receiving end of severe humanitarian abuses will have an entirely different perspective of proportionality, and whether or not a particular act is somehow deemed to be necessary to halt the atrocities being conducted against them. They have little interest in what means are used. They just want an end to the abuse being inflicted upon them.

## Utilitarianism and Humanitarian Intervention

Fredrick Rosen and David Cooper claim that Utilitarianism is the view that we are obliged to maximise utility. Utility has been classified variously as happiness, pleasure, wellbeing or 'preference satisfaction'.[46][47] Whatever the precise understanding of

---

46  Fredrick Rosen, 'Individual Sacrifice and the Greatest Happiness: Betham on Utility and Rights,' *Utilitas* 10, no. 2 (1999): pp. 130–32. Rosen's article attempts to counter the conventional view of utilitarianism with respect to the distribution of utility. In doing so, he considers the most common criticism of utilitarianism. That is, utilitarianism allows for, and may even require, the sacrifice of some members of society in order to increase overall happiness. See Ross Harrison, 'Rosen's Sacrifice of Utility,' *Utilitas* 10, no. 2 (1999): pp. 159–61. Harison disagrees with Rosen's analysis and he supports the conventional view of utilitarianism that individual sacrifice is required for overall utility.

47  David Cooper, *Ethics. The Classic Readings* (Massachusetts: Blackwell Publishers, 1998), p. 194.

utility, utilitarianism recommends that there should be as much of it as possible. It also holds that utility is the sole ultimate good so that all else that is good has value only to the extent of promoting utility. Robin Barrow summarises John Stuart Mill's theory of Utilitarianism as the assignment of moral goodness or rightness to only one kind of consequence – effects on overall well-being. [48]

Utilitarianism contends that an action is morally right, indeed obligatory, if it produces good or maximum utility for all person affected by the action. Most utilitarians will say that NATO action in 1999 to stop Serb atrocities against the Kosovars was morally justifiable because it halted gross human rights abuses in the tiny Yugoslav state. Coercive intervention, in this case, could be said to have ultimately produced a good utilitarian outcome.

There is an important moral distinction about what is good and what is best. I have argued previously that the NATO air campaign in Kosovo did not achieve the best possible outcome. Significant numbers of Kosovar casualties resulted from the international community's refusal to use ground troops. A 'good' utilitarian outcome in this case could have been much better had ground troops and overwhelming military force been used. The fundamental idea of utilitarianism is that the moral rightness of our actions is determined by the effects these actions have on the well being of others and ourselves.[49] Utilitarianism is not a single theory, rather it refers to a cluster of theories that are variations on a theme. Richard Frey proposes that this theme revolves around acts and their consequences, and it involves at least five components. [50] An outline of his argument is as follows;

> Firstly, there is the consequence component. This is where the rightness or wrongness of an act is tied to the production of good and bad consequences. Some utilitarians say that there is something inherently good or bad in particular acts because of the sorts of outcomes these acts produce. Others argue that acts are not themselves good or bad, but that outcomes will primarily determine goodness.

NATO action in Kosovo was morally flawed, not because the use of force is wrong (although some people will say that the use of force is always wrong) but because limiting the assault essentially to air power alone resulted in many Kosovar casualties. By most reasonable cost/benefit calculations – utilitarians strongly favour such calculations – the

---

48   Robin Barrow, *Utilitarianism: A Contemporary Statement* (Vermont: Edward Elgar Publishing Company, 1991), p. 39.

49   Bernard Arthur Owen Williams, *Morality: An Introduction to Ethics, Harper Essays in Philosophy* (New York,: Harper & Row, 1972), p. 93.   Contemporary philosophical thinking suggests that there exists act-consequentialism and rule-consequentialism. This book essentially deals with, and refers to, act-consequentialism.

50   Richard Frey, *Utility and Rights* (Minneapolis: University of Minnesota Press, 1984), p. 4.

introduction of large numbers of ground forces supported by a massive air campaign would have reduced the overall numbers of people killed in Kosovo.[51]

It is true that this action would most likely have cost interventionist casualties, but surely not nearly as many as the 100,000 missing, presumed dead, Kosovars or the forced displacement of a further 850,000 men, women and children. In the end, the lives of the Kosovars were deemed by NATO and the international community to be less important than interventionist lives.

Secondly, there is the value component. This is where the goodness and badness of consequences is evaluated by means of some standard intrinsic value of goodness. For example, few people would disagree that torture is wrong, violent aggression is wrong and not doing anything to stop such activities when they could be stopped is wrong. Similarly, most people would say that saving human life is a good thing to do and that helping others in desperate need is good. Therefore, Serb atrocities against the Kosovars was wrong and the international community's desire to stop such atrocities was morally right.

Thirdly, there is the range component. This is where the consequences of acts affect everyone and not just the agent in the determination of moral rightness. NATO's decision only to use air power against the Serbs in Yugoslavia in an effort to oust Slobodan Milosevic was morally flawed when applying the range criteria. Not only did bombing downtown Belgrade not immediately stop Serb atrocities against the Kosovars, but Serbs who were not directly involved in the killing campaign in Kosovo bore the brunt of the NATO attacks.

Elliot Abrams argues that 'We refused to interpose our troops between the Serbian soldiers and their Kosovar civilian victims. We chose instead a means that guaranteed very low American casualties, at the price of vastly inflating the damage done in Serbia and Kosovo. In the context of a 'humanitarian' intervention, this was a problematic choice. It was not novel, for we have been doing this in the Balkans all along: too little too late.'[52]   For big-picture utilitarians this may not morally be a problem providing overall utility was enhanced. They will argue that eventually Milosevic was forced to withdraw his troops from Kosovo as a result of NATO action.

This ignores the important differentiation between what is unavoidable and what is unnecessary. One could argue that the loss of some Kosovar, interventionist, and Serb lives as a result of a blitzkrieg approach to intervention in Kosovo would have been unavoidable but necessary to get the job done in a much shorter time frame. According to this line of thinking, the large loss of Kosovo lives as a result of relying on air power alone was avoidable and unnecessary when the use of ground troops could have reduced the overall death rates.

The fourth component is the maximising principle. One should seek to maximise that which the adopted standard of goodness identifies as being intrinsically good.

---

51   Australian Broadcasting Commission News Report, 'Nato Will Not Use Ground Troops,' (1999).

52   Elliot Abrams, 'Just War. Just Means?,' *National Review* 51, no. 12 (1999): pp. 16–18.

The humanitarian outcome of international intervention in Kosovo was not the best possible outcome because NATO refused to use ground troops, utility was not maximised and many people died.

Finally, the fifth component is the welfare element of utilitarianism. Robert Goodin says that welfare-utilitarians talk about the satisfaction of interests rather than mere preference satisfaction.[53]   This means that welfare utilitarianism would suppress short sighted preference satisfaction in favour of protecting people's long term welfare interests. 'Ideal utilitarians' – those centred on a notion of preference satisfaction – would say that NATO action in Kosovo did what it was supposed to. It stopped Serb atrocities being conducted in Kosovo.

Welfare-utilitarians will disagree about the enhancement of utility in this case. They will say that not only should the Serbs have been stopped from conducting their ethnic cleansing activities in Kosovo but that more generalised welfare issues such as shelter, sustenance, protection from further violence and so on are equally important. These must receive as much, if not more, attention by those who believe that a moral obligation to help those being seriously abused exists.

Welfare-utilitarians propose that there must surely be more to utility than what people immediately want for happiness. This is done by abstracting from people's actual wants, in a particular moment in time, to the more generalised welfare interests giving the entire notion of utility the broader appeal of having some practical content and reality. Individual and immediate happiness is important, but equally so is the broader notion of welfarism.

Utilitarianism sits comfortably with the basic notion that cross-border military intervention on humanitarian grounds may sometimes be required. Applying the consequence component means that if military intervention is not undertaken then significant numbers of people will probably die. The welfare element of utilitarianism is concerned not only about the numbers of people involved but how these people will suffer or die.

Entire communities and social structures are directly at risk if humanitarian abuse is allowed to continue unabated. The utility component refers to maximising accepted standards of goodness for the sake of the greatest number of people affected by the act of military intervention. Many critics of utilitarianism are concerned that the theory is overly permissive. Some are concerned that it is overly demanding. The concern is that, rather than follow the so-called rules of ethics that utilitarians claim are important, they resort to their own kinds of cost/benefit calculations that allow them to make exceptions here, there and everywhere. Nicholas Fotion outlines some of the core criticisms of utilitarianism that relate to these cost/benefit calculations as follows;

A promise is a promise, but if the calculations show that more benefit will come from not telling the truth then the truth need not be told. Truth telling is truth telling, but if the

---

53   Robert Goodin, 'Utility and the Good,' in *A Companion to Ethics*, ed. Peter Singer (Oxford: Basil Blackwell Ltd, 1991), pp. 243–45.

calculations show that more benefit will come from not telling the truth then the truth need not be told. Killing is killing, but if....Well, you get the picture.[54]

Some utilitarians will say that the so-called permissiveness of this ethical theory is actually a positive aspect of utilitarianism because this makes it possible to morally reconcile the use of extreme measures in order to satisfy a greater overall utility. For example, on the final night of Gulf War I and within hours of the cease fire, two US Air Force bombers dropped specially designed 5,000 pound bombs on a command bunker fifteen miles north west of Baghdad in a deliberate attempt to kill Saddam Hussein.

It could be said that this act did not conform to the intent of proportionality, which holds that in cases where the use of force is justified it cannot be employed in absolutely any measure. Yet it did conform to the idea that, while minimal force should always be used, some military tasks may require a disproportionate degree of minimum force to be applied in specific circumstances.[55] The utilitarian is therefore able to morally justifying such a raid.

Precisely targeting Saddam Hussein away from the civilian centres of Baghdad also conforms to the notion of discrimination according to Just-war theory. That is, force is morally justified if it can be employed in a discriminating manner.[56] Ignoring for a moment the likely death of Hussein's accompanying military entourage, the bunker cleaners, the children playing outside the bunker door and other civilians near the structure, one could justifiably claim that discrimination was being applied during this military operation.

Any others killed as a result of this attack on Saddam Hussein would be seen as tragic but unavoidable collateral damage. It could also have been much worse if the attack was carried out in the centre of Baghdad where Hussein was more vulnerable. The U.S. Air Force took the position in certain briefings that Iraqi civilians were not entirely innocent. Gerald Draper points out that in one such briefing, a senior Air Force officer defended this position on the grounds that '[Iraqi civilians] do live there, and ultimately the people have some control over what goes on in their country.' [57]

Again, the utilitarian position has considerable flexibility in how it deals with such matters. The idea of proportionality in response is an important one, although it is difficult to pin down exactly what this means. For example, one could use an act for act rationale as a basis for a proportional response. If Hizballah guerrillas fire

---

54   Nicholas Fotion, 'A Utilitarian Defence of Just War Theory,' *Synthesis Philosophica* (1997): p. 208.

55   Robert L. Phillips, 'Just-War Theory,' in *Life and Death. A Reader in Moral Problems*, ed. Louise Pojman (Singapore: Jones and Bartlett Publishers, 1993), pp. 482–85.

56   Ibid., p. 484.

57   Kai Draper, 'Self-Defence, Collective Obligation, and Non-Combatant Liability,' *Social Theory and Practice* 24, no. 1 (1998): pp. 57–81. See also, Barton Gellman, 'Storm Damage in the Gulf: U.S. Strategy Went Beyond Strictly Military Targets,' *Washington Post, National Weekly ed*, 8–14 July 1991.

mortars into Israel then the Israeli Air Force responds by carrying out a bombing raid on guerrilla training bases just outside Israel.

Another approach is to try to look at the larger picture. Sending in the NATO air force to bomb the Serbs into submission was, to some utilitarians, a proportionate response to the relentless Serb atrocities being committed to non-Serbs throughout Yugoslavia. Proportionality is not just about the excessive use of force. It is also about the inadequate use of force. Therefore, international action against the Serbs in Kosovo was not proportional because an inadequate level of force was applied against the wrong targets. I develop this theme later in this chapter.

The matter is further complicated by specific acts of atrocities where one would be hard pressed to come up with some sort of morally appropriate, proportional response. Different sorts of atrocities and war crimes shock people to varying degrees that will lead to different perceptions about what is and what is not morally proportional as a response option. The U.S. President, Bill Clinton told the British Prime Minister, Tony Blair, 'If people saw (the Serbs) tying groups of 15 people together and setting them alight, they would wonder why we didn't flatten the place.'[58]

There should be two important preconditions on having a permissive approach to an ethical stance on humanitarian intervention. Firstly, whatever moral theory is applied it must primarily consider the welfare of those suffering human rights abuse and the welfare of those likely to suffer abuse in the future if belligerents are not stopped. Secondly, the moral position must not only consider the plight of those being or likely to be abused (the world is full of concerned citizens considering others) but it must actually do something to successfully alleviate such suffering – and it must do it quickly.

*A Two-Tiered Model of Utilitarianism*

One may intuitively be affronted by the use of violence to address severe human rights abuse, but at the same time rationalise that unless force is used many people will needlessly suffer and die. William Shaw and R.M. Hare calls this a 'two-tiered model of utilitarianism'.[59] Hare argues that there are two basic levels of ethical thinking. The intuitive and the critical.[60]

His approach supports the view that it is possible to ethically rationalise undertaking certain acts during conflict as being necessary despite concern about the actual morality of carrying out such acts. At the intuitive level, our moral thinking responds to a commonsense view of right and wrong. It is commonsense to most people that torture, illegal killing and rape are wrong. Commonsense not because of some 'irrational instinct' but because the outcomes of these acts really are terrible

---

58 'The Morality of Warfare: Is Closer Necessarily Worse.'

59 William Shaw, *Contemporary Ethics: Taking Account of Utilitarianism.* (Oxford: Blackwell Publishers, 1999), p. 159.

60 Richard Hare, *Moral Thinking : Its Levels, Method, and Point* (Oxford: Oxford University Press, 1981), pp. 25–27.

and they do not enhance utility. We are non-critical in our thinking processes about moral issues and in everyday life it works well most of the time. Most people intuitively consider that killing, ethnic cleansing, rape and torture to be morally abhorrent acts.

When intuitive thinking is deemed to be unsatisfactory or inadequate then a second level of moral thinking is said to apply. For example, during war soldiers must kill, therefore an intuitive obstruction to killing must be overcome. Nicholas Fotion et al refer to Hare's utilitarian theory. This is the critical level of moral thinking where moral decisions are made according to 'logic and facts'.[61] Those who support this approach to moral thinking suggest that intuitive thinking is applied first, but when the moral choices become too difficult a second, more critical level of morals thinking kicks in. Either this second level subsumes the first or the first level just switches off.

There is another possibility. That is, neither level is subsumed nor switched off instead they both work together. At the so-called critical level one could rationalise killing another person despite being instinctively morally appalled at having to do so. For example, suppose that someone was physically attacking you and your family with the clear intent of killing you all. Assume that the attacker will actually kill you if you do not kill him or her. There are two possible response options you could take. You may decide not to resist physically because you are appalled at the thought of violence, and you simply could not bring yourself to kill another human being. In this case the attacker kills you and then your family.

The second option, if you have the means, is to kill the attacker. You could, of course try to disable the attacker but your chances of survival (and your family's survival) will be much less against a stronger and determined belligerent. At the critical level of morals thinking you morally justify your actions as self-defence, survival and protection of the family unit. Essentially you have rationalised that you must take another life in order to save your own life and the lives of your family. This is despite the fact that you may be morally appalled at having to make such a choice. At the instinctive level you are appalled, but at the rational level you do what you must to protect your family.

The application of a two-tiered approach to morals thinking is a useful adjunct to the utilitarian's moral view of life for two reasons. Firstly, it is not practical to calculate the consequences beforehand of every moral choice we need to make. It is not practical because of all the conflicting thoughts of competition, hurt, love, desire, thoughts of vengeance, lack of time to decide and so on which would influence, perhaps detrimentally, our moral choice and effective utility. It is more realistic to be initially guided by a broad set of commonsense principles that have been proven over many decades simply to be good.

Secondly, there are times when reacting intuitively (for example, you are intuitively against aggression and violence) may actually produce a morally

---

61   Nicholas Fotion and Gerald Elfstrom, *Military Ethics Guidelines for Peace and War* (London: Routledge and Kegan Paul, 1996), p. 13.

unacceptable outcome. That is, we do have a moral obligation to protect those who are totally dependent on us for safety and security. So, if we stand back and allow them to be abused or killed because of our initial instinctive reluctance to use force to stop the abusers then we have failed in our moral duty of care.

At a critical level where reflective and considered thought is brought into play there is a moral justification for using lethal force even when intuitively we are reluctant to do so. This justification could be a desperate humanitarian situation where intuitive morals thinking must be complemented by critical thinking for the greatest utility. That is, in order to save large numbers of people from being abused or killed, military intervention must take place.

A valid criticism of the two-tiered approach to morals thinking is that it may be altogether too convenient to subsume our intuitive morality for the sake of a more ideologically palatable moral choice. We may call this an application of logic or addressing the facts but we still end up, as the previous example shows, killing others. It is possible to be morally appalled at having to kill another human yet we may also feel morally justified in doing so. We may have no option other than to use lethal force in order to enhance overall utility, but this does not mean that we are any less morally appalled at having to use such force in the first place. In this case, both tiers of morals thinking are present and they work together.

We may be appalled at the requirement to use lethal force to stop ruthless belligerents from killing and torturing their victims, but at the same time we rationalise that unless we respond in this way, many innocent people will die. The need to use lethal force in order to stop atrocities from happening causes a great deal of moral anguish in a civil society.

## Humanitarian Obligation: Scope and Limits

If morality is generally defined as the overall promotion of some good then obligation could be thought of as an outcome imperative. This means that there is a binding requirement or promise as to duty. A moral obligation involves a requirement or duty to promote overall good. Empathy has an association with moral obligation although it is usually considered in an aesthetics context. Collective and personal altruism is primed by empathy, which results in a sense of moral duty but, as Nancy Sherman points out, in terms of the formal discourse of humanitarian intervention, empathy is not a clear player.[62]

Nevertheless, in morality, as in daily life, empathy or its absence affects our conduct towards others. Noel Preston directly links empathy and compassion. He argues that being human means being ethical (and therefore most humans have at least a measure of empathy and compassion to the welfare of others) otherwise we

---

62  Nancy Sherman, 'Empathy, Respect, and Humanitarian Intervention' (paper presented at the Joint Services Conference on Professional Ethics, National Defence University, Washington D.C, 30–31 January 1997).

are mere robot imitators of those around us.[63]  Mere imitation is clearly not the case for most people where individualism takes on its literal meaning.  Many humans also have a strong sense of community and collectiveness but this is different from blind herd instinct where individualism is mostly totally subsumed.  Empathy is an important primer to moral obligation.  Without empathy it is much more difficult to rationalise an obligation to help others.

Ralph Ross proposes that we have a fundamental moral obligation to behave in certain ways to others no matter how we feel about them and the likelihood of behaving toward them as we ought hinges on our feelings about them.[64]  But, as he points out, there are limits to the extent of empathy.  Empathy between feudal lord and serf, or master and slave is different compared to the empathy commonly shared (or assumed) between those of equal social rank.  Despite variations to the degree of empathy felt between humans few would reasonably argue that some empathy or connectiveness does not exist even if one is master and the other serf or slave.

If one subscribes to the notion that there are at least some universal humanitarian ideals – protection of the weak, care for those in need and retribution for violators of humanitarian law – then allowing extreme human rights abuses to continue challenges the fundamental notion that we live in a caring and humane world in the first place.  Time or distance should not be a barrier if we say that the welfare of other human beings is important.  We cannot morally argue that just because we live in Australia the humanitarian crisis and brutalities in Africa are irrelevant simply because of our distance away from the conflict area.  Extreme humanitarian abuse is wrong whether we live in Australia or Africa.

Forcible humanitarian intervention is fraught with danger.  The risks are not only of conflict casualties but that interventionist forces may find themselves reacting to political and strategic imperatives that have little to do with why they intervened in the first place.  In a less than ideal world, political and strategic imperatives all too often supersede humanitarian intent. The timing of humanitarian relief efforts is crucial.

UN operations in Somalia, Bosnia Herzegovina and Northern Iraq focused the attention of the international community on the possibility of using force to resolve situations of humanitarian crisis.  Yet the United Nations, paralysed and ineffectual during the Cold War, is just as confused about its role as a peacekeeper in the post-Cold War period.

The UN's overall management of military intervention for humanitarian reasons has been abysmal.  The Security Council did not intervene in Rwanda where over one million helpless people were killed, it did very little to confront the Bosnian Serbs during the first three to five years of the Balkan's war, and it refuses to address the conflicts occurring in Liberia or Chechnya – just to name a few dismal failures.  In Somalia, the UN sponsored forces lashed out, killing hundreds in a politically

---

63  Preston, *Understanding Ethics*.

64  Ralph Ross, *Obligation. A Social Theory* (Michigan: University of Michigan Press, 1970), p. 181.

motivated reactive response which had little to do with why they were there in the first place. They then departed in a huff, leaving the Somali people to their fate.

Julia Groenewold et al argue that the humanitarian action (UNOSOM) clearly failed in Somalia because no one understood what the troops were there for.[65] There is almost invariably an incompatibility between, on the one hand, prosecuting those guilty of war crimes and, on the other hand, reconciling the factions involved in the conflict. The American efforts in Somalia to capture and punish Aideed for his role in a June 1993 ambush that killed twenty-four Pakistani peacekeepers and the violent clashes with Aideed's supporters that resulted from these efforts are a good illustration of a recurrent dilemma that peacemakers face in resolving civil wars.[66]

### Realists, Pacifists and Others In-between

The ethical dilemmas of cross-border military intervention for humanitarian reasons are many and varied. Realists question the basic premise that morality has anything to do with military engagement in the first place and they say that this type of intervention in another state's affairs contravenes the notion of independent statehood. Many pacifists object to the use of military force on the assumption that physical force creates more problems than it tries to solve, and that it is morally wrong anyway to use directed force.

Just-war theorists and utilitarians support a view somewhere in the middle. That is, sometimes it is morally appropriate to use force, particularly in response to threat, but at other times it is not appropriate where the anticipated solution or outcome would cause more harm than good. Brian Orend outlines a useful synthesis of Kant's Just-war theory.[67] This section will address these three fundamental positions because they form useful moral and non-moral responses to questions about whether the international community should consider intervening in another state's affairs for altruistic reasons.

Realists are people whose interest is focused on things they consider to be actual or real as distinguished from abstractions. They claim a practical rather than a moral view of human behaviour, and they say that we should be more interested in representing things as they really are rather than as we think or would like them to be. Michael Smith proposes that many realists argue that moral claims such as 'torturing people is wrong' and 'helping those in need is right' are in error because when we engage in moral talk we presuppose that rightness and wrongness are features that acts are capable of possessing. Realists say that it is not possible for acts to possess

65  Julia Groenewold, Eve Porter, and Mâedecins sans frontiáeres (Association), *World in Crisis. The Politics of Survival at the End of the Twentieth Century.* (New York: Routledge, 1997), pp. 100–15.

66  Evans Ernest, 'The Clinton Administration and Peacemaking in Civil Conflicts,' *World Affairs Policy Journal* 159, no. 119 (1996): pp. 1–2.

67  See Brian Orend, 'Kant's Just War Theory,' *Journal of the History of Philosophy* 37, no. 2 (1999): pp. 323–53. for a comprehensive overview of Kant and Just War theory.

such features.[68]   Their focus is on interests – specifically national interests – rather than ideologies, values or beliefs.

Pacifists support a policy of establishing and maintaining universal peace. They adhere to the idea that violence is morally wrong and therefore unjustifiable; and that international disputes must be settled by arbitration rather than by conflict. Just-war theorists contend that military engagement and conflict generally is morally justifiable providing certain criteria are satisfied. They believe in ROE, an appropriate response, formal declarations of war by legitimate authorities, that engagement must have a high likelihood of success, and that the consequence of conflict should be that it benefits more people than it harms.

The Just-war theorists' moral thinking is in many ways similar to the utilitarian view of the world.   Similar in outputs and similar in the sorts of factual considerations taken into account, although not in fundamental principle.   The three positions presented in this chapter are not a defence of these particular philosophical stances. They are moral views defended by others and they have convergent practical inputs that are applicable to situations where military intervention is morally justifiable. My focus is on welfare utilitarianism and in applying it rigorously in defence of human rights.

*Realism and Military Intervention*

Extreme realists reject the notion that ethics and morality have any place during military engagements at all.   In effect this is a position of moral nihilism.  The claim that morality has no place in war is ambiguous.   Richard Wasserstrom argues that the claim may be descriptive, analytic or prescriptive but it is not definitive.   It would be descriptive if it were true that matters relating to conflict consistently end up being decided solely on grounds of national interest or expediency.   This clearly is not the case for every conflict, and it is particularly not the case for revolution or civil conflict where a confusing mixture of ethnic, religious, or ideological reasons is the primary imperative for conflict. [69]

The analytic point is not that morality ought not be used in war but that it cannot be used. This position is difficult to defend if, as at least some realists say, morality actually does exist outside of conflict.    Realists have a dubious answer to this problem by maintaining that military engagement somehow nullifies morality.   The prescriptive claim – the national interest, not morality, ought to determine policies in respect to conflict – is also difficult to come to grips with.   For example, the primary objective of dropping the atomic bombs on the Japanese cities of Hiroshima and Nagasaki during World War II (WW II) was ostensibly to limit potential allied casualties during the closing stages of the war.[70]

---

68   Michael Smith, 'The Blackwell Guide to Ethical Theory,' in *Blackwell Philosophy Guides*, ed. Hugh LaFollette (Oxford, UK ; Malden, Mass., USA: Blackwell, 2001), p. 15.

69   Richard Wasserstrom, *War and Morality* (California: Wadsworth, 1970), pp. 80–81.

70   Ibid., p. 83.

Yet, to say that this was only done to satisfy the requirements of the national interest assumes that there was no moral or ethical impediment to sending many tens, perhaps hundreds of thousands of allied troops to certain death or injury in an invasion of the Japanese mainland if these weapons had not been used. The stark separation of national interests and ethical imperatives in this way is difficult to defend if one asserts that human life has, at least on some occasions, a moral value.

Realists believe they have good reasons for sometimes excluding military conflict from the realms of morality. For example, some realists hold that war represents the cancellation of 'contracts' and practices that encourage nations to be civil to each other during peacetime. This means that moral bounds and limits on behaviour during times of conflict are cancelled and so morality itself has no place in war. [71]

Others contend that it is not meaningful nor realistic during conflict to say, '…do not kill…' when opponents are doing their level best to kill you. Military conflict, they say, is a loss of control of behaviour and we are not able to apply the same moral constraints to our behaviour as we did during peacetime.

The realist position may be challenged by the example of how prisoners-of-war (POWs) are treated. That is, POWs are usually not automatically killed despite the extra burden of care and responsibility they place on their captors. If, as realists suggest, morality truly has no relevance in military conflict then prisoners should be eliminated. This would save the resources expended in feeding, treating, sheltering and constraining them.

Realists give all sorts of military or strategic reasons as to why this final solution should not occur. They argue that protection – they would not use the term humane treatment – of enemy prisoners is important so that if one's own military forces are captured they will receive reasonable treatment in return.

Prisoner exchanges, they say, have nothing to do with being humane. They are conducted in response to political pressures. At the end of conflict there is simply no point in keeping another state's citizens locked up so they should be released. They also say that they would not just eliminate enemy POWs simply because there is no actual political or strategic benefit to doing so.

These are logical arguments but they cannot be applied in every case. For example, a determined and ruthless belligerent may not be concerned at all about the supposed political or strategic benefits of humanely treating their POWs. Even if some POWs are categorised as being useful for some purpose, the remaining POWs are not usually then just eliminated. The question of how belligerent states treat the civilian populations of their opponents also challenges the realist position. It is generally not a deliberate political or ideological aim to kill anyone and everyone opposing the dominant group. This does not mean that mass killings of a vanquished opponent do not occur but the intent to totally annihilate a particular group is extremely rare.

---

71 These realists are known as 'Contract Realists'. See Nicholas Fotion, *Military Ethics: Looking Towards the Future* (California: Stanford University, Hoover Institution Press, 1996), p. 10.

There are some exceptions. Nazi Germany was quite prepared to apply a final solution to what they saw as their 'Jewish problem' by the deliberate and systematic elimination of Jews, and there are similar parallels in the genocide conducted in Rwanda in 1994. However, these are exceptions to human behaviour rather than the rule. Even in some of the most vicious ethnic, religious, or tribal disputes, such as those in the Balkans, the Sudan, Sierra Leone and Afghanistan the elimination of entire populations did not occur.

The overused term 'ethnic cleansing' does not automatically mean killing every man, woman, and child opposing one's regime or ethnic group. It may simply mean forcibly expelling a particular ethnic group from one region to another. Deliberate genocide (the elimination of an entire ethnic or tribal group) is an extreme aberration in human behaviour. Despite deliberate policies of absolute genocide being rare events, as long as opponents exist they must be a threat or a potential threat to belligerents. It would seem logical to eliminate the threat by eliminating the problem – if morality is not an obstruction or a restraint.

Realists may think that this is going a bit far. They will say that they can live with threat or potential threat; it's just a matter of neutralising the threat. The concept of threat management and threat neutralisation is important to realists. A senior Australian Army officer, with over 30 years military experience in many parts of the world, suggested to me that the ideal military outcome is actually a standoff or stalemate between opposing military forces. In such a circumstance, he argued, people actually do not need to die.

He envisaged two sides of comparable military strength 'facing each other down'. Both sides would see that an attack by either side would not be advantageous. This would result in a standoff until the two opponents grew tired of looking at each other then apparently they would pack up and go home. He used the example of the two Koreas locked in stalemate for over forty years after the Korean War to support his case, but he admitted that they have not yet packed up and gone home. He added that conducting conflict in this way has nothing to do with the strange idea of morality in war. It's simply a matter of the appropriate application of military logistics and strategies, and recognition of the costs/benefits involved in the business of warfare.

There are major difficulties in applying the standoff idea to situations that involve deliberate human abuse. Even realists agree that humanitarian abuse actually does occur but, as this is a little too close to a moral position, perhaps they would call it the unnecessary wasting of human lives. The problem with the standoff idea is that although abusers may be reluctant to attack an opponent who is equal or superior in strength this in no way restricts their activities against the weak and the defenceless. If realists are concerned about the unnecessary wastage of human life then the standoff idea does not work very well at all. From the perspective of the abused, of course, the standoff idea is irrelevant.

How would realists react to the call for cross-border military intervention on humanitarian grounds? They would respond by asking what's in it for them. If no clear or immediate benefits are apparent they will question the rationality of exposing their citizens to great danger for no apparent reason. In March 1999, Douglas

Bandow, a senior fellow at the Cato Institute, presented a typically pragmatic and realist view on NATO's involvement in Kosovo.

He argued that Yugoslavia hasn't attacked the U.S. It hasn't threatened American citizens. It isn't even the worst human rights offender around the globe. He points out that, in January 1999 more people were killed in Sierra Leone than in Kosovo in 1998. More people were murdered in one massacre in Afghanistan in December than died in Kosovo in 1998. As many people died in one three-day battle between Tamil guerrillas and the Sri Lankan government in 1998 than in Kosovo the entire year.

> Indeed though Slobodan Milosevic is a demagogic thug, the behavior of his government towards Albanians looks not unlike that of America's ally Turkey towards the Kurds. Ankara uses U.S.-supplied weapons to kill Kurdish guerrillas and level Kurdish villages; some 37,000 people have perished over the last decade…America should set the Europeans free to make their own decisions and bear the resulting consequences. Let the members of the European Union, with a combined GDP of $8 trillion, population of nearly 400 million, and armed forces of more than one million sort out the problems of the Balkans. That is, if they believe doing so to be worth the cost.[72]

This type of realist paradigm rejects humanitarian intervention because others are doing equally if not even worse things to human beings so why do anything at all. Providing the home land is secure, why worry? The real question is if one's homeland is unfortunate enough not to be secure and one's citizens are being viciously brutalized, deliberately and continuously, does this mean that citizens in these places have no right to expect any outside help? Realist do not handle this sort of bland question too well because only those who are safe and secure have the luxury of dismissing humanitarian efforts as somebody else's problem – if it is really a problem at all.

Brian Orend argues that, in terms referring specifically to conflict, realists believe that it is an intractable part of an anarchical world system; that it ought to be resorted to only if it makes sense in terms of national interest; and that, once conflict has begun, a state ought to do whatever it can to win. So, he says, if adhering to a set of just-war constraints hinders a state in this regard, it ought to disregard them and stick soberly to attending to its fundamental interests in the pursuit of power and security.[73]

Most realists would dismiss calls for assistance from outside their own state or group unless such intervention has a direct bearing on the comfort or survival of their own citizens. They would cite conflicts of sovereignty, lack of relevance to own group, unnecessary risk to own forces, the increased effort and resources their own group would need to expend for no apparent return, and so on as being reasons for why they should not militarily intervene.

One reason realists think this way has its roots in history. As the entities of states and concepts of statehood began to develop, the goals of war became economic,

---

72  Doug Bandow, 'Europe's Welfare Queens,' *Cato Institute* (1999).

73  Orend, 'Kant's Just War Theory.'pp. 323–324.

political and essentially state-centred. Plunder, more territory, and hegemony became the primary reasons for conflict. A particular characteristic of state sanctioned conflict was (and often still is) for the accumulation of material gain and for the benefit of the state's citizens.[74]

So, for states to become involved in military adventures for reasons not associated with the direct benefit of the state would seem absurd to the realist. Not only is there no material gain from cross-border military intervention for humanitarian reasons but this type of military action places at risk one's own citizens. Cross-border military intervention may be acceptable to realists for strategic or political considerations but not for humanitarian reasons. Realists do not recognise the existence of a moral position in war in the first place therefore, so why should they be morally concerned over the fate of those outside their own group?

The logic of realism is challenging. They say that they have no social conscience outside their own group but only during times of conflict. During times of peace, a social conscience for others outside their own group returns. Many realists complain about those 'moralising do-gooders' who interfere with the serious business of warfare. Lives would actually be saved, they argue, if the do-gooders would just stop placing ethical obstructions in the way of serious war making.

Although it is difficult to morally rationalise realism, this will not concern the realists in the least who will say that they do not need or want to be morally rationalised. Realists simply believe in looking after family and immediate group first, and that the rest of the world should look after itself. They believe that if they can keep the sanctity of their own little group secure all will be well with the world. However, the reality is that in these days of suitcase nuclear weaponry, backyard chemical and biological factories, and global weapon's delivery systems there is no such thing as group isolation.

The concept of the state itself is increasingly under threat from political, economic, environmental and social issues. To somehow exclude a notion of moral obligation for the welfare of other human beings is anachronistic. The realist position regarding military non-intervention for humanitarian reasons is immoral and not as realists assert non-moral. Realists, of course, will dismiss this view for the reasons previously outlined.

## The Non-interventionist Pacifist

There are as many different types of pacifists as there are realists. It is a challenge to pin pacifists down on precisely what their moral position is once the discussion moves beyond 'I don't believe in aggression or killing'. For example, there is a certain type of pacifist who says that it is only one's self that one has no moral right

---

74  Laurence Keeley, *War before Civilisation: The Myth of the Peaceful Savage* (Oxford: Oxford University Press, 1996), p. 11.

to defend, but one may legitimately fight in order to defend other people.[75] This pacifist would support cross-border military intervention for humanitarian grounds.

Other pacifists say that it is all right to physically defend oneself from direct physical attack, but that it is morally wrong to use physical force on others.[76] Some pacifists will not use physical force for any reason, against anyone, at any time. They hold the basic view that solving problems through the use of physical force is morally wrong.

Most dedicated pacifists maintain that war is immoral because no cause can justify the immense suffering inflicted on human beings.[77] Absolute pacifists maintain that all military conflict is immoral; they refuse to participate in any war; they will not serve in the military; and they will not work in any war related industries. They argue that war unjustifiably violates the most fundamental human right to life.

How would pacifists respond to the call for military intervention on humanitarian grounds? They generally reject the idea that military force should be used to intervene in another state's affairs – even for humanitarian reasons. They will argue that physical force of any kind threatens the life of others, is counterproductive to peace and harmony in the world, begets violence, and basically that it does more harm than good.[78]

The pacifist position has the problem of attempting to reconcile the likely destruction of self, family or group on the basis that a forceful reaction is somehow inherently morally wrong. Pacifists also do not address the problem of scale very well. This is not unique to pacifism. All plausible moral positions have a problem with the idea of scale. For example, if all human life is equal, individually unique and sacrosanct then it should make no difference whether one life is at risk or one million lives are at risk. Even some ardent pacifists, long known for their opposition to military conflict, have relented when faced with the sheer numbers of the dead and dying.[79]

Barbara MacKinnon quotes the pacifist William Sloan Coffin Jr in the New York Times on the 21st of December 1992 as saying,

> Moral isolation is simply not a defensible position for those opposed to war. Civil war and 'ethnic cleansing' are likely candidates for military intervention – if this is the only way to eliminate them.[80]

Drew Christiansen, S.J., a fellow at the Woodstock Theological Center and former director of the U.S. bishops' International Justice and Peace Office, noted

---

75 Jan Narveson, 'A Critique of Pacifism,' in *Life and Death. A Reader in Moral Problems*, ed. Louise Pojman (Singapore: Jones and Bartlett Publishers, 1993), p. 471.

76 Ibid., p. 472.

77 Preston, *Understanding Ethics*.

78 Barbara Mackinnon, *Ethics. Theory and Contemporary Issues* (New York: Wadsworth Publishing Company, 1995), p. 412.

79 Ibid.

80 Ibid., p. 413.

that Pope John Paul has himself said he is 'not a pacifist' and in fact that he supported the use of military force to end the conflict in Bosnia.[81]

Comments and views such as these imply that moral judgements are a matter of degree after all and not simply a matter of absolutes as many pacifists argue. Pacifism is not just a radical position but it is actually incoherent because it is self-contradictory in its fundamental intent. If killing others is inherently morally wrong then it is not possible to be selective about who is being killed to uphold this basic position. Pacifists also fail to adequately take into account the misery and suffering non-action will cause when they refuse to condone intervention to stop humanitarian abuses. This is despite their well-known views on the sanctity of each human life.

*Supporters of the Concept of a 'Just-war'*

Somewhere between the extremes of realism and pacifism sit the Just-war theorists and the utilitarians.[82]    Not all Just-war theorists are utilitarians. Some may be rights theorists where the moral principle is developed into an idealised people's choice situation involving natural rights, moral rights or human rights.[83]    Others may embrace consequentialism or utilitarianism where certain states of affairs are deemed to be good states of affairs depending on an outcome that brings the greatest happiness to the most number of people.[84]

There is no single statement of the conditions of a 'morally just war' that covers all Just-war theories but Fotion et al argue that there are three broad categories that could be used to morally justify military engagement. These are; response to aggression, a pre-emptive strike against imminent or likely aggression, and a response to the threats against the lives and well being of citizens of other states.[85] When considering whether or not any of these three categories justify the direct use of military force, two other groups of factors must also be taken into account. One is the requirement for proportionality in response to aggression. The other is the long term and wide ranging consequence of initiating conflict.

People sometimes talk about concepts of Just-war and limited war in the same breath. They draw parallels between the evolution of theories about limiting warfare in the 1950s to having some equivalency with the core doctrines of Just-war. I do not discuss such parallels nor do I discuss, except in passing, the concept of conducting a limited war. I agree that there is some commonality between the two theories in

---

81    'Shift in Stance on 'Just War' Perceived in Recent Statements,' *American Journal of Public Health* 180, no. 6 (1999): p. 4.  See also Roger Williamson, *An Ethical Framework – or Just Intervention in Some Corner of a Foreign Field: Intervention and World Order* (New York: St. Martins Press, 1998), p. 225.

82    For a varied and insightful analysis of the Just-war tradition see P Christopher, *The Ethics of War and Peace:An Introduction to Legal and Moral Issues* (New Jersey: Prentice Hall, 1994).

83    Kenneth Rogerson, *Ethical Theory* (Orlando: The Dryden Press, 1991), p. 239.

84    Scheffler, *Consequentialism and Its Critics*.

85    Fotion and Elfstrom, *Military Ethics Guidelines for Peace and War*.

that military engagement can be so awful as to warrant constraint on moral grounds. A shared notion of proportionality and discrimination during military engagement comes into play. However, I consider this link to be a tenuous one and not directly applicable to military intervention for humanitarian reasons.[86]

Just-war theory attempts to present a moral justification for military engagement. It tries to avoid risks of error in the moral dilemmas of fighting when one should not and not fighting when one should. Pacifists worry about the former and realists worry about the latter. Each absolutist prefers to ignore the existence of at least one of these risks. An ideal moral theory, to justify precisely the use of military force, would address when to act, when not to act and how to act. Such a perfect theory does not exist.

Despite these ethical quandaries, a moral society is still forced to make judgements about whether or not it is morally justifiable to use coercive force – even if it is for apparently purely humanitarian reasons. In attempting to justify such military engagement not only does the question of when to fight (just-cause or Jus ad Bellum) need to be addressed but also how to fight (just-means or Jus in Bello). These are different but not independent issues for the Just-war theorist to tackle. The decision of whether to fight should be influenced by consideration of the means used and the ultimate cost of engagement.

The theory of the just war provides a defence of the use of violence during conflict that parallels the common sense justifications for the use of violence by the state for a defence of domestic rights. The state's use of violence against external threats may be legitimate providing that the ends are deemed to be just, and that the means used to achieve these ends are proportional to the threat. Just-cause is not limited to the state responding to external threats. For example, domestic police violence may be legitimate providing it serves morally just and well-specified goals, and that it is constrained by rules acceptable to the society as a whole.

Just-war theorists are virtually unanimous in the belief that self-defence of the state may provide a morally just-cause for war but there is little agreement beyond that. Other candidates for the notion of a just-cause include defending another state against unjust external aggression, the recovery of rights that may have been lost during previous unjust aggression that was not resisted, the punishment of unjust aggressors, and the defence of fundamental human rights within another state against abuse by the government.

Just-war theorists claim that there are essentially three requirements that determine just-means or Jus in Bello. Firstly, there is the requirement to use minimal force in order to achieve one's objectives. Secondly, the expected bad consequences of conflict must not outweigh, or be greater than, the expected good outcomes of conflict. Thirdly, force may be directed only against persons who are legitimate targets of attack.

---

86 For a comprehensive analysis of the parallels between the concept of a Just-war and a limited war see William O'brien, *The Conduct of Just and Limited War* (New York: Praeger Publishers, 1981).

Just-war theory proponents argue that a war may be considered to be morally just if other core criteria are fulfilled. [87]     For example, a Just-war must be declared by a competent authority (the principle of legitimacy), and it must be for a just-cause (a good reason for military engagement).   There must also be a reasonable chance of success in conflict, military engagement should only be used after all peaceful means have first been exhausted (last resort), just-means must be employed and unjust means avoided during conflict (good intentions), and a military response must be in proportion to the provocation (proportionality).[88]

## Proportionality and Reasonable Likelihood of Success

This section further addresses the Just-war concepts of 'proportionality' and 'reasonable chance of success' because of their close relationship to the utilitarian position, and because of their direct relevance to humanitarian intervention.  The other criteria – last resort, legitimate authority, just cause and good intentions – are not absolutely utilitarian.  Some, such as good intentions, could be said to be at least partly utilitarian.  For example, although the individual targeting of Saddam Hussein during the Gulf War may not be considered by many to be a 'proportional response' – one individual being deliberately targeted by Coalition Forces – this attack could still be morally justified because it attempted to bring an immediate end to the conflict.  This would have saved many lives and much misery on all sides.

The issue of proportionality will be dealt with first.  The concept of proportionality means that the good we intend to do as a result of military engagement should be in proportion to the assumed bad event/s that caused us to engage in the first place. The common view is that excessive or unnecessary military force is not morally acceptable in the pursuit of this aim.  There is another view of proportionality that is particularly relevant to humanitarian intervention.  The ineffectual application of military force by interventionists who have the capacity, but not the inclination, to be effective is also morally wrong if one supports a literal interpretation of proportionality.  That is, not enough force is as morally wrong as too much.

There are two ways proportionality could be considered.  Firstly, it may be viewed in its most narrow sense.  A military response must aim to be robust and successful yet at the same time it must be proportionate in its application of force. This means that absolutely any level or type of military response is not morally acceptable.  Similarly, totally annihilating an opposition who is clearly defeated or needlessly making an opponent suffer is also unacceptable.

It would not have been morally justifiable for NATO to explode a nuclear device over Belgrade in an effort to destroy Slobodan Milosevic's military and civil

---

87   For an in depth discussion on Just-war theory see Robert Holmes, *On War and Morality* (Princeton, New Jersey: Princeton University Press, 1989), pp. 146–82.

88   Emmett Barcalow, *Moral Philosophy. Theory and Issues* (California: Wadsworth Publishing Company, 1994), pp. 329–30.

infrastructure. This act would be morally unacceptable as it would have caused unnecessary suffering not only to military personnel but also to many civilians.

The other way the concept of proportionality may be viewed is that one must consider the likely or assumed outcomes of military engagement and whether or not overall utility is enhanced as a result of such engagement. Enhancing overall utility means that the effect of the use of direct force must be considered not only from the perspective of how much damage is done to opposing military forces but also by how such military engagement impacts on those whom one is 'trying to save'. Other important considerations include the effect on the states and peoples living in regions around the area of conflict, and even how the outcomes of this action may influence the rest of humanity.

The international community should stop trying to convince potential belligerents that genocide and other crimes against humanity are morally wrong because this is mostly a waste of time. A positive moral outcome is achieved if belligerents are either physically stopped or their activities are halted through fear of immediate and substantial retribution by the international community. It is not necessary that they be morally converted but it is necessary that they be stopped.

The further the distance from the immediate area of conflict, the more difficult it is to determine what the humanitarian outcome of military engagement will be. In this way Just-war theorists and utilitarians draw an ethical line in the sand regarding how and when force should be used as a morally appropriate response to aggression. Just-war theorists and utilitarians must contend with the problem of intent verses the reality of military engagement.

Critics of Just-war theory will point out that for all the so-called projections and forward planning of military engagements there is little if any guarantee that whatever military response is undertaken it will be successful or that it will be proportional. Again the example of international action in Kosovo may be used to reinforce this point. NATO action during the seventy-eight day air campaign in Kosovo was not a proportionate response for at least two reasons.

Firstly, NATO action was not an adequately robust response to more than a decade of deliberate Serb aggression and atrocities in the Balkans. Secondly, there was a very real possibility (subsequently proven to be correct) that Serb forces would immediately start killing as many Kosovars as possible if NATO attacked using air power alone. NATO's military response was not 'proportional' to the threat. [89]

NATO should have used ground troops to stop the Serb attacks in Kosovo. Airpower alone took too long and it did not quickly stop the killing. NATO action did not do what it specifically intended to do which was to stop Serbs killing and displacing Kosovars. One outcome of the air campaign was that approximately

---

89 For an alternate view on Serb involvement in the Balkans, and a Serb perspective on the NATO air campaign during the 1999 Kosovo conflict see, S Stojanovic, 'A Serb's View of Nato's Bombs,' *Free Inquiry* 9, no. 13 (1999): pp. 10–11.

8,000 Serbs and perhaps up to 100,000 Kosovars were killed.[90][91]   Prior to the NATO action, approximately 2,500 Kosovars had been killed in Kosovo.

More than ten years of Serb military and police action in the Balkans attest to Milosevic's determination for ethnic cleansing, so there should have been no confusion by the international community as to the Serbs intent in Kosovo. There was little doubt that as soon as NATO militarily intervened, the Serbs would apply a scorched-earth policy in the province. Military force should have been relentlessly directed at Serb forces in Kosovo. Instead the air campaign was largely centred on command and communications systems, water and power supplies, and army and police barracks in downtown Belgrade.

Targeting individual military forces in Kosovo was technically very difficult using air power alone. An overwhelming NATO sea, ground and air campaign should have been launched directly against the Serbs in Kosovo. This would have been a robust, proportional response to the desperate humanitarian situation in the Balkans.

The Coalition Force's Gulf War I campaign showed how successful a technologically superior, highly determined and massive military response against a well prepared and ruthless opponent can be. Such a response should have taken place in Kosovo. The good NATO and the international community intended to do in Kosovo was not in proportion to the Serb atrocities and ongoing aggression which caused NATO to intervene in the first place. In this case, overall utility was not enhanced.

So, in the end response to aggression may be out of all proportion to that which is considered to be morally appropriate under most circumstances, yet it may still be considered to be morally the right thing to do. To further add to the complexity, humanitarian interventionists must not only be prepared to apply proportionate force to counter threats against themselves but they must also consider the welfare of those whom they hope to rescue. There is no moral point in applying a proportional response against belligerents when those whom you wish to rescue are all dead because you took too long.

The dropping of atomic bombs on densely populated civilian cities in Japan during WW II and the Allied air campaign of obliteration bombing over Germany cities during WW II are examples of the disproportionate use of military force. Unconfirmed reports that Muslim fighters sent salvos of mortar rockets into the crowded market places of their own people in Srebrenica – to force the international community to attack the Serbs – suggests that the notion of proportionality may sometimes be justified using the concept of criticality in morals thinking. That is, it

---

90   Refer to Chapter 5 for a detailed account of the NATO action against Slobodan Milosevic's Serb forces. Also see Emma Daly, 'Arithmetic of Death That Does Not Add Up,' *The Independent*, 1 May 1996. for overall Balkan's war death estimates.

91   M McDonagh, 'A Just War Also Has Its Dark Sides,' *New Statesman* 12, no. 570 (1999): p. 1.

may be intuitively morally wrong to conduct such acts but the ultimate rewards may be greater than the initial costs.

Utilitarians who say that only ends not means are important may argue that the obliteration bombing of civilian cities is morally wrong but that it is still possible to justify such an act if it stops an even greater humanitarian disaster from occurring. This is a short-term view because the use of disproportionate force has unforseen consequences, which may ultimately cause more harm than good.

The second utilitarian-like principle, stated at the beginning of this section, is the idea that military engagement may be morally justifiable if the engagement is undertaken with a high likelihood of success. Success in this case equates with improved utility. Looking at the Kosovo example, it is difficult to morally justify NATO action on this basis. Selectively bombing Yugoslavia to make them capitulate failed, but more importantly it had no real chance of success in the first place. Unless one is prepared to be absolutely ruthless in bombing campaigns (meaning that entire cities and their inhabitants must be destroyed) there is very little likelihood that those on the receiving end will give up.

Germany bombing London, Coventry and other cities during WW II did not make Britain surrender. Allied bombing raids over Hamburg and Dresden in Germany did not stop Hitler. The Coalition's selective bombing of Baghdad did not remove Saddam Hussein, and sending Hizballah rockets into Tel Aviv will not make the Israelis withdraw from the West Bank and Gaza Strip.

The NATO bombing campaign in Yugoslavia did bring an end to Serb action in Kosovo but only after many lives were lost. One could make all sorts of predictions and projections about what could have happened to the Kosovars if NATO had not conducted the air campaign but the reality is that many thousands, perhaps tens of thousands, of Kosovars died at the end of the seventy-eight day bombing campaign.

NATO action in the Balkans did not come with a high likelihood of success because history repeatedly tells us that wars are not won with air power alone.[92] William Hawkins compares the military strategy against the Serb's in Kosovo with the Vietnam war. The air strategy in Kosovo had similarities with American force strategy used during the Vietnam War where individual targets were subject to presidential approval. In the early weeks of the air campaign, NATO strikes were limited to below the 44th parallel, well away from the Serbian capital and heartland. It was a campaign of gradual pressure meant to persuade, not win. It proved powerless to stop the Serbian army and police from killing thousands of Kosovars and driving most of the population out of the province.[93] Very little has been learned from the Vietnam war experience.

Insurgency, civil war, revolution, and other types of non-conventional warfare are particularly challenging to the just-war theorists because there are no definitive

---

92 Douglas MacGregor, *Breaking the Phalanx: A New Design for Landpower in the 21st Century* (Connecticut: Praeger, 1997), p. 17.

93 William Hawkins, 'Imposing Peace: Total Vs Limited Wars, and the Need to Put Boots on the Ground,' *Parameters* 30, no. 2 (2000): pp. 72–82.

answers to the issues of competent authority, just cause, right intentions, let alone 'reasonable chance of success'. Just-war and just-means are very rubbery concepts in these types of conflicts.

Identifying who the protagonists are, and defining what a competent authority is supposed to be, is extremely difficult. A morally just-cause may be difficult to define when one tribe or ethnic group keeps referring to a real or imagined wrong committed centuries ago. The idea that one can judge whether intervention has a reasonable chance of success when entire populations are involved in some vicious ethnic or civil conflict beggars belief.

## A Concept of Rights: Human Rights

Much is made about the concept of human rights, particularly in democratic western societies, but a truly moral society must do more than articulate a range of values that it sees as being relevant to the human condition. This is a good start but we must be prepared to support and defend such values. This may need to be done by force when other means do not or will not work.

It could be argued that the idea of human rights must take into account different cultural, ethnic, or religious requirements and that the universality of such rights may be challenged. However, all humans have a right to the essentials of life. Adequate food, shelter, and freedom from abuse are essential rights. These rights, in particular, could be deemed to be universal rights. Even mass murderers have these basic rights although, if they do not stop killing or abusing others, their fundamental right to life is challenged in some societies.

Different cultures have differing views on the rights of their people to have access to education, to be involved in political participation, to travel freely within or outside their state's borders and to marry whom they wish. These are important social issues but they are not life and death issues. Human rights are a reinstatement of a much older theory about the source of moral value inculcated in the doctrines of natural law and natural rights. The idea of human rights is not confined to Western liberalism and it cuts across many political, ethnic, ideological and religious boundaries. Rights themselves are concepts sometimes enshrined in legal protocols that societies bestow on individuals and groups.

Fundamental to the notion of natural rights is that men and women are entitled to make certain claims by virtue simply of their common humanity.[94] This view has been both supported and denied, depending on the philosophical leanings of those who are prepared to consider questions about fundamental human values. An appeal to human rights is said to be an appeal to the values of freedom and equality among humankind. The notion of human rights developed from an even earlier concept known as the Rights of Man. Human rights, Margaret Macdonald proposes;

---

94    John Charvet, 'Fundamental Equality,' *Utilitas* 10, no. 3: pp. 337–40. Also see John Rawls, *A Theory of Justice* (Cambridge: The Belknap Press, 1971), pp. 504–12. For an opposing view regarding equality of human worth.

...safeguard and restore, where necessary, the Rights of Man, those ultimate points at which the authority and social differences vanish, leaving the solitary individual with his essentially human nature, according to one political theory, or a mere social fiction, according to another.[95]

Human rights are based on an assumption. The assumption is that humans have a unique and special sense of being which translates directly into notions of worth and value. The idea of human rights is an attempt to articulate this special sense of being into something more than a simple recognition of sentient existence. This something more includes ideas of value and worth in conjunction with human uniqueness. Humans have a special ability not only to value themselves but also to value other humans. We recognise this ability in the conventions of human rights.

Like all constructed and assumed rights, human rights are not immutable. Some, even the 'essential ones', may be subject to restoration or removal if people deliberately violate humanitarian ideals. For example, murderers are censured by incarceration and, in some societies, by execution. Their right to freedom or life may be removed by a society that does not accept this individual's right to wantonly take another life.

Some will say that human rights cannot be lost; that they may only be violated or abused. Therefore, those who violate the human rights of others desecrate human life and act without right. The counter argument is that those who act to deter or punish these particular violators, according to international laws and conventions, are not themselves violators of human rights rather they uphold fundamental human rights by constraining or removing the rights of belligerents who have demonstrated complete contempt for the rights of others.

The common view of human rights is usually centred on the plight of the abused, but the position of those doing the abusing and of society generally also needs to be considered. Society has the right and a moral obligation to curtail the activities of abusers because their activities are not acceptable in a civil and humane community. This is a moral condition rather than simply a legal position.

H.L.A. Hart proposes that a theory of rights can be derived from the minimum content of natural law. This is also known as the minimalist approach to rights. That is, given a number of basic generalisations about humankind, it is possible to deduce certain rules of conduct without whose observation (at least to some degree) social order would collapse.[96] Such rules of conduct recognise that humans are essentially vulnerable beings so there should be some rules about violence, property and goods must be protected, and so on. Those who support a minimalist approach focus on the fundamental requirements for a civilised existence. They do not appeal primarily to the universal equality notions that are integral to the more common view of human rights.[97]

---

95  Macdonald Margaret, 'Natural Rights,' in *Human Rights*, ed. Abraham Melden (California: Wadsworth Publishing Company, 1970), p. 41.

96  H.L.A. Hart, *The Concept of Law* (Oxford: Clarendon Press, 1961), p. 189.

97  Ibid., p. 196.

For example, in past slave-owning societies the slave was more of an object of use than a subject of rights.[98]   This type of minimalist approach suggests a very selective application of human right's theory.  It excludes a section of the community (in this case slaves) as not even being fully human.  The selectivity argument in the minimalist's application of human rights commonly excludes certain sections of humanity from rights theory.

The problem with this position is that it is a very small step to view some sections of humanity as being less than human, even non-human.  Ethnic and racial hatred neatly fits into this view of the world.  Nazi Germany frequently referred to people with mental disabilities, Jewish people and gipsies as being sub-human.  The minimalists are at one end of the human rights spectrum.  At the other end are the maximalists.

Maximalists argue that human rights should have primacy over all other rights. They support the idea of universality and equality of human rights to reflect maximisation of natural law.  Robert Nozick argues that this means that the rights of all individuals have primacy over the rights of states and institutions. [99]   Individual rights are assigned to fulfil the principles of co-operation within that society.  Some maximalists arrive at the point of universality of human rights, but only if social justice, fairness, and so on are enhanced.  Others begin with the notion of social justice and fairness then extend it to individual human rights.

Exercising the right is the activity that connects the subject of the right to the object of the right, but this is more than simple connection and claim of right.  Exercise of a right may include assertion and demand, claim, seeking protection against infraction or demand for compensation.  Rights are usually held against someone or something. An important indicator of a right is the existence of a mutual relationship between duty and right.  The attribution of a right is meaningless without the possibility of a correlative duty resting somewhere.

The idea that rights are bound to correlative duties is important because this suggests that rights are more than just something one can get away with.  To say that Might equals Right is an assumption, not a justification, because there is no correlative duty.   R.J.Vincent proposes that to justify a right a certain wider social acceptance of the importance of the right is required.[100]   Entitlement then rests on social acceptance of the claim of right.  This social acceptance of the justification of a right may be based on custom, culture, convention or contract.  Coalition Force action during Gulf War I was considered rightfully justified by many in the international community based on Iraqi violation of UN resolutions.

Whether Coalition action was truly rightfully justified is open to question as anti-war groups, the Iraqis themselves and some states did not agree at all with either the

---

98   Ibid.

99   Robert Nozick, *Anarchy, State, and Utopia* (Oxford: Blackwell Publishers, 1974), p. ix.

100 R.J. Vincent, *Human Rights and International Relations* (Cambridge: Cambridge University Press, 1986), p. 9.

Coalition action or the UN resolutions. However, with some qualification, according to Vincent, social acceptance of the justification of a right does not need to be a full one hundred percent. [101] A majority generally will do.

So far, this section has focused on the idea of individual rights, but states and groups are often considered to have rights as well. Human rights can take on collective as well as corporate forms. Peter Jones claims that this means that what is fundamentally important to human beings may also relate to goods and bads that people experience collectively rather than individually:[102] A further division is discernible amongst those who distinguish between group rights and individual rights. That is, the reality of the conceptual difference between individual human rights and group rights does not mean that there should be any antagonism between the two forms of rights. Some group rights, such as the rights of cultural minorities, closely complement individual human rights.[103]

The reasons that lead us to ascribe rights to individuals are also reasons why some people recognise certain forms of group rights. Human rights may be conceptually distinct from group rights but the same underlying values and concerns unite the two sorts of rights. One should not, however, take the connectivity between individual and group rights too far because this may lead to competition between individual rights and the rights of artificial constructs such as a state or an organisation. Traditionally, a major purpose of the doctrine of human rights has been to protect individuals from the power of groups and states.

Institutionalised power or state rights should not have precedence or primacy over individual human rights because this doctrine risks the very purpose of safeguarding individuals against the predations of groups. The argument for the primacy of individual rights over state rights is an important one and it will be further explored later.

James Nickel proposes that human rights have a number of salient characteristics as conceived in twentieth century documents such as the Universal Declaration Twentieth-century human rights documents.[104] One characteristic is that they are an assumed right and, according to convention and much contested legal definition, they are high-priority norms whose pursuit may be considered to be mandatory. The universal approach to human rights contends that they exist independently of recognition or implementation in the customs or legal systems of particular states. These rights may not be fully effective rights until legally implemented or formally recognised in their entirety; nevertheless, they clearly exist as standards of convention.

Human rights are important norms. They are sometimes strong enough as normative considerations to prevail in conflicts with contrary national norms. This

---

101 Ibid., p. 8.

102 P Jones, 'Human Rights, Group Rights, and Peoples' Rights,' *Human Rights Quarterly* (1999): p. 80.

103 Ibid.: p. 90.

104 James Nickel, *Making Sense of Human Rights* (California: University of California Press, 1987), p. 3.

was the case in East Timor although it took 25 years for human rights issues to come directly to the fore. Human rights norms justify international action on their behalf (admittedly very selectively and then only sometimes) should violations be seen to occur. The maintenance of human rights, even at the prima facie level, implies duty for both individuals and governments. These duties, like the rights to which they are linked, are said to exist independently of acceptance or recognition. Governments and people everywhere are therefore obligated not to violate a person's rights.

The rights theorist, Vincent suggests that rights could be thought of as consisting of five main elements: The subject of the right, the object of the right, the exercise of the right, the bearer of the correlative duty, and the justification of the right. [105] The subject of the right or the right-holder may be an individual, a group, a region, a state or a culture. The object of the right is the actual claim of right. For example, I (subject) claim a right to work (object) undisturbed.

Some claims of right may be considered as trumps because they outrank ordinary interests and, most importantly, they may override the utilitarian calculation of group advantage. Such a trump right may be that I claim a right to life. Some rights are more important than others and some trumps outrank and override lesser trumps. So, if the object of a right is the right to life then this is a trump compared to the right for me to work undisturbed.

My right to life is a trump that outranks my ordinary interest of working undisturbed because it has a higher value base. This is important because sometimes the trump of a right (for example, the person being subjected to human rights abuses) may override a state's rights to sovereignty. This is one utilitarian calculation relative to group advantage where the individual has trump rights over state sovereignty.

This then raises the question of a citizen's moral obligation to conform to the requirements of the state and how far such a moral obligation goes. It also raises the question of the legitimacy of states. Many people live in states that they would not voluntarily consent to obey but this alone does not make a state illegitimate.[106] It means that many states are unjust so we must try to make them just and to make them serve our needs.

The crux of the issue, regarding military intervention for humanitarian reasons, is whether state sovereignty could be considered to be an ordinary interest when compared to a human right to life. In a civilised world the human right to life must override state's rights. The hierarchical status of some rights may change their position on the ethical values ranking scale depending on the conduct of the subject of the right. If someone commits an inhuman act (an act, lawful or unlawful, which is an affront to common humanity and common decency) against another individual or group then his or her personal trump of the right to life or freedom may be taken away.

---

105 Vincent, *Human Rights and International Relations*.

106 Ronald Dworking, *Taking Rights Seriously* (London: Duckworth Press, 1977), pp. 5–10.

The individual may or may not devalue their own right to life or freedom, but others in a civilised community may forcefully remove such rights. Some will disagree that different rights have different values or that one may lose or gain a right depending on one's actions. They prefer a simpler view of life where everyone has the same basic human rights forever, regardless of conduct. I do not support such a view.

Maximalists would support the view that everyone retains some basic human rights regardless of how they treat others. The attraction of such a position is its universality and its simplicity, but one must challenge the idea that it is possible to ignore how people conduct themselves in relation to an assumed right. A fundamental flaw in the argument that individuals or groups retain personal human rights, no matter what atrocities and violence they commit against others, is that the rights of the abused and the rights of society to live in a world free from violence are either not adequately taken into account or they are not taken into account at all. The rights of the abused and the right of civilised society to live violence free should be trump or essential rights compared to a belligerent's rights.

Up to this point, I have discussed the notion of humans having rights that may be removed or reinstated depending on how a civil community values human behaviour. I have argued that all humans have some essential rights by virtue of their humanity but this does not mean that such rights are immutable. The Declaration of Human Rights is a convention that outlines the values of civilised human behaviour. This charter articulates what is and what is not considered to be acceptable human behaviour. It is based on the idea that the welfare of humanity is enhanced if these protocols are followed.

## Non-forcible Intervention: Natural Disaster Relief and Giving Aid

Humanitarian intervention by the international community may also be required as a result of a natural disaster, such as flood, famine, fire, drought or earthquake. This type of intervention is usually conducted with the willing participation of most parties. Natural disasters may be long term as well as short term. The international community is frequently asked to help out when critical food shortages occur as a result of inefficient food distribution systems, inappropriate food management practices, or unsustainable agricultural practices.

Natural disaster relief programs are usually much more palatable to the international community because there is low physical risk to interventionists. The few dollars we individually contribute to various relief funds does little to threaten our comfortable lives and we usually do not place our own citizens at too much risk. However, not everybody believes that giving humanitarian aid is necessarily a good thing. Giving aid to all who apparently need it does not necessarily address the many underlying problems of why such aid is required in the first place. Even immediate disaster relief is not immune from this line of thinking.

This line of thinking is as follows. People unable or unwilling to move away from frequent drought or flood areas (Bangladesh is one example) cannot survive without reliance on humanitarian aid. Therefore, to keep supplying such aid encourages these people to stay where they are. Joseph Fletcher argues that in situations where human reproduction has outstripped productivity, to give food aid without making serious inroads into increasing local production simply increases the population and increases the number of starving people. He says that this produces a net loss of life and a net increase of human misery.[107]

There are concerns that global food production cannot keep pace with increasing populations. This creates a moral quandary and a simple lifeboat analogy makes the point. If the world's food lifeboat can only hold ten or fifteen people then to allow the swimming hundreds to clamber on board is illogical and morally wrong because those trying to clamber aboard will overturn the boat and everyone would die.[108]

There are two fundamental problems with this type of argument against the giving of aid, particularly food aid in a world supposedly running out of food. Firstly, the reason people are starving in the world today is not because there is not enough food to go around. The reason people starve is because food is not distributed equitably. It is factually incorrect to say that there can never be enough to go around when resource rich countries pay their farmers not to produce food in order to maintain artificially high market values for produce. 85 percent of the world's income is earned by 23 percent of the world's population and over 80 percent of the world's food production is consumed by 20 percent of the population.[109]   We have the capacity to manufacture enough food lifeboats.

Many developing countries in serious need of humanitarian aid require much more than food. They also need medicines, doctors and hospitals, education, clean drinking water, access to clean energy, and farming practices that are productive and environmentally sustainable. A small reduction in global military spending would pay for such programs.

Dr. Oscar Arias in his paper presented to the UN on December 14, 1995 pointed out that 12 percent of the developed countries annual military expenditures would pay for the cost of basic health care for the world's entire population, provide immunisation for all children, eliminate severe malnutrition and provide safe drinking water for all.[110]   The problem is not an inability to increase global net production. The problem is inequitable and inappropriate distribution of resources.

---

107 Joseph Fletcher, 'Give If It Helps, but Not If It Hurts,' in *World Hunger and Moral Obligation*, ed. William Aiken and Hugh LaFollette (New Jersey: Prentice-Hall Publishers, 1977), p. 106.

108 William Aiken and Hugh LaFollette, *World Hunger and Moral Obligation* (New Jersey: Prentice-Hall Publishers, 1977), p. 2.

109 United Nations, 'Human Development Report 1991,' (Oxford: Oxford University Press, 1991): p. 4.

110 Oscar Arias, J Friedman, and C Rossiter, 'Less Spending, More Security: A Practical Plan to Reduce World Military Spending'.' (paper presented at the Capitol Hill Symposium, U.S. Senate, 15 December, 1995).

Secondly, any moral position that says that it is acceptable to allow starving populations to starve must be challenged. Those who support the lifeboat view actually go a step further in their analogy when they argue that it is actually immoral not to let the swimming hundreds drown because the alternative is that everyone will drown if those in the boats allow those in the water to clamber on board. This is the survival of the fittest rationale where only the strong prevail, and it has little to do with a wider view of ethical behaviour.

## Individual and Collective Duty

I have proposed that the international community has a moral obligation to defend and support human rights. But to many people there is significant disputation about the limits to such obligation, and what the interplay is between individual and collective duty. I argue that military intervention for humanitarian reasons should be reactive to a sense of duty above that of the individual or the state interest.

If we consider obligation to be closely related to a moral imperative then we should recognise that the application of a moral position may be subject to more than just self-interest. This does not exclude the individual self rather it recognises the existence of moral obligation over and above self. Utilitarians, for example, say that we have moral obligations not only to ourselves but also to others. The practical difficulty is determining which has primacy.

One distinguishing feature of ethics is that ethical judgments are often universalisable. That is, ethics requires us to go beyond simple self-awareness to include family, friends, organisations, states, and even humanity as a whole.[111] Universalisability forbids racism, nationalism and other isms from entering into moral assessments.[112] By contrast, egoism is essentially concerned about welfare of self.

Universalisability is about taking a wider view or perspective regarding moral obligation. If this idealised view of morality is accepted then it is not unreasonable to suggest that we are morally obliged to be responsive to the humanitarian requirements of those who have the most need. This is the fundamental ethical position I apply to the notion that military intervention ought sometimes to be undertaken for altruistic reasons – and that it ought to be undertaken despite some risk to one's own citizens.

Risk itself is relative and subject to degree, so how does one attempt to conceptualise how much moral obligation an individual or a society has? Is such obligation even quantifiable? One way is to consider intervention based on altruism, which is the principle or practice of promoting the welfare of others. Altruistic intervention is intervention by external agencies that have no political or strategic

---

111 Singer, *Practical Ethics*.

112 Douglas Lackey, *The Ethics of War and Peace* (New Jersey: Prentice Hall, 1989), p. 4.

relevance to the intervening state. Intervention, in this case, is primarily based on humanitarian concerns.

The reason I define altruism in this way is that I am attempting to eliminate as much as possible the usual raft of other arguments against intervention. Arguments such as; '...it is not in the national interest, there is no political or economic advantage, we did not cause the humanitarian problem in the first place so we have no responsibility...', and so on. These issues are further discussed in Chapter Four, Objections to the Ethical Principles and Applications.

Altruistic intervention is based on the idea that moral obligation extends past the immediate concerns a state may have regarding its own interests. If it is possible for the all-encompassing national interest argument in particular to be put aside for the moment then many of the moral reasons not to intervene are eliminated. A moral obligation to intervene is dependent on the idea of moral permissibility. It would be difficult to argue that there is a moral obligation to militarily intervene in another nation's affairs if it were not morally permissible. Yet, moral permissibility does not automatically mean moral obligation or duty. The next section directly addresses the concept of permissibility and its relationship to moral obligation.

### Permissibility and Moral Obligation

Military intervention may be morally permissible providing a range of conditions are met. This does not mean that it is obligatory. [113]    The nexus between what is apparently permissible and what is obligatory is problematic but it may be considered as follows. For example, if I am subjected to an unprovoked attack then I am morally justified in physically defending myself, providing I have no other option except to resort to force. Although I am morally permitted to react with force, I am not actually obliged to use force to defend myself because it is always open for the holder of a so-called right to waive that right. I may, for whatever reason, choose not to react and allow myself to be attacked.

If I promise to defend my friend from attack then not only do I have a moral justification to go to his or her aid, but I am also morally obliged to do so because of my personal commitment to his or her welfare. In this case I am obliged to act because of my commitment to my friend's defence. There may be a range of reasons (not all of which are purely altruistic on my part) why I should promise to defend my friend in the first place. It may simply be a matter of survival for us both. If we unite to protect each other from external aggression then perhaps we stand a better chance of fending off attacks and deterring future attacks.

On the other hand, I may have purely altruistic reasons for offering to defend my friend.   One of these may be that I cannot bear to stand by and watch him or her

---

113 Michael Walzer, *Just and Unjust Wars : A Moral Argument with Historical Illustrations* (New York: Basic Books, 1992), p. 236.

being attacked when I feel that by direct intervention I am able to stop the attack. The prospect that I may suffer injury to myself if I carry out my moral obligation to defend my friend also needs to be considered from an individual moral standpoint. If there is a high probability that I may suffer significant injury and I still decide to intervene then I have made a decision that exceeds my personal moral obligation for intervention.

Peter Singer would say that at this point I have reached my level of marginal utility. [114] He elaborates on the concept of marginal utility by further fine tuning a response as being a strong or moderate version of marginal utility. This makes the entire concept even more complex than it really needs to be so I will not dissect his variations to the central theme. Suffice to say that marginal utility is the level at which I would cause as much suffering to myself as I would relieve by my defence of others. Conversely, if it is in our power to prevent something bad from happening, without thereby sacrificing anything of comparable moral importance, we ought, morally, to do it.[115 116] This is consistent with the moral principle of minimal altruism.

The idea of permissibility and moral obligation is important for humanitarian intervention. If the international community professes deep concern over severe human rights violations, and it says that such violations are unacceptable in a civil society, then a clear moral obligation exists to stop these atrocities. Unlike the earlier individual example, if there is a risk of injury to intervening forces the moral obligation to intervene remains the same. This is because individuals within groups do not have the same moral choices as individuals by themselves. People belong to groups for the benefit such collectiveness brings, and in return for these benefits individuals have obligations to the group as a whole.

Mathew Hanser argues that preventing a person from being saved is morally on par with letting die, which infringes on a victim's positive rights. Regardless of whether the positive or negative rights of the victim are being infringed upon, from a humanitarian perspective it cannot be morally right to stand back and to allow such suffering and death to occur by inaction, procrastination, or the incorrect action. He makes a good point (morally speaking) when he says that doing nothing is as morally wrong as doing the incorrect thing.

A moral requirement for the international community to act to stop atrocities from occurring exists because inaction will significantly increase the overall levels

---

114 Peter Singer, 'Famine, Affluence and Morality,' in *Philosophy, Politics and Society*, ed. Peter Laslett and James Fishkin (Oxford: Basil Blackwell/New Haven Yale University Press, 1987), p. 33.

115 Peter Singer, 'Famine, Affluence, and Morality,' in *World Hunger and Moral Obligation*, ed. William Aiken and Hugh LaFollette (New Jersey: Prentice-Hall Publishers, 1977), p. 24.

116 Peter Singer, 'Famine, Affluence, and Morality,' *Philosophy and Public Affairs* 1, no. 1 (1972): pp. 229–43.

of suffering and death.[117]   My moral responsibility as a stated citizen may require me to sometimes subsume my individual safety and comfort requirements for the sake of others in greater need.   The extent to which individual requirements are subsumed by the group's requirements or visa versa is a complex issue, but most people accept that in everyday life we must sometimes put a group's needs before our own.

If members of the international community take human rights seriously (enough to ratify and endorse them) then there is at least some moral obligation to ensure the effective exercise of these rights.   Human rights are the claim of all of humanity on all of humanity. [118]   If all human life has value, we are individually and collectively morally obliged to protect such life.   This is even if that is at some cost to our group or ourselves.

## The Vexing Problem of Ends and Means

How people conduct themselves to achieve a particular goal could be considered means with ends being the outcomes.   Military intervention for humanitarian reasons is a means to an end.   An everyday example of the relevance of means is in the application of reasonable force to uphold the law.   For example, most democratic societies would not accept police officers shooting a shoplifter who ran from a crime scene.   This is not considered to be a reasonable use of force.   Law enforcement officers would be expected to give chase to physically apprehend the perpetrator, even though there is a greater chance that the shoplifter will escape and an increased risk of injury to the officers.

Everyone has a vested interest in this idea of means.   Means are important in law enforcement because society responds to criminal acts depending on how such acts are carried out as well as the outcome of the act.   Criminals are interested in means if only because society's notion of punishment is closely linked to how the lawbreakers go about their activities.   Victims of crime relate to means because their suffering is relative to how the crime is conducted.

Society responds to criminality by awarding different punishments to different crimes.   Robbery with violence is more severely punished than robbery without violence.   The point is not whether the crime involves physical or non-physical violence causing trauma to victims – both cause trauma – but that the act of violence in conjunction with a crime is treated differently by society than crime without violence.

When considering means and ends, Peter Singer presents the case of Oskar Schindler, the now famous German industrialist who saved the lives of many Jews during World War II.   Oskar Schindler ran a factory in Cracow, Poland during World

---

117 Mathew Hanser, 'Killing, Letting Die and Preventing People from Being Saved,' *Utilitas* 11, no. 3: p. 277.   Hanser has the view that like killing, preventing people from being saved is the same as doing them harm and it infringes on the victim's negative rights.

118 Kok-Chor Tan, 'Military Intervention as a Moral Duty,' *Public Affairs Quarterly* 9, no. 1 (1995): p. 31.

War II. He assembled a labour force of Jewish inmates from concentration camps and ghettos at a time when Polish Jews were being sent to death camps. This was a labour force considerably larger than his factory actually needed.

He used a variety of strategies, including bribing members of the SS and other officials, to protect his workforce. Schindler spent his own money to buy black market food to supplement the meagre official rations he obtained for his workers. By these methods he saved the lives of about 1,200 people. Singer suggests that Schindler's means were justified because in the end he saved 1,200 people.

These means were morally good acts that resulted in morally right outcomes. In this particular case, the ends justified the means. The view that there is a direct correlation between means and ends is not without its critics. For example, means are subject to moral judgements other than those associated with outcomes or ends; therefore, the ends in some cases may not be used to justify the means. This is a generalised approach to the problem because it depends on which means are used to produce which ends.

The challenge facing those who are prepared to take a moral position on means and ends is that ideas of right and wrong mean different things to different people. It is not incomprehensible to believe that the Germans rounding up the Jews during World War II morally justified their activities to themselves.

The means and ends of humanitarian intervention are of vital interest to the abused. If the 'end' results in a significant reduction, perhaps the elimination, of death and suffering during a humanitarian emergency then there is a powerful argument that says that the means used to achieve such ends have merit. This argument is further enhanced if the means used are proportionate, suitably discriminate in targeting those who are responsible and conducted according to international law.

Consequentialists will say that the sole criterion for decision-making is that the intended actions must have the effect of producing a greater balance of good consequences over bad ones. An act is right if, and only if, it produces at least as great a balance of good over evil as any available alternative. From this logical sequence derives the maxim '…the ends justify the means.'[119]

A problem with generalising about means and ends in this way is that the even the best intentions or means will not necessarily produce the best outcomes. It depends on which means are justified by which ends. Those being abused will say that any means to stop the abuse are acceptable, but the international community still needs to consider the wider ramifications of the use of force to resolve these issues.

When discussing means and ends some important questions relating to the degree of abuse arises. For example, is the likelihood of military intervention based on the degree of abuse and how does the degree of abuse affect the means used to try to stop the abuse? Military intervention is more easily justified, and therefore more likely, when the degree of abuse is high. This does not mean that it is morally acceptable

---

119.Haass, 'Reinhold Niebuhr's Christian Pragmatism: A Principled Alternative to Consequentialism.'

for small numbers of people to die, but the reality is that many deaths and much suffering usually occurs before military intervention is even considered.

Degree of abuse is also important because it focuses attention on potential outcomes. If many lives are at serious risk then there are many lives that potentially may be saved by direct intervention. The question of scale of abuse and the level of outrage it generates has direct relevance to means and ends. The higher the level of abuse, the more likely (possibly) the international community will forcibly respond.

It is difficult to define when or if a particular humanitarian disaster or type of violation falls into a so-called severe category. Levels of international concern are not a suitable benchmark for such judgements. The following section address how the international community responds to perceptions of degree of abuse, and it proposes a method of defining and valuing levels of outrage.

## Levels of Outrage

Degree of abuse is often a proportionate measure of the number of people abused. However, the level of outrage over abuse is not the same as degree of abuse. The level of outrage over a particular incident may be high yet the degree of abuse may actually be small. Killing five Red Cross workers would cause a high level of international outrage compared to killing five suspected terrorists.

A sense of international outrage is usually very selectively applied to specific humanitarian circumstances. It is also generally short lived and it relies more on an observer's immediate feelings of revulsion or shock regarding a particular act. This is not an objective appraisal of the seriousness of the situation. There are a many examples that demonstrate the fickleness of international outrage over humanitarian issues. [120]

In 1998, Kofi Annan stated that the ongoing humanitarian crises in the Sudan, Sierra Leone and Afghanistan could not be described as anything but severe, yet international interest has not reflected the urgency of humanitarian need in these regions. [121] There is little if any change in many of the poorest and most oppressed African states today. Other humanitarian disasters continue unabated. Chechnya, Rwanda, Burundi, Uganda, Tanzania, Sierra Leone and the Democratic Republic of Congo (formerly Zaire) are all current humanitarian disaster areas – to name just a few. Millions of human lives are at imminent risk of famine, malnutrition and disease. The lack of western or most other press coverage of these tragic events demonstrates the selectivity of the international community's attention span regarding humanitarian crisis.

The sense and degree of outrage expressed by the international community about particular incidents is generally short lived. Constant priming by the mass media

---

120 Community Aid Abroad OXFAM Australia, 'Desperate Times: War and Famine in Sudan,' *Horizons* (1998).

121 Deen, 'Politics: Un Laments World's Two Forgotten Emergencies.'

is required to maintain levels of concern, even levels of interest. The international community needs to be more objective in how it perceives the seriousness of humanitarian crisis. A method of valuing patterns of behaviour, which lead to serious human rights abuses, is required. Valuing such patterns of behaviour provides an objective yardstick. This is more rational than a momentary instinctive moral outrage to justify forcible intervention.

## Valuing Patterns of Behaviour: When Should We Intervene?

To value a pattern of behaviour a number of interrelated standards of appraisal may be used. Valuing patterns of behaviour means to judge whether specific acts by individuals, groups or governments have reached a level of severity to warrant international intervention. Where possible, the following standards of appraisal should be used together.

Firstly, there is the natural law position. This contends that there are a number of self-evident convictions about what is right and what is wrong. Torture is abhorrent to most people regardless of whether specific laws exist to prohibit the practice. It is abhorrent regardless of whether the international community formally declares such practices to be morally wrong. Deliberately withholding food or shelter, rape, ethnic cleansing, genocide and war crimes are all unacceptable according to natural law.

Secondly, international law specifically outlaws extreme human behaviour such as rape and torture. International law is indicative of the standards of natural law. Both natural law and international law are responsive to degree of abuse, and not just to the pattern of behaviour itself. Thirdly, the human rights charter and associated conventions are a guide as to what is generally considered acceptable human behaviour.

Fourthly, violations may be considered as severe depending on the degree of pain or suffering they cause, and depending on the numbers of people harmed. A situation may be judged as being of 'severe concern' if large numbers of people are harmed and they are deprived of the necessities for life. It is not possible to determine an absolute numerical threshold of what the term 'large numbers of people' means, but it is possible to link numbers of people harmed to some level or degree of concern.

Although the human statistics of abuse are an important gauge to the level of outrage generated by specific acts – they are often used as a threshold determinant of severity of abuse – statistics alone should not be the primary instigators for level of outrage. A level of international concern regarding serious humanitarian abuse is not only about numbers killed or harmed. It is also about who is affected and how the abuse is carried out.

Finally, if serious abuse is ongoing and instigators do not stop their activities then the case for forcible intervention is much stronger. A problem with using this by itself as an objective yardstick for intervention is that those who deliberately conduct humanitarian abuses simply stop and start their activities depending on international reaction. Abusers clearly understand that the international attention span is very limited. If they momentarily halt their activities then the international community's political will to act and public moral outrage will usually simply disappear. Slobodan Milosevic and Saddam Hussein repeatedly demonstrated such brinkmanship skills when dealing with the international community.

Standards of appraisal are most effective when used in conjunction with each other. Natural law, international law and human rights conventions form an objective yardstick to help the international community to decide the severity of abuse, and whether or not intervention in another state's affairs is warranted. Intervention may be justified where many people are severely abused, the abuse continues regardless of international expressions of outrage, and efforts to reconcile the conflicting factions are repeatedly unsuccessful.

# Chapter 2

# Plausible Interventionist Strategies

The international community currently sometimes reacts when situations of humanitarian abuse are deemed to be severe enough to warrant armed intervention. This apparent severity is usually not objectively based rather; isolated incidents tend to act as triggers. These in turn may instigate some sort of international response.

NATO's Deliberate Force air strikes against the Bosnian Serb Army (BSA) were a direct response to the BSA shelling of a market place in Sarajevo on 28 August 1995. Graphic pictures of the shelled market place, and the many dead and wounded citizens of Sarajevo, resulted in NATO action. The subsequent use of overwhelming military force by the international community finally ended Serb activities in and around Sarajevo.

The response to the many severe cases of humanitarian abuse ranges from inaction to various attempts at mediation or peacekeeping. I have argued that the difficult question of *when* or *if* to intervene should be primarily focused on the plight of the abused. The ramifications of intervention (or non-intervention) to the wider human community must also be considered. The needs of the many (those being abused) must take priority over the needs of the few (those considering intervention). If overall utility is to be maximised, as utilitarians argue, then the needs of the majority have precedence.

Third party intervention is warranted when the suffering of the abused occurs regularly, the abusers will not permanently cease their activities, or when there is a high likelihood that the abused will either die or be seriously harmed. Such outcomes are not impossible to observe or measure when the activities of belligerents are monitored.

Other important considerations such as; risk to intervening forces, economic and political costs/benefits of intervention, the morality of using force to settle disputes, the strategic capability to intervene, and national interest concerns are of vital interest to potential interventionists. These must also be considered then balanced against the plight of the abused.

## The First Step: Determining Responsibility

A challenge for the international community is to identify precisely who is responsible for carrying out deliberate and ongoing, extreme human rights violations. It is not impossible to identify the leaders and instigators of such violence. They are the ones who incite their followers to commit criminal acts, and they are the ones who through control or acquiescence incite such activity.

Over 1 million Tutsis and Tutsi sympathisers were shot, stabbed, clubbed, set alight or beaten to death by rampaging mobs of Hutus in Rwanda in 1994. There is no great secret or confusion over who orchestrated and conducted these atrocities. Eric Markusen, a professor in the Department for Holocaust and Genocide Studies at the Danish Institute for International Studies said that, 'In Rwanda, the genocidaire [perpetrators of genocide] killed 75 percent of the Tutsi population, and they announced their plans beforehand.' He added that many of the accused on trial in Arusha had been heard making public speeches advocating the murder of Tutsis.[1]

Amnesty International reported that those directing the killings were supporters of the former single ruling party, the Mouvement Republicain National Pour la Democratie et le Developement (MRND), the Republican National Movement for Democracy and Development. This organization's youth wing, known locally as the Interahamwe ('They who attack together'), were directly responsible for organising and leading many of the Hutu mobs during the genocide.[2]

Also directly responsible for the many organised massacres in Rwanda, was the Coalition Pour la Defense de la Republique (CDR), Coalition for the Defence of the Republic. This was an exclusively Hutu political party with a youth wing known as the Impuzamugambi ('They who have the same goal'). The CDR and the Impuzamugambi orchestrated a violent campaign against any Hutus who supporting the sharing of power with the Tutsi-dominated rebel Rwandese Patriotic Front (RPF).

Supporters or sympathizers of the MRND and CDR in conjunction with members of the security forces carried out the massacres in Rwanda during 1994. The Presidential Guard, the Gendarmerie, the regular army and the local government police were all involved in the killing. Most of the killings were politically motivated. They were specifically aimed to destroy the population groups viewed as potential supporters of the RPF and the multi-ethnic parties opposed to the MRND and CDR. Identifying who is responsible for such crimes against humanity is important because the international community is extremely reluctant to intervene in another state's affairs unless it can distinguish 'good guys' from 'bad guys'.

Michael Walzer supports the notion that [we] are extraordinarily dependent on the victim/victimizer, good guys/bad guys model. He seriously questions whether any very forceful intervention is politically possible without it. One of the reasons for the weakness of the UN action in Bosnia, he argues, has been that many of its representatives on the ground do not believe that the model fits the situation they have to confront. They are not quite apologists for the Serbs, who have (rightly)

---

1    Stacy Sullivan of the Institute for War and Peace Reporting, 'Milosevic and Genocide: Has the Prosecution Made the Case?,' *Guardian Unlimited*, 27 February 2004.

2    Amnesty International, 'Rwanda: Mass Murder by Government Supporters and Troops in April and May 1994, Ai Index:Afr 47/11/94,' (Amnesty International: The International Secretariat News Service, 1994).

been condemned in many UN resolutions, but they do not regard the Serbs as wholly 'bad guys' or as the only 'bad guys' in the former Yugoslavia. And, Walzer adds, this has made it difficult for the UN to justify the measures that would be necessary to stop the killing and the ethic cleansing.[3]

This is part of a moral simplification process or moral minimalism where complicated internal conflicts must be reduced to notions of right and wrong, good and bad before it becomes politically viable for the international community to intervene. This approach to international affairs has both disadvantages and advantages from a humanitarian perspective. An important disadvantage is that the international community simply does not know what to do (therefore, it generally does nothing) when just about everyone turns out to be part of the wrong/bad team. This is often the case when it seems that entire populations are involved in conducting atrocities against each other. One criminal act leads to another, and revenge and retaliation form a vicious circle of violence.

In all instances, those who lead or encourage others to commit criminal acts should be identified, and they must be held morally and legally accountable for their actions. If it is just not practically possible to apprehend and try some of these criminals then we must censure such individuals and groups in the strongest possible terms. All legal means of bringing them to justice must be relentlessly pursued.

One advantage of moral minimalism is that simple notions of right and wrong are useful as intuitive moral prompts to encourage international attention, and then maybe intervention. Unlawfully killing, raping, torturing and otherwise deliberately abusing people is clearly wrong; therefore, stopping such abuse must be morally obligatory according to minimalist thinking. Potential interventionists seek to identify possible friends from likely foes before intervening. Even on the rare occasions when intervention is said to be purely for humanitarian reasons, the international community must still go through the laborious but necessary process of friend/foe identification. However, it should instead be concentrating on who is being abused and who is doing the abusing. Australia's intervention in East Timor in 1999 is an example of this friend/foe quandary.

Much is made about Australia's common bond with the East Timorese. They helped Australian soldiers in Timor during WW II at great personal risk. The East Timorese are our friends, we said. We must help them. The dilemma for Australia is that it also has substantial diplomatic and economic ties with Indonesia. Whether these links mean that Australia sees Indonesia as a regional 'friend' may be debatable, but such associations have clearly influenced the time it took for Australia to respond to serious violations of human rights by Indonesia in East Timor.

Identifying who is individually responsible for instigating extreme human rights abuses is not impossible. Those who aggressively pursue their ideological and political goals in an unlawful manner with minimal or no constraints are directly responsible for crimes against humanity. They frequently incite their supporters to

---

3    Michael Walzer, 'The Politics of Rescue,' *Social Research* 62, no. 1 (1995): p. 53.

carry out morally abhorrent acts and they condone activities considered by most of humanity to be unacceptable. They must be held accountable for their actions.

Allocating responsibility in this way could be challenged. Adolf Hitler and Joseph Stalin enjoyed wide spread popular support before, and even after, they began orchestrating what we now consider to be atrocities. Their supporters did not consider them to be war criminals. So, being classified a war criminal depends to a significant extent dependant on which side of the fence you are on.

This ignores an important moral point. Allocating responsibility for human rights abuses is not about whether a particular population supports such activity or if unacceptable human behaviour is sometimes, for whatever reason, somehow 'popular'. It does not matter who committed an atrocity on whom or why. It is the act itself that determines culpability during humanitarian abuse not the reason behind the act. This applies equally to belligerents as it does to interventionists.

The many third parties who directly or indirectly support crimes against humanity must share responsibility for these crimes. Those who look the other way and those who express concern over human rights violations but then do little to address the problem are all responsible. The international community frequently expresses deep concern over violations of human rights, but it must assume a greater responsibility for the compliance and enforcement of international law. This was not done during the Balkan's conflict and it is not being done in many places around the globe today.

Why were Serbs permitted to repeatedly bomb, mortar and shell the UN declared safe-areas around the Muslim enclaves of Srebrenica, Sarajevo, Tuzla, Zepa, Gorazade and Bihac? Serb action caused extensive civilian casualties and significant suffering. Why are no Serbs held responsible for such blatant and illegal acts? Why is no one in the UN held responsible for failing to properly defend the 'safe-areas' against these Serb attacks? In these cases, there is culpability on all sides.

Failing to stop serious humanitarian abuses supports the murderous activities of belligerents. Criminal acts perpetrated against the helpless must be addressed not only by parties involved in conflict but also by the international community as a whole. Everyone is responsible for allowing severe violations of human rights to continue. Neither a struggle for independence nor a declaration of war morally justifies crimes against humanity. Simply being in a conflict situation or retaliating against some real or imagined feud between parties also does not justify this type of human behaviour.

It is increasingly difficult to keep crimes against humanity an absolute secret in this age of swift global communications. Responsibility for humanitarian abuse resides with political and military leaders who conduct or condone atrocities. It also resides with the international community for failing to effectively address gross violations of human rights.

## Military Intervention in Support of Humanitarian Objectives

Military intervention by the UN (or by anyone else) to alleviate a humanitarian situation is a contentious issue because there is a practical limit to what a force of arms can accomplish in the sphere of humanitarian relief. A force of arms in this sense refers to direct military action, and not military logistics or support activities assisting others. Such action will achieve very little in the medium to long term if follow-up mediation, diplomacy and other non-violent humanitarian assistance does not occur.

The military needs clear political and strategic directives, realistic mission goals and achievable military objectives before forceful intervention should even be considered. Today's military forces are trained and equipped to protect their own citizens, but they are not well prepared to deal with the complexities of another state's internal conflicts. Where political systems are in chaos and identification of friend from foe is difficult, perhaps impossible, military forces have great difficulty in carrying out their humanitarian mandate. These practical, day-to-day problems for the military increase exponentially if their political masters are not sure what the political, strategic or humanitarian goals are or should be. Domestic support is important for those intending to intervene but military intervention cannot hope to be effective if it is based primarily on daily approval ratings.

Then there is the challenge of reconciling military objectives with humanitarian objectives. The simple answer is that humanitarian objectives should come first, but unless clear political goals are in place direct humanitarian intervention will quickly degenerate into a tit-for-tat exchange between interventionists and belligerents. Military intervention in Somalia during 1993–94 is only one such example. In December 1992, Operation Restore Hope was an international effort to restore law and order to Somalia and to ensure the delivery of humanitarian supplies to the starving Somali population. Leadership of the operation was turned over to the UN in May 1993. The UN undertook a much more ambitious program of nation-building and disarmament but was militarily totally unprepared for such an ambitious project. After more than two billion dollars had been spent by the international community and 130 peacekeepers had died trying to carry out the UN mandate. The UN withdrew in March 1995 and the mission to Somalia was judged a failure.[4]

The military has a crucial role in humanitarian affairs, and it is not limited to fixing bridges, guarding food convoys, or being a logistics packhorse. The logistics and support role of the military is an essential one, and it should be used much more extensively, but the military is uniquely equipped and trained to apply the force of arms. The quandary is how and when this force should be applied. If and why it should be applied is as much a moral problem as it is a diplomatic and political problem. The how and when of coercive intervention are tactical and strategic issues for the military to resolve based on parameters outlined by their political masters.

---

4    F.M. Lorenze, 'Operation Restore Hope,' *Parameters* (1996): pp. 52–62.

Military interventionists initially need to take on the role of peacemaker in order to create an environment where peacekeeping and peace-building may be effective. The traditional UN convention of only entering another sovereign state when invited, and then only as lightly armed observers and monitors, has encouraged belligerents to mouth platitudes and to make promises of peace whilst continuing on with atrocities.

The international community should not entertain the idea of policing or peacekeeping until belligerents stop the abuse and the killing. If they refuse to stop then suitably armed peacemakers must intervene. To expect UN peacekeepers to keep the peace in situations where there is unrelenting and deliberate violations of all the norms of human behaviour is unrealistic and dangerous. There is no peace to keep.

An important issue when considering using the military in humanitarian situations is the need for collective decision making about how, when and where military force is to be used. Such decision-making is best left to a representative humanitarian organisation such as the UN. Current thinking is that the military should only be used (if it is used at all) as a last resort option, but we need to reconsider this approach. Constraining the use of external force only to a final option response allows genocide and the other crimes against humanity a free reign up until the point of forceful intervention. Richard Haass argues that the just war requirement of last resort he finds ill-advised, mainly because its observance may mean the loss of surprise and the loss of initiative. And when force is used, he says, '…it is better to err on the side of using more rather than less.'[5]

Endless diplomatic manoeuvrings and negotiations, long-term economic sanctions and trade embargos, closing embassies and so on, are all quite irrelevant to those facing immediate extermination or serious deprivation. This is a short-sighted approach to tackling humanitarian crises. Even if the killing and torture was to stop for the moment, as soon as the interventionists leave the atrocities will usually start again. Those who favour contingency planning, diplomatic engagement, mediation, dialog between conflicting parties, and other longer-term strategic planning to address serious human rights abuses will not be convinced that the use of force is of much practical use in these circumstances.

Longer term plans and strategies to tackle humanitarian issues are important, but it is a mistake to reject forcible intervention outright in the hope that such strategies will just materialise or simply to assume that they will be effective. The UN and the developed world have been implementing long-term solutions and contingency planning on the African continent for over 60 years but the humanitarian crises have increased not lessened. Many hundreds of thousands of people have died and suffered waiting for diplomacy, contingency planning and all the rest of it to work.

Alternatives to military intervention should be fully supported if they have a realistic chance of being effective. What they must not do is to simply provide a

---

    5    Richard Haass, 'Intervention: The Use of Military Force in the Post-Cold War World,' *Foreign Affairs* 73, no. 6 (1994): p. 168.

more morally palatable alternative to the use of force when the use of force could be more effective. Cross table conferences, 'ceasefires' and embargos must not end up as mere diplomatic exercises with indefinable outcomes resulting in barely a pause to the abuse. Each day such strategies are in place and not working increases human death and suffering.

Third party military intervention is specifically intended to be for a short time only and it must be fully supported by follow-up mediation and diplomacy. Its primary goal must be to immediately separate and disarm conflicting parties to protect civilians and non-combatants. This type of intervention will not, and is not intended to, solve the many complex and difficult problems inherent with humanitarian crises. What it can do is immediately stop the killing and severe deprivations so alternatives to the coercive use of force – mediation, dialog, cross table talks, sanctions, and diplomacy – have an opportunity to work.

Yves Sandoz, the ICRC Director for Principles, Law and Relations proposed that international intervention should be based on three principles central to the provisions of humanitarian law.[6] Firstly, a party to a conflict does not have the right to starve its adversary's population. It must allow free passage for international relief consignments intended for that population when such assistance proves necessary. Secondly, parties to a conflict have an obligation to supply all civilians under their control (including their own population) with food, medicines and other items essential to their survival. Thirdly, should the conflicting parties be unable to supply a needy population with basic essentials then they must accept international help to deliver such assistance to territories under their control.

These three principles reflect some of the requirements of humanitarian law as contained in the 1949 Geneva Convention and their Additional Protocols of 1977. They recognise the rights of victims to receive assistance in international and non-international conflicts. Should any of these three principles be violated then compliance must be imposed – by force if necessary. Violation of human rights is more than withholding food and other supplies to a needy population. Unlawful internment and execution, torture and deliberate policies of ethnic, racial, cultural or religious persecution also require direct intervention by the international community. The requirement for forcible intervention will depend on whether mediation with the conflicting groups immediately proves to be successful or not.

The make up of interventionist military forces is an important issue. Multinational military forces under the control of the UN, a regional security organization such as NATO, or a combination of the two groups intervening on behalf of the international community are the best organisational outcomes for coercive intervention. Which states should participate, what contributions are required, who should manage the command and control aspects of the humanitarian mission, and who should have

---

6    Yves Sandoz, Director for Principles, Law and Relations of the ICRC,. 'The Right to Intervene on Humanitarian Grounds: Limits and Conditions'. (paper presented at the Committee of Foreign Affairs and Security of the European Parliament, Brussels, 25 January 1994).

overall political and strategic control of the operation are all crucial aspects of the planning process.

The make up of such a military force is not just a matter of which combination is militarily the most suitable because many other factors will influence the force composition. Domestic support, the structure and competency of the intervening forces, capacity to finance the cost of the operation, and the longer term strain to economic and diplomatic relationships between participants are all issues that must be addressed.

Domestic support is an important factor underpinning potential intervention. Currently, many of the major powers are in a relatively weak domestic political position so, unless national security is directly threatened, states are very reluctant to participate in foreign military missions. Many political leaders also genuinely doubt whether outside military intervention would actually benefit the states in trouble.

Developing nations, particularly those who have previously been under colonial rule, are very suspicious of the so-called merits of foreign military intervention. They view such intervention as a direct violation of national sovereignty, and they are rightly concerned that this could lead to exploitation even if the stated objective initially is to protect human life. This is because forcible intervention historically has had unclear mandates with vague, often indefinable objectives.

The UN and the international community must provide a clear mandate and concise mission objectives for the military. It is not the military's role to define the broader strategic mission objectives or to develop their own mandates for intervention. This leads to mission-creep where mandates and objectives keep changing. Under these circumstances, there is the danger that force may be used for reasons that have little to do with why the military is supposed to be there in there in the first place.

Developed countries are reluctant to become involved because they would have to bear most of the cost for the operation. In most democratic countries, involvement in a military operation that could have significant economic and human costs generates complex domestic debates. The debates usually centre on how resources are allocated, what the risk is to interventionists, and what the relevance of such involvement is relative to their own national security. Few leaders will risk their political futures on participating in some foreign military adventure (no matter how apparently desperate the humanitarian situation) without overwhelming domestic support.

Domestic support usually depends upon at least three important factors. Firstly, there needs to be a general acceptance that some sort of moral obligation exists to intervene in the first place. Intervention will not proceed without either the national interest being at risk or the existence of a moral imperative to stop the atrocities. Secondly, people need to be convinced to move past the stage of proclaiming concern to actually doing something quickly and effectively to stop serious human rights violations. This is the most difficult stage of the process to be overcome. Much concern with little action is usually what occurs.

Thirdly, after a decision is made that it would be morally right to act, and that something needs to be done immediately, the important decision about what to do must be addressed. If, at any of these three stages, strong domestic support cannot be generated then intervention in humanitarian crises will (at best) probably end up being restricted to handing out food parcels, medicines and blankets, and expressions of outrage.

One way to generate domestic support for the possible use of coercive force is for politicians to focus on the consequences of inaction as applied to their own state's welfare. The destruction of entire communities, massive movements of displaced persons, possible disruption to international commerce, and the disruption to regional security and trade could all be viewed as outcomes that may seriously affect the national interests of states external to the conflict area.

Environmental concerns should also not be discounted as a prompt for the international community to at least begin to try to resolve humanitarian crises. The deliberate sabotage of the oil wells in Kuwait caused extensive damage to the marine environment in the Persian Gulf. Environmental damage from a nuclear exchange or a biological weapons attack between two warring factions is not likely to be limited only to the belligerents in the conflict – the consequences would be global.

The UN has a pivotal role in military intervention for humanitarian reasons. It is generally perceived as being a caring, humanitarian organisation that has played a notable, and often very difficult, part in the maintenance of international peace since WW II. UN resolutions and decrees based on humanitarian law add a measure of legitimacy to military action. The legitimacy of forceful military intervention is itself a crucial factor to encourage the participation of some of the more reluctant nation states to become involved in international peacekeeping or peacemaking efforts.

## *The Role of Third Parties in International Conflict*

Joseph Starke proposes that third parties currently become involved in external armed conflict in a number of ways. [7]   For example, a state may declare itself neutral. Other states involved in the conflict do not have the legal right to attack a state that declares itself to be neutral. This type of 'involvement' in conflict is recognised in the Laws of the Hague and Geneva. Bulgaria, Greece, Hungary and Albania declared themselves to be neutral from the Balkan conflict.

Another scenario is where a third party is recognised by international law as being an interventionist. The accepted legal sense of this term is that the party is not a belligerent in the conflict rather it is involved in the rescue of nationals, Services Assisted Evacuation (SAE), protecting people within no-go zones, securing the free passage of humanitarian aid, and so on. This category involves parties who act as observers, monitors of the peace (or ongoing conflict if there is no peace), and supervisors of the distribution of humanitarian aid. These are known as the interpositionary force or the peacekeepers. The UN frequently provides observers, cease-fire monitors and military interpositionary forces for peacekeeping purposes.

---

7    Joseph Starke, *Introduction to International Law. 10th Edition*, 10th ed. (London: Butterworths Publishing, 1989), p. 130.

I have argued that there is a crucial role for a fourth group. These are the peacemakers. The peacemakers' job is to enforce a ceasefire by immediately stopping belligerents attacking their victims. Peacemakers must ensure that all heavy weapons are either destroyed of permanently removed from the area of conflict. They must close down compounds that illegally restrain people.

Peacemakers should not be interested in whether belligerents will *allow* their heavy weapons to be removed, whether they will *agree* to the central conditions for a ceasefire, or whether they are *prepared to release* illegally detained persons. The peacemaker's primary purpose is to make these things happen. The role of peacemaker is further discussed later. It is quite likely that one party may need to fulfil both interventionist and interpositionary roles. The UN had interpositionary ground forces in the Balkans protecting the distribution of humanitarian aid and supervising protected zones. At the same time, UN sanctioned interventionist air forces enforced no-go areas, bombed ground forces and shot down Serb aircraft. The UN carried out both roles simultaneously.

*Traditional Functions of the Peacekeeper*

The traditional functions of peacekeeping are observation, fact-finding, disarmament/ demobilisation, human rights monitoring, election/referendum monitoring, and humanitarian assistance. The traditional view is that the UN should always be neutral, non-partisan and that it must seek consensus from all parties before attempting to carry out humanitarian objectives.[8][9]  The following briefly outlines the traditional peacekeeping functions.

Observation. The dispatch of small numbers of unarmed observers to trouble spots with the consent of the conflicting parties. This usually occurs after a cease-fire has been agreed to. Sometimes the presence of the observers may be negotiated as an integral part of the cease-fire. Fact-finding. Again, only small numbers of personnel are involved. The UN mission to Tajikistan (UNMOT) involved fact-finding, observation and conflict status reporting to try to determine which side breached the many cease-fires.

Supervision. The supervisory peacekeeping role usually involves the placement of a much larger, lightly armed military presence of several thousand troops. Supervisory tasks include the securing of a cease-fire and occasionally, with the consent of all parties, the withdrawal of conflicting troops to positions occupied by the parties before the cease-fire was instigated. A model for this operation was UNEF I established between Egypt and Israel in 1956.

Disarmament/Demobilisation.   This is a much rarer occurrence of the peacekeeping process in that it signifies a willingness of the conflicting parties to lay down their arms. Combined with the notion of consensual peacekeeping,

---

8    Dennis Jett, *Why Peacekeeping Fails* (New York: St Martins Press, 1999), pp. 1–19.

9    Marrack Goulding, 'The Evolution of United Nations Peacekeeping,' *International Affairs* 69, no. 3 (1993).

the supervision of peaceful settlement may progress through disarmament and/or demobilisation. The Contra rebels agreeing to voluntary demobilisation in March 1990 could be considered to be an example of UN instigated disarmament processes in action. Although this probably had as much to do with the right-wing opposition securing victory in the elections against the left-wing Sandinista government as it had with any efforts of the ONUCA mission.

Human Rights Monitoring. The UN Observer Mission in El Salvador was set up to verify that the parties to the long-running civil war between the US backed government and the left-wing Farabundo Marti National Liberation Front (FMLN) comply with the human rights accord they both signed at San Jose in July 1990.[10] The UNOSAL mission's primary task was to monitor compliance with the San Jose Agreement.[11]

Election/Referendum Monitoring. After UNAVEM I had successfully supervised the withdrawal of Cuban troops from Angola in June 1991, UNAVEM II was created following the Lisbon Agreement of 31 may 1991. An important part of the UNAVEM mission was the supervision of the Angolan police force who monitored the election process.[12] The elections were held on 29 and 30 September 1992 under UNAVEM II's election monitoring processes.

Humanitarian Assistance. The efforts of UNPROFOR in Bosnia Herzegovina reflect a recent increasing trend for UN missions to become directly involved in humanitarian assistance. UN Involvement in East Timor is another example. Humanitarian assistance includes the provision of food and other essential basic necessities for life. It may include the monitoring of safe havens for protection of civilians and other non-combatants.

## Expanded Peacekeeping, Peace-Enforcement, and Peacemaking

In 1992, the Secretary-General of the United Nations, Boutros Boutros-Ghali, submitted his Agenda for Peace at the request of the Security Council. The document hinted at an expanded peacekeeping, peace-enforcement and peacemaking role for the UN. Boutros-Ghali fundamentally underestimated what is involved in such activities, and the terminology used in the document did not define the UN role. He incorrectly used the term 'peace-enforcement' to refer to actions aimed at maintaining a cease-fire and at actions to re-instate a failed cease-fire.

I recommend that the Council consider the utilization of peace-enforcement units in clearly defined circumstances and with their terms of reference specified in advance...Just as diplomacy will continue across the span of all the activities dealt within the present report, so there may not be a dividing line between peacemaking and peacekeeping.[13]

---

10  United Nations, 'Document S/21541,' (1990).

11  United Nations, 'Un Security Council Resolution 693, 46 Unscor,' (1994).

12  United Nations, 'Document S/22627 Additional 1,' (1991).

13  Boutros Boutros-Ghali, 'An Agenda for Peace. Preventive Diplomacy, Peacemaking and Peace-Keeping.' (paper presented at the Summit Meeting of the Security Council, New

Donald Snow points out that this interpretation is quite different from the US Force's Joint Staff view that there needs to be a clear distinction between peace-enforcement and peacekeeping. The Joint Staff view is that peace-enforcement is the physical interposition of armed forces to separate ongoing combatants to create a cease-fire that does not yet exist. [14] This means that management and supervision of cease-fires is a role of the peacekeeper whereas peace-enforcement requires that the conditions for a cease-fire must first be created.

The interpretation of the difference between peacekeeping and peace-enforcement is an important point. The problem remains that the term peace-enforcement still implies that there is some sort of peace existing in the first place to enforce. In 1995, Boutros-Ghali again presented his Agenda for Peace. The term peace-enforcement now disappeared from his rhetoric and he talked about peacemaking and peace-building.[15] The UN had developed a range of instruments for controlling and resolving conflicts between and within States. The most important of them, according to the Secretary-General, were preventive diplomacy and peacemaking; peace-keeping; peace-building; disarmament; sanctions and so on. 'The first three can be employed only with the consent of the parties to the conflict.'[16]

There is still a fundamental problem with this revised interpretation of peacemaking in that the term is used in connection with the idea of preventive diplomacy. This blurs the distinction between making peace and keeping peace. Peacemaking is not about preventive diplomacy. It is about making peace when preventative diplomacy has failed. Peacekeeping and peacemaking must not be seen as being the same or even similar operations. Peacemakers should be clearly seen for what they are. They are interventionist military forces that have a mandate to make peace where no peace exists.

Most importantly, peacemaking is not just about creating cease-fires between belligerents. Peacemaking must also address the terrible outcomes of humanitarian abuse. All prisoner-of-war camps must conduct their operations in accordance with the requirements of the Geneva Conventions. Civilian holding camps violate international law and they must immediately be closed down and their occupants repatriated. All impediments to the transportation of humanitarian aid must be withdrawn. The free movement of humanitarian aid workers within the conflict areas must be without condition and without obstruction. Conflicting parties must be disarmed. There is little point in enforcing an immediate cessation of hostilities with the result that belligerents remain armed to the teeth waiting for interventionist forces to withdraw.

---

York, 17 June 1992).

14  Donald Snow, 'Peacekeeping, Peacemaking, and Peace-Enforcement: The Us Role in the New International Order' (paper presented at the US Army War College Fourth Annual Strategy Conference, 24–25 February, 1993).

15  Ibid.

16  Boutros Boutros-Ghali, 'Supplement to an Agenda for Peace: Position Paper of the Secretary-General on the Occasion of the Fiftieth Anniversary of the United Nations,' (New York: United Nations, 1995): p. 7.

Heavy weapons, offensive weapons platforms and all WMDs must either be confiscated or destroyed. Once the cessation of armed hostilities has been realised, the peacemaking mandate should be withdrawn and peacekeeping should take over. Peacemaking combat and force projection elements should then be removed from the theatre of operations to encourage diplomacy and conciliation efforts.

Conciliation efforts may be hampered if the peacemakers and the peacekeepers are essentially the same group, so ideally the peacekeepers should be nationally independent from the peacemakers. If the choice is either a single multinational force carrying out both functions or no action at all, then a single multinational coalition of forces should carry out both the role of peacemaker and the role of peacekeeper.

The decision to pursue either a peacemaking or a peacekeeping strategy must be a humanitarian decision endorsed by the UN. If the UN is incapable of making such a decision (not an outlandish suggestion judging from its past performance) then a multinational collective of concerned states must make the decision to intervene. NATO action in Bosnia Herzegovina is an example of such intervention.

Individual states may need to act on their own if a multinational collective of concerned states cannot come to a consensus about what to do regarding a serious humanitarian situation. This is a highly undesirable final option for military intervention. Despite the undesirability of states acting unilaterally Tanzania intervened to stop Idi Amin in Uganda in 1979, Vietnam intervened in Cambodia in 1979, and India intervened in East Pakistan (now Bangladesh) in 1971. This was declared to be the lawful use of force to '...end practices considered shocking to the human conscience'. [17]

The international community has not fulfilled all its humanitarian obligations just by peacemaking and peacekeeping. War criminals must be ruthlessly pursued and brought before an international court of justice, destroyed civil infrastructures must be rebuilt and the delivery of essential humanitarian aid must continue. These are critical elements of any attempts to use force to address widespread and deliberate abuse.

To effectively address gross violations of human rights, peacemaking, peacekeeping, the active pursuit of justice, and the immediate delivery of essential humanitarian aid to those who need it are crucial elements of an overall interventionist strategy. Peacemaking cannot be effective if those who conduct atrocities remain armed and free. Peacekeeping cannot work if there is no peace to keep in the first place, and neither peacemaking nor peacekeeping will ultimately be judged successful if all that is left is a scorched earth and a traumatised society.

*Peacemaking in Kosovo: A Military Success, a Humanitarian Disaster*

The international community was aware of the rapidly escalating Serb violence against the Kosovar people from at least January 1998. In early 1998 dozens of civilians were killed in the Drenica and Racak regions. Surely no one could have been surprised that Yugoslav forces were continuing their ethnic cleansing policies

---

17  Groenewold, Porter, and Mâedecins sans frontiáeres (Association), *World in Crisis. The Politics of Survival at the End of the Twentieth Century.*

in Kosovo. This was after the many Serb atrocities conducted throughout Bosnia Herzegovina for most of the past decade.

Map 1 shows the province of Kosovo and southern Yugoslavia, Macedonia (a former republic of Yugoslavia) and Albania. Map 2 is a map of Kosovo and its location within Yugoslavia proper.

The international community had more than enough warning, regarding Serb activities in Kosovo, and there was adequate time to militarily prepare for intervention. Each day and each hour was crucial to the survival of Kosovars who were relentlessly being pursued by the Serbs. The eventual use of air power against the Serbs in Kosovo was a militarily success but a humanitarian disaster. Intervention should have included ground forces to support the air campaign. There were a number of military challenges to be overcome such as a difficult mountainous terrain, poor road access, limited entry points to launch a ground assault and so on but nothing which would rule out the use of ground forces by highly mobile assault forces as being militarily impossible.

Was such action feasible as a strategy to significantly improve the humanitarian plight of the Kosovars? Yes, it was providing intervention was overwhelming and immediate. NATO action was neither. An understandable fear of possible interventionist casualties, and the lack of a coherent international political framework for intervention, resulted in air power alone being used to try to break the political will of Slobodan Milosevic. This strategy meant that Serb tanks, artillery, and mortars could simply continue with their destruction of Kosovo's civil infrastructure. Serb troops did not halt their ethnic cleansing activities.

The NATO air campaign was a humanitarian disaster because for eleven weeks bombing downtown Belgrade did nothing to stop Serb activity in Kosovo. The use of air power alone as a military strategy is itself fundamentally flawed because it cannot take or hold territory. Taking and holding territory is vital because otherwise opposing forces will dig in, wait out a particular air strike then emerge to conduct business as usual.

NATO estimates of damage to Serb forces in Kosovo were highly inflated and not substantiated even after the conflict.[18] Of course, the Serbs did suffer casualties but not enough to dissuade them from attacking the Kosovars. Only by immediately and simultaneously overwhelming the Serb forces by air attacks and ground force assaults could the international community hope to stop the atrocities from continuing.

A combined air and ground assault directly against the Serb military and police units operating in the province is what was required in Kosovo. There was no point trying to destroy the network of command and control systems of the Yugoslav Army and police because the military units on the ground in Kosovo operated as autonomous entities. They were not reliant on tactical control from Belgrade.

---

18  Ryan Lizza, 'The Numbers Game,' *The New Republic* 221, no. 3/4 (1999): p. 16. NATO estimated over 150 of the 300 Serb tanks in Kosovo were destroyed, however reporters travelling all over the conflict areas after hostilities had ceased reported seeing only one destroyed tank.

**Map 2.1 The Province of Kosovo and Southern Yoguslavia**

**Map 2.2 Kosovo**

Bombing the police headquarters, military barracks, power and water supply infrastructures, and the television stations in Belgrade was militarily irrelevant to the Serb forces in Kosovo.[19]

The initial assault should have been a one week, overwhelming strategic and tactical bombing campaign to eliminate Serb air defences and as many artillery, tanks, mortar positions and troop concentrations as possible. This posed a particular problem for NATO because the Serb forces were well dispersed among the civilian population. This made an overwhelming ground assault even more important. The Washington Post reported that General Wesley K. Clark, the supreme allied commander in Europe, called together British and U.S. officers at NATO headquarters in Mons, Belgium, to poll their views on various ground options.

Not all the military, and certainly not all in the White House Administration, favoured the use of ground troops but in Mons, the senior military staff gave Clark a stark assessment: 'If you want to induce the Serbs to leave Kosovo, you are going to have to use ground forces to do it,' in the words of one officer. 'We all felt very strongly we would have to go to a ground option, and that we needed to begin deployment of U.S. and allied forces for that purpose as soon as possible, knowing what the timelines were for an invasion before winter.[20] By mid-May, Clark had come up with a preliminary plan for an attack from the south by 175,000 troops, mostly through a single road from Albania. But political imperatives, and military strategic problems with the actual transportation of large numbers of ground troops into Kosovo ultimately defeated the 'Wes Plan'.

NATO forces should have parachuted quick reaction and special forces into Kosovo to take and hold strategic choke points. This would be in readiness for the immediate insertion – over both air and land – of light to medium NATO armour and significant numbers of ground troops. The U.S. 101st Air Assault Division could have staged an assault from Italy directly into Kosovo.[21]

US Generals claimed that NATO could assemble up to 40,000 ground troops to protect Kosovar civilians '...within days', and they continually warned about overestimating Serbian military strength.[22] Possible NATO troop entry points into Kosovo could have been through Albania, Bulgaria or Romania, or through Macedonia. Maps 3 and 4 are maps of Albania showing possible entry points into Yugoslavia.

As such a strategy was never finally considered by NATO (except at the very end of the air campaign) we will never know whether these states would have agreed to NATO's military build-up on their territory, or whether they would have agreed to being a launch pad for military operations into Kosovo. None of these countries

19  Abrams, 'Just War. Just Means?.'

20  Dana Priest, 'Kosovo Land Threat May Have Won War,' *Washington Post*, 19 September 1999.

21  'The Ground War Scenario,' *The Economist*, 29 May 1999.

22  Patrick Moore, 'U.S. Generals Say Ground Forces Could Protect Kosovars,' *The Balkan Report* 3 (1999).

**Map 2.3 Albania**

actually ruled out the possibility of NATO forces gaining access to Kosovo through their territories.

NATO air supremacy meant that round-the-clock close-air support for the initial and subsequent waves of ground forces was possible. Close air support is where battlefield commanders are able to call on helicopter gun-ships and other air assets to respond to enemy entrenchments or attacks. Guided Tomahawk missiles launched either from the Adriatic Sea or from aircraft, backed up by air-to-ground missiles fired by helicopters and ground attack aircraft, would quickly have overwhelmed any entrenched Serb resistance.

Very few states today would be able to resist NATO's massive fire support tactics, and the strategic insertion of well armed and highly trained, quick reaction forces. Within two to three weeks NATO should have been able to take all the major strategic choke points in Kosovo. They could then have immediately followed this initial assault with the insertion and deployment of significant numbers of ground troops.

This is the highly successful Blitzkrieg method of conducting military operations. Blitzkrieg style military operations are never about conducting air campaigns on their own. They are about conducting a ferocious air campaign, which is directly and immediately supported by troops on the ground to mop up, and to take and hold ground. Enemy resistance is either bypassed then later dealt with or it is immediately overwhelmed.

The Serb's weakness was in their extended supply lines from Yugoslavia proper into Kosovo, their 1960's military equipment, obsolete soviet style military training, no air protection for their forces in Kosovo – NATO Special Forces had disabled the Yugoslav MIGs prior to the air campaign – and the doubtful enthusiasm of their conscripts operating in the province.

The fact that Serb forces had only ever been militarily successful against civilians and a rag-tag bunch of Kosovo Liberation Army recruits means that they had no experience confronting well-armed and highly trained troops with the resources of the NATO war machine. Few military analysts seriously considered that Serb forces had the capacity to resist a determined air and ground assault by NATO.

## Making Peace and the UN

The international community will not continue to provide finances for the multi-billion dollar operating budget of the UN if the organisation repeatedly proves itself as being hopelessly inept at addressing the more difficult humanitarian situations around the globe. The UN cannot limit its operational procedures to observation, fact-finding, supervision and monitoring.

Multinational action in Somalia, in Bosnia Herzegovina, in Kosovo and UN involvement in East Timor indicates that the international community is prepared, at least sometimes, to use military force to stop extreme human rights abuses. The UN needs to review its interventionist policies. On the one hand, the Secretary General

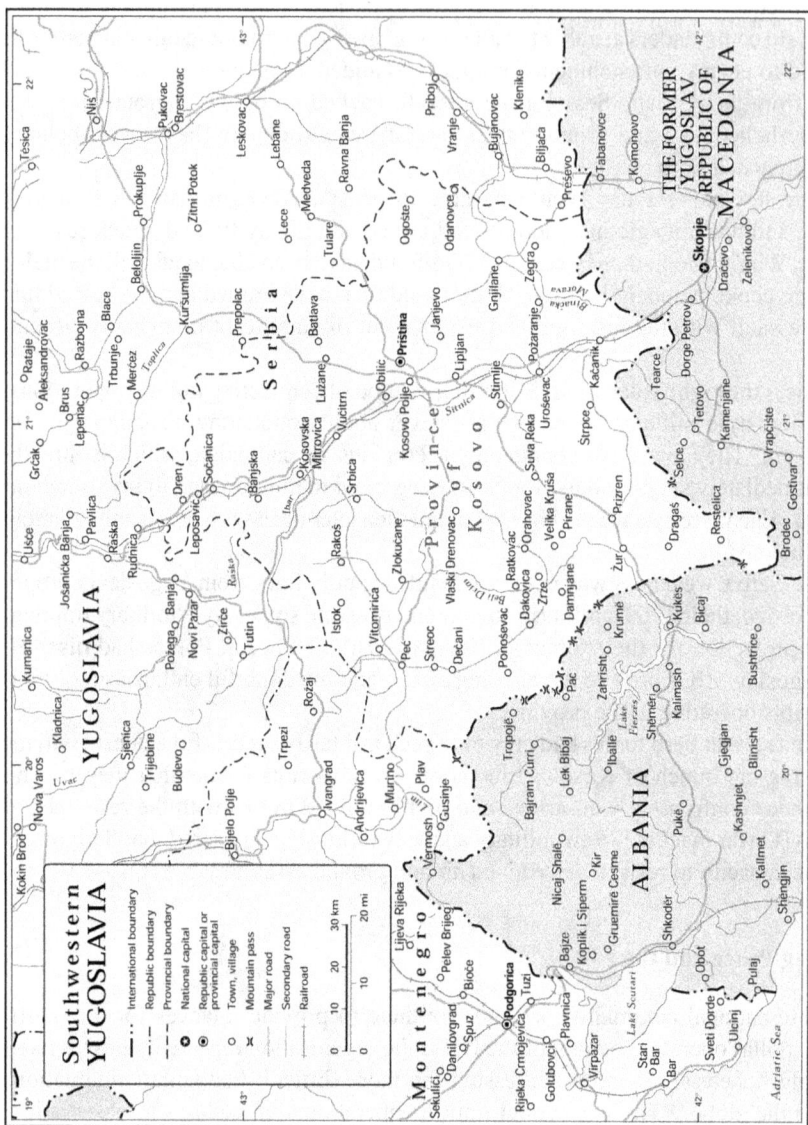

**Map 2.4 Albania and Southwestern Yugoslavia**

admits to the expanded role undertaken by the UN, but then he chides Member States for the use of force in situations other than for 'self-defence'. The UN cannot have it both ways. Either it supports the coercive use of force in some humanitarian situations or it reverts to a purely self-defensive role to protect the peacekeepers.

The UN did not change its peacekeeping strategy in Bosnia Herzegovina until just before authorising NATO military intervention in mid 1995. The reason for this late change of strategy is fully discussed in Chapter Five *Ethnic Conflict in the Balkans – A Case Study*. The French-preferred option of having UN troops on the ground to do the peacekeeping was abandoned for the US-preferred option of using NATO air strikes to enforce an immediate cessation to hostilities.

Repeated UN Security Council resolutions mandated the use of force by UNPROFOR, but only to ensure the safety of UN troops delivering humanitarian aid. A clear mandate to protect civilian populations in Bosnia Herzegovina was never given.[23]  Following the shelling of Sarajevo on 28 August 1995 – graphic pictures of the 37 dead and many wounded were transmitted live around the globe – NATO's Deliberate Force air strikes reacted against the BSA. Ninety targets in 23 areas were hit and, after two weeks and 850 bombing missions, the BSA having defied the UN for over three years had been knocked out.[24]

The reality in Bosnia Herzegovina was that the UN proved incapable of carrying out its peacekeeping mandate. Its so-called safe havens collapsed one after another. Srebrenica, Sarajevo, Tuzla, and Zepa turned into collecting pens of humanity and productive killing zones for the Serb Army. Atrocities continued unabated despite thousands of UN observers and monitors.[25]  Only when the Member States of the UN in desperation turned to NATO for military intervention did the heavy guns of the Serb Army cease firing and the mass killings stop. The hurried authorisation by the UN for NATO to act as peacemaker only came after intensive international pressure.

The Secretary General was overly optimistic when, in his concluding remarks in his 1995 Agenda for Peace, he said that;

> There is no reason for frustration or pessimism. More progress has been made in the past few years towards using the United Nations as it was designed to be used than many could have predicted.[26]

200,000 dead in Bosnia-Herzegovina and more than 2 million refugees in the region do not bear out his upbeat assessment of UN performance. The role of peacemaker is fraught with danger and military intervention by force of arms should only be undertaken with extreme caution. The imposition of military force is a risky but

---

23  Groenewold, Porter, and Mâedecins sans frontiáeres (Association), *World in Crisis. The Politics of Survival at the End of the Twentieth Century.*

24  Ibid., p. 133.

25  Ibid., pp. 127–29.

26  Boutros-Ghali, 'Supplement to an Agenda for Peace: Position Paper of the Secretary-General on the Occasion of the Fiftieth Anniversary of the United Nations.'

crucial strategy to address humanitarian situations where accepted norms of human behaviour have been abandoned.

This is clearly a difficult and complex undertaking, but it should not be postponed until the situation degenerates so badly that only overwhelming revulsion by the international community finally prompts action. This is currently how many man-made humanitarian disasters are handled. Peacemaking may be applied in a range of different strategic and tactical situations but the bottom line must always be that belligerents must stop the killing and unlawful deprivations. Military intervention means the forceful protection of safe-havens or diplomatic missions. There needs to be a clear distinction regarding the role of the peacemakers, and the difference between peacemaking and peacekeeping.

If safe-havens (currently misnamed because most of them are anything but safe) are attacked then a swift and decisive military retaliation by the international community must be the response. If diplomatic and peacekeeping missions are threatened or attacked then again forceful military retribution must be the response. The setting up of undefended safe-havens or diplomatic dialog with totally intractable conflicting parties is a waste of time if the killing and atrocities do not stop.

In some cases, this can be much worse than just a waste of time, as Rony Brauman of MSF points out. He presents the example of the Ethiopian crisis in 1985. The Ethiopian famine of 1984–85 resulted in the forced migration of over 800,000 people from the northern regions to the south. 200,000 died in the process. Non-government organizations (NGOs) including MSF set up a number of aid camps, which attracted many hundreds of thousands of refugees.

These undefended and neutral camps provided the human bait for the Ethiopian military forces of Colonel Mengistu. The feeding centres had become traps and killing grounds. The conflicting militias requisitioned even the trucks and cash given by the international community. This was ostensibly to speed up the forced migration. MSF is scathing in its criticism of international apathy to the conditions in the camps and by the lack of UN action over the systematic killings in the aid centres. Brauman said, 'As had occurred in the Second World War, the neutrality of the humanitarian organizations provided a benign facade for totalitarian power.'[27]

*Challenges to the Peacemakers*

There are at least three major issues involved in peacemaking. Firstly, the international community must not expect that the imposition of external military force in humanitarian situations will somehow solve differences between conflicting parties. These groups are often involved in complex ethnic, cultural and ideological conflicts some of which go back centuries.

Secondly, the efforts of the peacemakers will often be violently opposed. Casualties must be expected and a protracted fully-fledged military campaign may be needed to

---

27  Groenewold, Porter, and Mâedecins sans frontiáeres (Association), *World in Crisis. The Politics of Survival at the End of the Twentieth Century.*

stop a determined belligerent. Thirdly, peacemaking forces need specialised military structures, training, and resources from the international community in order to fulfil their role. Each of these points will be dealt with separately.

Military intervention is not a cure-all for international strife. The goal of peacemaking is not to solve deep-seated ethnic, ideological or other problems between intractable parties. The goal of peacekeeping is to immediately bring a halt to the ethnic cleansing practices, genocide and unlawful deprivation of people so that the differences between the belligerents may be aired and addressed outside the killing fields.

Until the killing stops nobody will be able to begin to address deep-seated political, racial or ideological differences, much less 'solve' them. Conflicting parties ultimately must solve their own problems. Neither peacekeepers nor peacemakers can do this for them. When the killing and serious abuse stops and the belligerents are disarmed, then another type of strategy is needed. This is a vital time for mediators, intermediaries, peacekeepers, diplomats, international law enforcement officers and human rights lawyers to become involved. When the guns and killing factories fall silent, then is the time to develop some sort of platform for reconciliation. Medium to longer-term resolution to serious international conflict will not occur without this second phase taking place.

There is currently a tense stand off in Mitrovica (a small but strategically important town in northern Kosovo) between the minority Serbs and the ethnic Albanians. What is happening in this small town is an example of the lack of planning and foresight by the international community regarding what it needs to do after forcible intervention.[28]

Mitrovica and points north are the only bits of Kosovo where ethnic Serbs (perhaps 50,000 of them) have stayed on in significant numbers since NATO troops took charge. The far north is the only place where Serbs are able to escape ethnic Albanian revenge. For Albanians, northern Mitrovica is the only place where the cleansing of non-Serbs continues. Map 5 shows the location of Mitrovica in northern Kosovo.

Sandwiched between these two protagonists is the UN peacekeeping force, which once again is mandated to observe, monitor and to maintain a ceasefire. Serbs and ethnic Albanians have clashed a number of times in Mitrovica, and they are barely able to stop themselves from an all out assault on each other.[29]

There is no second-phase strategy about what to do with the Mitrovica powder keg other than to try to keep the opposing groups physically separate. Poorly armed UN troops are used as the separators. The hope is that Serbs and the ethnic Albanians will just somehow learn to live together in some sort of peaceful coexistence. Most notably, the international mediators, diplomats, and human rights lawyers are conspicuous by their absence. In July 2004, HRW outlined the near-complete collapse during the crisis of Kosovo's security institutions—the NATO-led Kosovo

---

28  'Kosovo Untamed,' *The Economist*, 26 February 2000.
29  Ibid.

Force (KFOR), international civilian police from the U.N. Interim Administration Mission to Kosovo (UNMIK), and the locally-recruited Kosovo Police Service (KPS) in Mitrovica.

Another major problem for interventionist forces is the risk of casualties. Peacemakers and interventionist powers must expect casualties, sometimes heavy casualties, as a result of peacemaking. It is illogical to expect otherwise. Most military professionals understand such realities. Some Western societies unrealistically expect very low, even zero, casualties from military action. This is a worrying trend. Worrying, not because one should not care about casualties but because being fixated with the idea that somehow there must be no casualties in a lethal conflict environment is plainly irrational.

The only way to guarantee that interventionists will not suffer casualties is either to immediately withdraw from a conflict area or to conduct a war by remote control. Hence, the attraction of only using air power and long range weaponry. Usually, all that the military asks is that they are given lawful commands to carry out their military objectives and that they have the means to do so. Authorisation and ratification of military action by the UN are such lawful commands.

If the military suffers casualties in pursuit of its objectives then it will deal with these losses as it has done throughout history. By forbearance, fortitude, and faith in their political masters that what they are dying for has some point. Increasingly the idea of consideration for a wider community is expanding to include most of humanity.

The third major challenge for peacemaking is that such forces must have appropriate training and resources to carry out their mandate. These resources are available. The international community has military forces with enough firepower to wipe out the population of the globe many times over. Trillions of dollars are spent annually on military infrastructures. The international community needs to redirect a small portion of this military might into upholding international law. Complaints by the UN about lack of military resources to do its job are not because those military resources do not exist. It is because inadequate resources are allocated to the important job of peacemaking and peacekeeping.[30]

There are many other challenges for the would-be peacemakers. For example, who will command such a force? The command and control aspects of peacemaking should be left to a professional military organisation, or a coalition of military forces, authorised by the UN. This may be a military force structure such as NATO or a coalition group such as the 40 states who participated in the Gulf War against Iraq. Competent command and control is vital to any peacemaking endeavours.

A clear and workable mandate for peacemaking is required. The UN has already set some early precedents. In 1950, the Security Council authorised a group of Member States to undergo enforcement action in the Korean peninsula. In 1990, forceful military intervention was authorised by the UN for the Coalition Forces in

---

30   Strobe Talbott, 'The Crisis in Africa: Local War and Regional Peace,' *World Policy Journal* 17, no. 2 (2000): p. 23.

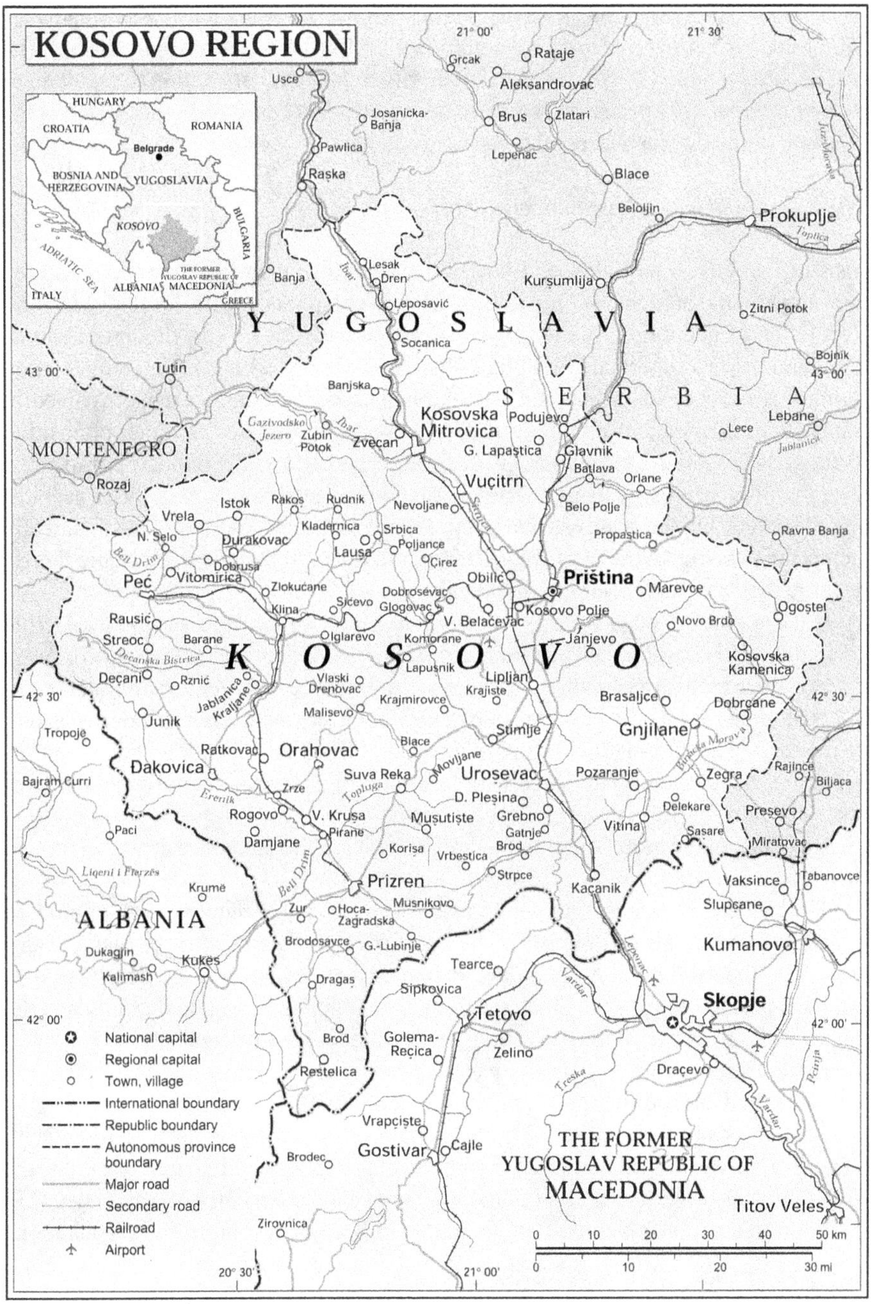

**Map 2.5  Kosovo Region within the Former Yugoslavia**

the Persian Gulf. Somalia, Rwanda, Haiti, Bosnia Herzegovina, Kosovo and East Timor are further examples of UN authorisation for the use of military force. The UN Security Council (UNSC) has the authority to take military action to maintain or restore international peace and security under Article 42 of the Charter. This is the mandate to instigate a peacemaking strategy.

*The Role of the UN in Humanitarian Wars*

Insisting on UN impartiality and non-partisan involvement in international affairs and not having procedures in place to ensure compliance with Declarations and Resolutions encourages humanitarian abuse worldwide. For the international community to assume that it will be effective in simply telling belligerents to stop fighting is unrealistic and naive. It is unrealistic because belligerents involved in intra-ethnic, ideological or religious conflicts aim to conquer as much opposition territory as possible. They aim to kill and injure, sometimes to eliminate completely, as many of their opponents as possible. Such views are at odds with the concept of a civil society, but the reality is that many groups and some entire nations fanatically support these objectives. Women, children, the old and the infirm are prime targets because they are the easiest to kill or subdue.

If these soft targets are eliminated then it is very difficult to sustain a guerrilla campaign. This is a simple equation in ethnic war. Belligerents in these types of wars are not interested in cease-fires, safe-areas, diplomatic intervention, humanitarian aid, sanctions, or world opinion unless they interfere with their ethnic cleansing processes. The international community has difficulty accepting these realities because it believes in compliance with rules and regulations, neutrality and at least some concern for the plight of fellow human beings. These perspectives are entirely alien to some of the more brutal protagonists involved in humanitarian abuses around the globe.

The UN must adapt its interventionist procedures to the requirements of modern humanitarian disaster situations.[31] The primary requirements must be that all sides must stop the killing, stop the unlawful imprisonment and stop the deprivation of innocent people. One of the greatest failings of the international community and the UN in the Balkans was not protecting the declared safe-areas and protection zones in Bosnia Herzegovina.[32] The UN has never accepted responsibility for declaring a safe-area then abandoning its inhabitants to belligerents.

Safe-areas are not safe simply by declaration. Recent history is filled with examples where the international community declares the existence of safe-areas only to find that the presence of humanitarian organizations provides the bait. Aid distribution centres and civilian protected areas become killing traps. Declarations

---

31   Jett, *Why Peacekeeping Fails*.

32   S Zifcak, 'International Human Rights and Humanitarian Law' (paper presented at the Vice Chancellor's Symposium, Griffith University Key Centre for Ethics, Law, Justice & Governance, Queensland Parliament House, Australia, 18 August 2000).

of safe-areas, safety zones, protected zones, no-fly zones and so on all have the same basic problem. Belligerents do not respect their sanctity.

They do not respect the poorly armed Blue Helmets within these zones, and they treat with contempt the multitude of unfulfilled threats not to interfere with humanitarian activities in the region of conflict. Those who deliberately violate the so called sanctity of a UN declared safety area would think twice if any violation of a protected zone resulted in an immediate, effective military response from the international community.

Those who are prepared to commit appalling crimes against humanity must be made to understand that their conduct is not acceptable to civilised society. From 1991 to mid 1999, the efforts of the UN and the international community to end the conflict in Bosnia Herzegovina and Kosovo did not convince the main protagonists that their conduct was unacceptable until they were forced to stop as a direct result of NATO action. Hundreds of thousands of defenceless people were killed, many more injured and millions displaced as a direct result of the international community's inadequate response to the appalling humanitarian situation in the Balkans.[33]   I have argued for a more forceful and direct strategy to stop international humanitarian abuse. Military intervention is sometimes the only way to stop the killing.

## Conclusion

Interventionists need to have specific ROE to manage the how of intervention. However, to justify intervention in the first place a broader perspective is needed. The international community needs to directly support a generic, broad based range of values which should affirm coexistence, tolerance and respect for all.

Insistence by the international community that all peoples adhere to the requirements of the Charter for Human Rights would be a positive start. If the Charter is deliberately violated, and violators refuse to heed international directives to stop the abuse and the killings, then a strong moral case exists for immediate action by the international community. The international community has not demonstrated any coherent logic or moral consistency regarding why intervention is warranted in some cases and not in others. There is little difference in the on-the-ground human suffering and deprivation between countries such as Kosovo, Albania, Rwanda, Cambodia, Somalia, East Timor and Afghanistan. Yet the international response to each of these humanitarian crises was not the same.

Some man-made humanitarian disasters, such as Rwanda and Cambodia, are just ignored until the deaths reach into the millions. Even then very few perpetrators are held accountable. If the international community declared genocide in Bosnia Herzegovina as sufficient grounds for international military intervention then it is

---

33   Human Rights Bureau of Democracy, and Labor., 'Bosnia and Herzegovina Country Report on Human Rights,' (US Department of State, 1998): pp. 1–35. The report estimates that during the war nearly 17,000 children were killed, 35,000 wounded, and over 1,800 permanently disabled.

blatantly hypocritical to ignore the clearer and considerably more severe genocide in the Sudan.

Similarly, the US determined that the breakdown of the Somali government merited American intervention while officials ignored the crisis in Rwanda after the 6 April 1994 assassination of President Habyarimana. Demands that US troops protect democracy in Haiti are inconsistent with the international community's indifference toward the suspension of democracy in Algeria when Muslim extremists were poised to win elections in 1992.

There are many other examples that show the inconsistency in international approaches to humanitarian concerns. The international community repeatedly tries to impose a set of rules for belligerents to follow based on incorrect premises. Firstly, that belligerents will do as they are told. Secondly, that protagonists care about international opinion.

No safe-havens should be declared unless the international community is fully prepared to enforce compliance on all parties to respect such declarations. The US strongly opposed the idea of safe-areas in Bosnia Herzegovina because they considered them to be glorified concentration camps for Bosnian Muslim refugees. They feared that such places would end up as semipermanent Beiruts. The US President called the enclaves shooting galleries and refused to let American troops join the UN forces to patrol them.

Coercive military intervention should have one primary goal. It must immediately bring to a halt the killing and extreme abuses suffered by helpless people. The rights and wrongs of the situation, who originally did what to whom, and any other attempts at justifying such appalling human conduct are all irrelevant to immediately stopping the atrocities. What is relevant is that the killing must stop.

Chapter 3

# Humanitarian Law and Military Intervention

## Introduction

Humanitarian law has become a complicated set of rules dealing with a variety of legal issues. Six major treaties with more than 600 articles and a complex mesh of customary law rules place restrictions on the use of violence during conflict. Despite many complications and complexities, humanitarian law may be summarised into what the International Court of Justice (ICJ) has called in the Corfu Channel Case (Case concerning Military and Paramilitary Activities in and against Nicaragua), 'elementary considerations of humanity' and 'fundamental general principles of humanitarian law'. Hans-Peter Gasser, former Senior Legal Adviser at the ICRC outlines these fundamental principles as follows;

Firstly, persons who are not taking part in hostilities must be respected, protected and treated humanely.[1] They must not be discriminated against and they must be given appropriate care. Secondly, captured combatants and other persons must be treated humanely. They are to be protected against all acts of violence, and in particular against cruel and/or unusual punishment or torture. If these persons are placed on trial they must be subject to internationally accepted judicial procedure. Thirdly, the means and methods of warfare are not unlimited. Superfluous injury or unnecessary suffering is not acceptable. Fourthly, armed forces shall clearly distinguish between civilian populations, and civil infrastructures and military objectives. Neither civilians nor civil infrastructure are to be the targets of military attack.

The legal issues surrounding the use of forcible interventionist strategies are more complex and more challenging than non-coercive, non-forcible means of delivering humanitarian assistance. It is not just that coercive intervention involves the use of force that makes it significantly more difficult to implement. It is because of the dangerous, sometimes lethal, environment interventionists must operate in.

Military intervention for humanitarian purposes must conform to the requirements of international law, which means that there are a number of legal and quasi-legal restraints on how such a campaign is conducted. A civil and humane society does

---

1 Hans-Peter Gasser, 'International Humanitarian Law and the Protection of War Victims,' (Geneva: International Committee of the Red Cross, 1998): pp. 1-7.

not condone the unbridled use of force, the use of weapons that cause unnecessary suffering, or deliberate scorched earth policies by interventionists.

A significant problem for the international community is that international law is fragmented and obtuse regarding humanitarian intervention. Geoffrey Robertson points out that human rights conventions have traditionally been particularly unsuitable as legal entities because they are a list of values, not rights in law.[2]  Even a so-called right declared in a treaty or other convention may not be recognised or enforceable in law.[3]

It is vital that there is a legally recognised convention that directly addresses issues such as genocide, aggression, war crimes, crimes against humanity and so on.  One such broad convention, for all its imperfections and unwieldiness, is known as international humanitarian law.  People may say that responding to humanitarian crises should simply be based on a moral imperative to relieve the suffering of those in need.  The problem is that in this cynical and pragmatic world such imperatives are not enough to prompt the international community into action.  Humanitarian laws and conventions provide an important legal platform that supports the moral argument that not all conduct during conflict is acceptable.  Certain types of behaviour are totally unacceptable regardless of culture, ideology, religion or historical precedent. International law is important to the development of a global civil society.

This chapter addresses the relationship between military intervention for humanitarian purposes and international law; and how the notion of human rights is often used to justify cross-border military intervention.  It will address the question of whether human rights have a basis in law.  The issue of whether or not military intervention can be legally justified to support human rights is further addressed in Chapter Four *Objections to the Ethical Principles and Applications.*

## Working Definitions of International Laws and Conventions

A great deal of confusion exists regarding exactly what international law, humanitarian law, and human rights are; and what these types of laws and conventions are supposed to regulate.  The following are some broad working definitions of the terms natural law, human rights, international law, humanitarian law and the laws of conflict. These definitions are not exclusive.  My aim in presenting my working definitions in this way is for consistency.  I use the same terms throughout this book because I am attempting to avoid the confusion of overlapping terminology when discussing conventions, protocols, laws and rights.

Figure 1 shows a conceptual schematic interrelationship between convention and law.  The term 'convention' means an agreement or accord between parties. A convention is usually not a law unless it refers specifically to an international

---

2    Robertson, *Crimes against Humanity. The Struggle for Global Justice.*   Robertson argues that many over optimistic lawyers incorrectly consider that the Universal Declaration is by now part of international law.

3    Ibid., pp. 74-76.

```
┌─────────────────────────────┐        ┌─────────────────────────────┐
│      NATURAL LAW            │───────▶│   EARLY CODES OF BEHAVIOUR  │
│ Also known as customary or  │        │          IN WAR             │
│ natural rights and conventions│      │ For example; the Chivalric Code│
└─────────────────────────────┘        └─────────────────────────────┘
```

NATURAL LAW
Also known as customary or natural rights and conventions

EARLY CODES OF BEHAVIOUR IN WAR
For example; the Chivalric Code

INTERNATIONAL LAW
Laws that govern civil society.
For example; The Law of the Sea and International Aviation Laws

HUMANITARIAN LAW
Detailed and very specific rules and regulations that are supposed to regulate behaviour between combatants, and between combatants and non-combatants and civilians.
For example; the Geneva Conventions and Protocols

HUMAN RIGHTS
Derived from 'Natural Law' and 'Natural Rights'.
For example: The Universal Declaration of Human Rights and The Covenant on Civil and Political Rights

LAWs OF ARMED CONFLICT
Also known as 'Laws of War'. Rules, Protocols, and Conventions that relate specifically to the conduct of warfare and conflict

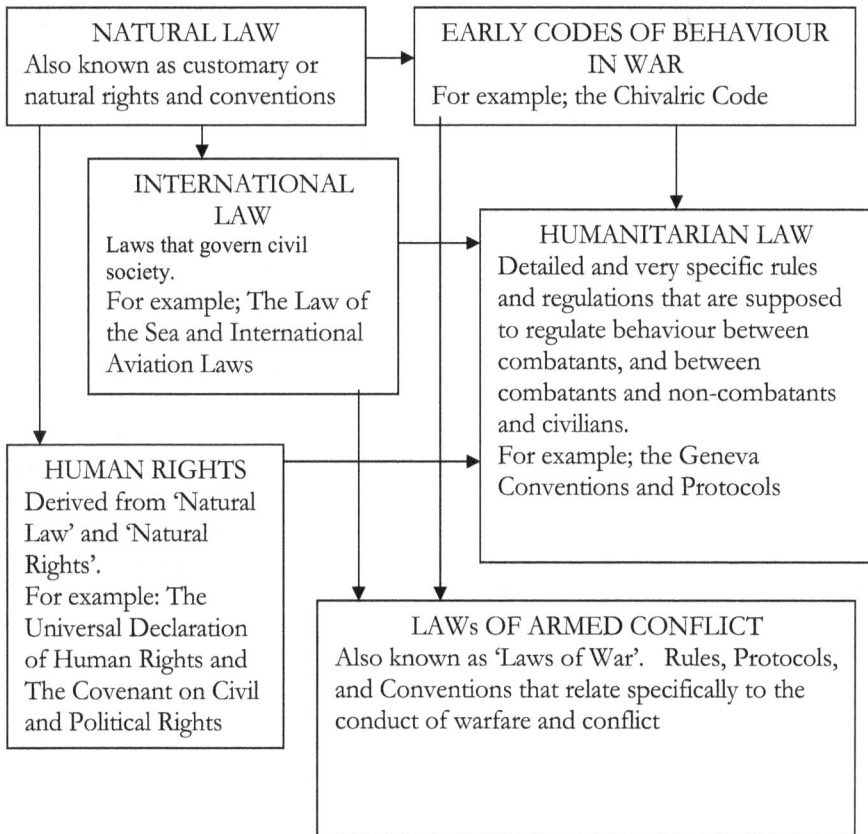

**Figure 3.1   Diagrammatic Relationship Between International Law, Humanitarian Law and Human Rights**

agreement that has achieved a legal status. The Geneva Convention is one example. The term protocol in used in a similar way. The term 'international law' refers to a body of rules that govern how the world community operates. International laws regulate air traffic, international trade, diplomatic and consular immunities, and extradition of offenders from one country to another. Legal protocols are being developed for medical research, space exploration and exploitation of the resources on the seabed.

I frequently talk about humanitarian law. Some use the term 'international humanitarian law'. Both terms relate to a unique body of international law that attempts to apply some sort of rules to how the victims of conflict should be treated. Victims of conflict include combatants, non-combatants (such as stretcher bearers and military medical personnel) and civilians. I am particularly focused on humanitarian law and its relevance to civilians.

Most societies recognise rules of conduct that try to limit the barbarity of violent conflict and humanitarian law consists of a combination of international law and human rights conventions. It attempts to legally codify human rights protocols into international law. The Geneva protocols and conventions are examples of humanitarian law. The laws of armed conflict are sometimes known as the humanitarian laws of war or just the laws of war. These are further categorisations of humanitarian law consisting of international rules governing the conduct, means and methods of conflict specifically relating to military operations. These laws tend to be exclusive of conventions not relating to military matters.

Recognising a right in law is a complex business. Historically, the legal process of recognising a right in law has required a law to be declared first and then a right, according to this law, has been inferred. There are a number of other requirements for a right (or a law) to have legal weight. These will be discussed later in this chapter. The development of human rights has been the reverse of this process. The Universal Declaration of Human Rights was declared in 1948, but this was not based on law. The Declaration was a list of duties and promises relating to how human beings should treat each other. The legal status of such perceived rights has been challenged ever since.[4] The quandary of international law and how and why it should be applied is demonstrated by current concerns about the so-called 'war on terrorism'.[5] The following is an example of some of these concerns and what to do about them.

## The Problem with International Law and Terrorism

The relationship between international law and terrorism is subject to much conjecture and confusion. There is no internationally agreed set of legal protocols about how to deal with terrorism. Acts of terror have occurred throughout human history but at least one significant difference between terror in ages past and terror in the modern world is the global proliferation of WMDs and the likelihood – a high likelihood according to our political leaders – of these weapons falling into the hands of fanatics and extremists to be used against big, soft targets in the West.

Many states no longer believe that they should wait and respond only in self-defence after an act of aggression has occurred against them. This is because of concern over the sheer destructive power of WMDs. Casualties as a result of these types of weapons will not be restricted to thousands or even tens of thousands. Millions of people will be killed and injured if a nuclear device is smuggled into New York harbour and detonated. The deliberate targeting of civilians and non-

---

4    Ibid., p. 30.

5    John Janzekovic, 'Responding to Terror: The War That Is Not a War' (paper presented at the Australasian Political Studies Association, DUNEDIN , New Zealand, 28–30 September 2005). The following is an abridged excerpt from my paper presented at the APSA conference in New Zealand in 2005.

combatants by an aggressor is seen as an anathema in a moral society yet this practice is as old as warfare itself.

Many will say that terrorists deliberately target the weak and the defenceless, and they do not conduct their activities according to any rules of behaviour considered to be important to a civil or moral society. Therefore, this makes them different from conventional combatants who must adhere to the laws of war, ROE, and so on. The Judeo Christian Just-war theory attempts to morally and legally justify conflict. That is, killing in conventional conflict is deemed to be legal providing certain specific criteria or rules are adhered to. Unconventional conflict (terrorism, civil war and various other forms of asymmetric warfare) on the other hand is seen to have no rules, or at least no rules that are immediately apparent.

Political motivations are usually fundamental imperatives behind conventional and unconventional conflicts alike. However, whether or not political motivations are present cannot be the sole determinant that identifies terrorism. The legality or otherwise of different types of conflict must also be considered. Who or what determines legality in conflict? Is it a UN Security Council resolution, NATO action in Kosovo operating without a UN mandate, the rules of war based on Just-war theory, or is it authorisation by the American President and the Prime Ministers of Great Britain and Australia to form a 'Coalition of the Willing' and head off to war in Afghanistan and Iraq? All, some or none of these are at various times considered to be legal justifications to engage in conflict depending on what legal (and/or ethical) benchmarks are used.

The legality of all conflict, not just terrorism, is a very contentious issue. Liberators become invaders, saviours become oppressors, and freedom fighters become terrorists depending on which side you choose or are compelled to support. Certainly terrorism as we know it today is abhorrent and an affront to any notions of a civil and moral society. Equally abhorrent is shooting guided missiles from Israeli helicopter gun ships into crowded restaurants or market places in an effort to kill Palestinian extremists, and the use of cluster bombs and radioactive munitions in Iraq that will keep on killing and maiming the innocent long after the main protagonists have departed. The acceptability of a certain level of collateral damage according to the laws of war is quite irrelevant to those on the receiving end of these appalling weapons.

The idea of proportionality in conflict has always been an uneasy trade off to military necessity, and states and terror organisations no longer bother formally declaring war on each other. Now we openly declare our opposition to fundamentalism and extremism under the all encompassing banners of the 'war on terrorism' and threats to national security. Just War theory is particularly unsuitable when applied to asymmetric warfare or acts of terror. For example; determining who the lawful authority is that makes a so-called 'lawful declaration' for conflict when addressing targeted acts of terror is difficult if not impossible.

When trying to address strategies to combat acts of terror, modern law makers are severely challenged on many fronts. The need to construct effective anti terror legislation that does not wipe out civil liberties altogether, concern over the medium to longer term effects of legislation deemed to be critical by law enforcement agencies, and the need to consult and engage the community without totally alienating them with possible draconian security measures are all monumental challenges.

In the absence of an internationally accepted legal definition of terrorism we have come up with a swathe of ad hoc, poorly worded declarations about terrorism and terrorists. Vague fall back options of stopping terrorists (whoever they may be) from getting hold of WMDs or just 'spreading democracy' and 'dealing with rogue states' are inadequate substitutes as workable legal tools for a war on terror.

Those who conduct acts of terror aim to terrorise but their strategy is not just to conduct random terror. Extremist acts of terror are specifically intended to goad powerful opponents to respond in a certain way. The response by the U.S. and its allies against extremists flying airliners into high-rise buildings in America was to go to war in Afghanistan against the government backed Taliban who apparently supported Osam Bin Laden and his followers. This was quickly followed by the Coalition of the Willing's invasion of Iraq. The large scale mobilisation of conventional military forces against the elusive, largely covert operations of individuals and groups who conduct acts of terror is an unsuitable anti-terror strategy.

The war in Iraq was ostensively to stop the development of WMDs (none were found) by the 'rogue state', and to stop these weapons being passed onto extremists. Iraq passing WMDs onto extremists is a moot point on two counts. Iraq did not have WMDs to pass on and there is no evidence that even if they had such weapons that they would have passed them on. After nearly four years, these particular responses to the post September 11 terror attacks have been ineffectual in reducing the so-called 'global threat of terrorism'.

The Australian Government has stated that it is committed to the campaign to eliminate the global threat of terrorism and that the threat of terrorism to Australians is global.[6]    The term global threat of terrorism is a double misnomer. Firstly, individual acts of terror (despite the dreadful loss of life and suffering at ground level) do not threaten the security of the globe itself. What is threatened is the status quo that 20 percent of the globe's affluent population enjoy while 80 percent of humanity lives with abject disease, poverty and starvation. Humanity has always lived with acts of terror from individuals, groups, organisations and governments. Nothing new there.

Secondly, the word terrorism is a simile...an idiom...a metaphor that attempts to articulate – unsuccessfully – a particular human behaviour. Addressing the Helsinki International Federation of Human Rights conference in the Hague, Elisabeth Rehn (Stability Pact for South-Eastern Europe) claimed that it is impossible to define terrorism.[7]    Anna Goppel agrees that there is no internationally accepted legal definition of terrorism despite the term being commonly and regularly used. As a

---

6    Department of Foreign Affairs and Trade, 'Advancing the National Interest. Foreign and Trade Policy White Paper,' (Canberra: Australian Government, 2003).

7    Elisabeth Rehn, 'Human Rights: Terrorism,  Excessive Reliance on the Use of Force Does Not Stop Terrorism' (paper presented at the Organization for Security and Co-operation

result, she argues, the use of the term terrorism does not lead to a congruent concept of terrorism which could be enshrined in international law and commonly be used in the international community.[8]

Some eminent international lawyers say that a legal definition of terrorism is not required in the first place. Judge Richard Baxter, formally of the ICJ, in 1974 stated that;

> We have the cause to regret that a legal concept of 'terrorism' was ever inflicted upon us. The term is imprecise; it is ambiguous; and above all, it serves no operative legal purpose.[9]

According to Rosalyn Higgins terrorism is a term without legal significance. She argues that the term is at once a shorthand to allude to a variety of problems with some common elements and a method of indicating community condemnation for the conduct concerned.[10] Attempts to pin down what a terrorist or terrorism is flail at the difficulty of obtaining any sort of real consensus on the meaning of these terms never mind trying to find a coherent, internationally accepted legal definition.

The problem is that in a post September the 11th world, and in this 'New Age of Terror', legal confutations about who or what terrorism is serves only those fanatics who deliberately fly airliners into skyscrapers, place bombs in crowded clubs, or detonate bombs in crowded passenger trains – in New York, Bali, and Madrid. There should be no confusion about the criminality of these acts.

There is nothing new about even the best legal minds having great difficulty in defining some of the more extreme elements of human behaviour. On the international front, terms such as 'war crimes' and the 'crime of genocide' are specific behaviours that require legal definition, articulation, analysis and explanation before they can be dealt with according to some sort of internationally accepted law.[11] They require definition because they relate directly to a particular act that has a defined and specific outcome. But attempts to obtain an international consensus on an 'act of terror' or the equally ambiguous 'crime of aggression' or 'hate crime' are ultimately self defeating because they increasingly narrow down the legal definitions of criminality until the result becomes so specific that it is practically unusable in a court of law.

---

in Europe, Seminar in the Hall of Knights, The Hague, The Netherlands, 18 September 2003).

8    Anna Goppel, 'Defining 'Terrorism' in the Context of International Law,' (Melbourne: Centre for Applied Philosophy and Public Ethics (CAPPE), 2005): pp. 1–8.

9    Ben Golder and George Williams, 'What Is 'Terrorism'?' (paper presented at the Conference: Twenty Years of Human Rights Scholarship and Ten Years of Democracy, Centre for Applied Legal Studies and the School of Law, University of the Witwatersrand, 5–7 July 2004).

10   Rosalyn Higgins, 'The General International Law of Terrorism,' in *Terrorism and International Law*, ed. Rosalyn Higgins and Maurice Flory (London ; New York: Routledge : LSE, 1997), p. 28.

11   Rome Statute of the International Criminal Court, 'Setting the Record Straight: The International Criminal Court,' (United Nations Department of Public Information, 2002).

The threat today is not from groups attempting to generate a global version of the pan Islamic state but that extremists will actually get hold of WMDs and cause large scale death and destruction to further their aims. What is important is how the international community – in this instance loosely defined as those who are not rabidly extremist in their views – deals with acts of terror in this age of WMDs. The fact that the Western world, in particular the Coalition of the Willing partners the US and Britain, have enough WMDs of their own to wipe out most life on this planet many times over rarely enters into the discourse over concerns about WMDs.

States are introducing more and more draconian measures in order to deal with terror attacks in this 'new age of terror'. In Australia seventeen groups have been banned by the attorney-general. It becomes a crime punishable by up to 25 years' jail to be a member or receive funding or training from any of these groups. Under the Anti-Terrorism Bill (No. 2) 2004, anyone who associates more than once with a banned organization could be jailed for three years – even if the person did not know it was banned. Under some circumstances, journalists writing about even non-violent activities of such organizations, or people who communicated with those journalists about their stories, could be guilty of association.[12]

What is relevant is how a civil and moral society deals with criminality in all its manifestations. To dispense with the international laws and conventions and the common criminal code, and to try to come up with a totally new version of criminality called terrorism is reinventing the wheel, at best. At worst, this places those who commit such acts (and those who are suspected of committing such acts or those who are suspected to be even thinking about committing such acts) outside of any commonly accepted international or domestic legal framework. This has resulted in detainees being committed to institutions such as Abu Ghraib and Guantánamo Bay without any legal representation despite most of them not being formally charged with any offence.

The Guardian reports that the U.S. is preparing to hold terrorism suspects indefinitely without trial, replacing the Guantánamo Bay prison camp with permanent prisons in the Cuban enclave and elsewhere.[13]    The new prisons are intended for captives the Pentagon and the CIA suspect of terrorist links but do not wish to set free or put on trial for lack of hard evidence. Erwin Chemerinsky, Law Professor at the University of Southern California, points out that there is no authority in American or international law to hold these people indefinitely with no judicial process.[14]

Whether or not an act is criminal or terrorism also seems to revolve around the issue of intent. That is, if the intent was political then this should somehow be treated differently compared to any other form of motivation which could be deemed

---

12  Brendan Nicholson, 'Lib Slams Anti-Terror Law,' *The Melbourne Age Newspaper*, 27 June 2004 2004.

13  Julian Borger, 'Special Report Guantanamo Bay: Us Plans Permanent Guantanamo Jails,' *The Guardian*, Monday January 3, 2005 2005.

14  USA Today, 'Rumsfeld: Guantanamo Bay Suspects Held Indefinitely,' 9 November 2003 2003.

criminal. Flying an airliner into a building filled with people with the deliberate intention of making a political statement is a criminal act. The burden of proof lies in the act and in the rubble.

The Delaware Criminal Justice Council (DCJC) makes the claim that terrorism should not be confused with traditional warfare, and therefore terrorism cannot be considered to be a War Crime.[15] Terrorism is a political act. In war, they argue, the target is selected for its military value. In war, groups of people are selected for attack because the people themselves have some specific value and attacking the group will achieve a military objective. According to DCJC, in the case of terrorism the target group is of little account per se but the fact that they are killed is the point.

Delineating traditional war and terrorism in this way is misleading. In terrorism and war targets are selected for both military and political reasons. The same can be said for selecting particular groups for killing because they have a particular 'value' as a target. If the point that the DCJC is trying to make is that terrorism is just random, senseless killing then this must be challenged. It is true that terrorist targets are not usually able to shoot back but this does not make these random or senseless killings. The aim of these acts of terror is to strike at the foundations of a society by targeting its weak points.

The same rationale is also used in many conventional conflicts. For example, the citizens of Hamburg, Dresden and Kassel were firebombed during World War II by thousand bomber Anglo-American attacks. 100,000 civilians perished in Dresden alone; a city with no significant military targets that was located hundreds of kilometres from the battle front.

Acts of terror should be considered to be a criminal offence that violates international law. Leading lawyers support this view. Associate Professor Tim Lindsay of Melbourne University in Australia claims that there is good, strong evidence that the Bali Bombers did commit mass murder, and that they could be subject to prosecution for murder, equivalents to grievous bodily harm, and so on.[16] The Bali Bomber's defence lawyer Wirawan Adnan also stated that his clients were wrongly charged under anti-terrorism laws that were passed retrospectively. He added that his clients could be charged under the existing conventional penal codes under Article 340 first-degree murder, and that it was a mistake not to have done so in the first place.[17]

The criminality of acts of terror is an important consideration if those who carry out such appalling attacks are to be brought to justice in a court of law. This applies

---

15 The Delaware Criminal Justice Council, *The Nature of Terrorism* [Internet] (17 May 2005 2005 [cited); available from http://www.state.de.us/cjc/terrorism/nature.shtml.

16 Tim Lindsay interviewed By Mark Colvin ABC Radio, 'Bali Bombers Could Evade Jail,' (Australia: Australian Broadcasting Corporation (ABC) Radio National and PM, 23 July, 2004).

17 Wirawan Adnan interviewed by Eleanor Hall ABC Radio, 'Lawyer Says Australia Should Stay out of Indonesia's Justice System,' (Australia: Australian Broadcasting Corporation (ABC) The World Today Program, 25 August , 2004).

equally to indiscriminate mass bombing attacks during conventional warfare as it does to any other act of terror where the aim is to kill and maim the innocent. The question of who is 'innocent' and who is a 'legitimate target' is a difficult one. Terrorists of all persuasions will say that there are no innocents, their targets contribute to the war/conflict effort, and that their immediate targets provide succour and comfort to the primary targets. This is the rationale use throughout history to vindicate 'total war' where all conduct can be justified on the basis of military need that is itself closely followed or led by political imperatives.

International laws, conventions and common law do not have all the answers to deal with acts of terror. But the idea that we need to come up with a whole new set of home-grown parameters in the form of totally different laws that are intended to deal with the age old problem of indiscriminate killing is problematic. It is true that certain aspects of our current laws and conventions do need to be reviewed to more appropriately address terrorism but this has always been the case. Current international laws and conventions should be the foundations for changes to any new domestic criminal laws that aim to address the problem of terrorism at the local level.

Many states ignore or at best only pay lip service to international laws and conventions. Such legal tools against the scourge of terrorism are only effective if states are willing to support them. To take the extra critical step of ignoring international law and then different states attempting to come up with totally different domestic laws to directly address acts of terror is ultimately self defeating. The circumvention of established international laws and conventions that currently could directly address acts of terror as being a war crime, a crime against humanity or at the local level a simple criminal act such as murder is fraught with danger.

The danger (and the reality) is that this circumvention process has resulted in the establishment of a torture centre like Abu Ghraib and the indefinite incarcerated of individuals in places like Guantánamo Bay because these inmates are considered to be outside any sort of legal process. This does not excuse the abhorrent activities of extremists worldwide. Extremists violate many moral and legal conventions and modes of behaviour that are fundamental in a civil and moral society.

The laws of war that have served humanity (with varying degrees of success) for centuries are outdated and they need to be updated to respond to the realities of contemporary conflict. They were never intended to address asymmetric conflict in the first place. The concept of 'total war' is the ultimate path to moral decay where there are no rules, or the rules that are applied are tailor made to suit particular states at particular times. Applying self-serving rules and laws to terrorism will not stop terrorism.

## International Laws Governing Conflict and Intervention

Wars of unprovoked aggression are illegal according to Article 2(4) of the Charter of the United Nations. The charter, which is a formal document of international law, clearly states that the threat or use of force against states is unlawful except where the Security Council has authorised its member states to use such force in response to unprovoked aggression. Article 42 of the charter authorises UN member states to use force, '…as may be necessary to maintain or restore international peace and security.' [18]

A whole raft of international rules, protocols and conventions have been developed to deal with the reality of armed conflict. The apparent legality or illegality of conflict is an important consideration for external powers that are attempting to justify lawful military intervention. Despite all the practical problems of implementing and enforcing codes of conduct during conflict, the international community is bound by its own protocols and conventions to adhere to such codes of conduct. Whether or not they actually follow such protocols and conventions, and whether these are appropriate pre or post September 11th are separate issues entirely.

This raises a number of challenges for potential military interventionists. It is very important that intervening forces conduct themselves according to the requirements of international law. Intervening forces need all the legitimacy of action they are able to muster in order to maintain the political and strategic cohesion so essential to their operations. It is particularly important that they conduct their military operations in accordance with the so-called laws of armed conflict.

Another, even more difficult challenge, is to try to convince intractable belligerents and their supporters that they are subject to humanitarian law, whether they wish to be or not. There are four basic reasons in law why rules and conventions on conflict are as necessary today as when the UN first drew up its charter. Firstly, the Charter has not completely outlawed the use of force. States retain the right to individually or collectively defend themselves against attacks on their territories or on their independence.[19] As long as war itself is not absolutely declared to be illegal, rules and regulations governing how conflict is conducted remain necessary.

Secondly, civil wars and internal wars of insurrection are not covered by the Charter's prohibition on the use of force. Thirdly, Chapter VII of the Charter allows member states to collectively use force to restore international peace and security. Fourthly, wars and armed conflict keep occurring; therefore, there is a

---

18 Chapter VII, Article 42 of the UN Charter states, 'Should the Security Council consider that measures provided for in Article 41 would be inadequate or have proved to be inadequate, it may take such action by air, sea, or land forces as may be necessary to maintain or restore international peace and security. Such action may include demonstrations, blockade, and other operations by air, sea, or land forces of Members of the United Nations.'

19 Chapter VII, Article 51 of the UN Charter states, 'Nothing in the present Charter shall impair the inherent right of individual or collective self-defence if an armed attack occurs against a Member of the United Nations, until the Security Council has taken measures necessary to maintain international peace and security. Measures taken by Members in the exercise of this right of self-defence shall be immediately reported to the Security Council and shall not in any way affect the authority and responsibility of the Security Council under the present Charter to take at any time such action as it deems necessary in order to maintain or restore international peace and security.'

need to constantly monitor the conduct of military conflict and to apply some basic humanitarian rules and conventions to limit the effect of such conflict. The fourth reason is one of the most important from a humanitarian perspective.

International law should clarify the legal status of warfare, but this is very difficult to do in reality. Many protagonists do not formally declare that a state of war exists in the first place. They may proclaim that their military adventures are a response to threats against their sovereignty or their national interest. International law, particularly the UN conventions, has great difficulty in legally defining undeclared conflicts. For example; is a particular conflict classified as a counter-insurgency, civil war, terrorist activity, or guerrilla war; or is it just a response to some of these? The legal status of conflict/warfare is important because it guides international response options.

The UN did not legally sanction coalition action against Iraq during Gulf War I because of concerns over human rights violations. It was sanctioned as a response to Iraq violating the sovereignty of Kuwait.[20] Australia and twenty other countries sent military forces to the Gulf as a result of UN Security Council Resolution 678, which demanded Iraq's unconditional withdrawal from Kuwait by the 15 January 1991.

*Conventional Law Has Primacy Over Human Rights*

Conventional law (also commonly known as domestic or national law) is derived from these early ideas about the primacy of social convention over the rights of the individual. The modern progression has been that human rights are now gradually being proclaimed in law. One of the most important aspects of conventional law is in the prima-facie recognition of state sovereignty having primacy over natural law or human rights.

The international community is extremely reluctant to forcefully intervene in another sovereign state's affairs, even for important humanitarian reasons. All states fear that the concept of state sovereignty will no longer be sacrosanct. Territorial boundaries, which traditionally have been the cause of much conflict and dispute, would have a much diminished status in law if state sovereignty was not respected. State's are always concerned about threats, real or perceived, from external powers trying to expand their territories and influence.

There are many definitions of state sovereignty. Most of them come down to recognising a state's right to conduct its affairs free from outside authority or interference.[21] The legal outcomes of state sovereignty are a set of norms that embrace equality in the rights of states and non-intervention in a state's domestic affairs. This set of norms was enshrined in the UN Charter. The charter mentions human rights and the responsibilities of the international community in upholding

---

20 Ian Bickerton, *43 Days: The Gulf War* (Melbourne: The Text Publishing Company, 1991), p. 228.

21 Stanley Hoffmann, *The Ethics and Politics of Humanitarian Intervention* (Indiana: University of Notre Dame Press, 1996), pp. 12–16.

such rights. It also reasserts the principle of state sovereignty and the principle of consent. The Security Council is able to authorise external intervention under Chapter VII of the Charter in order to restore rightful sovereignty when a state's sovereignty is violated.

The intention of the legal norms of the principle of non-intervention is twofold. An important aim is to minimise intra-state conflict. The absence of state sovereignty is seen, if not already anarchical, then a sure road to anarchy. The other function is to preserve a state's autonomy. Governments argue that they must be able to carry out their internal functions and affairs without interference from outsiders.

Many humanitarians and others who are concerned about human rights abuses will challenge some of these assumptions. For example, internal conflicts and vicious intra-state squabbles over territory have always been a blight on human development *despite* the much-vaunted eminence of state sovereignty. Towards the end of the century, cultural, religious and ethnic conflicts are dominating international affairs. More and more people are being killed and abused. The concept of state sovereignty has not minimised intra-state conflicts. Humanity is increasingly subjected to more conflict, more suffering, more displacement and more death.

The legitimacy of the state system can no longer automatically be taken for granted in the modern world. Yugoslavia and Indonesia (along with many other belligerent regimes) wrongly assumed that they could do what they liked within their own borders. In these cases, the international community was not prepared to accept state sovereignty as a final defence against intervention by external powers.

Liberal normative political theories generally assume that peace and justice are the ultimate moral goals for political institutions, but it is questionable whether these goals are best served, or served effectively at all, simply by a system of states. Even if some states are able to advance the cause of peace and justice this does not automatically mean that the state system in general will conform to these goals. Some state systems are so morally corrupt that their moral if not legal legitimacy must be questioned. If their moral legitimacy is able to be challenged then so too should be their legal claim to state sanctity.

Supporters of statehood will say that the ultimate purpose of a state is for the benefit of its people. This ignores the fact that many governments deliberately victimise certain individuals or groups within the state. State sovereignty frequently does not protect its own citizens from violence and deliberate abuse. There must be a legal mechanism to override the sovereignty of rogue states, in order to protect the citizens of the state, if protection of a state's citizens is the ultimate point of statehood. The problem is that such a legal mechanism needs to compete with the primacy of national law.

Most conflict intervention has not been about humanitarian intervention until very recently. It is usually conducted in pursuit of some national interest goal or as a defence of state sovereignty. NATO action in Kosovo in 1999 and international action in East Timor in 1999 are two rare exceptions. Gulf War I was ostensibly about protecting the sovereignty of Kuwait with the added side bonus of maintaining the West's continued access to the world's richest oil fields. National interests – mostly those of powerful western states – were said to be at stake regarding Iraq's invasion of Kuwait.[22] Coalition action was never sanctioned for humanitarian reasons despite the many human rights abuses being conducted in Kuwait by the Iraqis. The ongoing severe human rights abuses directed against the Kurds of northern Iraq also did not prompt international intervention.

The US congress authorised the use of military force against IRAQ in order to implement UN Security Council Resolutions 660, 662, 665, 666, 667, 669, 670, 674, and 677. None of these Resolutions were even indirectly aimed at stopping human rights abuse.[23] In Bosnia Herzegovina, the international community took over four years to decide to forcefully act to stop humanitarian abuses. NATO and UN action in this case was not due to human rights abuses being committed daily by the Serbs and others. It was instigated because the UN was losing face and increasingly being seen to be irrelevant in the region.

The problem with the Balkans situation, and most other humanitarian crises, is not only that international law is inadequate but also that the international community usually subordinates human rights to conventional law. Conventional law should complement the idea of natural law and human rights. It should not be used as default justification for inaction on the basis that it cannot reconcile the rights of the individual over the rights of state.

*International Law and Humanitarian Law*

Humanitarian law has its origins in codes of conduct in warfare that goes back centuries. Cultures and societies throughout recorded history have developed a range of customs and codes that have applied specifically to the business of conflict. The purpose of these codes of conduct during conflict is to regulate behaviour between combatants, and between combatants and non-combatants. They were never intended to stop conflict or to make conflict illegal.

Humanitarian law aims to strike a balance between military necessity and the requirement to conduct military operations in a humane way. Humanitarian law may not seem very humanitarian to a human rights lawyer, but it does have the advantage of being reasonably precise in legal terms. For example, just because one of the conflicting parties is losing (or winning) the war does not mean that they no longer need to comply with basic standards of humanitarian law.

The difficulty arises when the losing party attempts to reconcile desperate conflict strategies (perhaps resulting in large numbers of civilian deaths) based on the idea of military necessity or military survival. A certain amount of collateral human damage is allowed for in humanitarian law. Again, the human rights lawyer would consider this to be abhorrent, but humanitarian law does not automatically reject civilian death and injury as being part of lawful military operations. The term 'collateral damage' is used in these circumstances.

---

22 Bickerton, *43 Days: The Gulf War.*

23 Ibid., p. 238.

Humanitarian law and human rights overlap each other in many areas. Both support the rule of non-discrimination, the right to life, the protection of the means necessary for life and the prohibition of torture and inhumane treatment. They both prohibit slavery. They differ in other areas where human rights are more generalised and humanitarian law is more specific. For example, human rights conventions specify the right of association and political freedom, neither of which are addressed in humanitarian law. Humanitarian law does not recognise any differentiation between civil, economic or social rights where human rights conventions do.

Humanitarian law concentrates on the most essential types of protection for human life during conflict. Increasingly the notion of human rights is being enmeshed into humanitarian law. This is because modern conflict increasingly involves civilians and non-combatants either as victims of the conflict or as participants in the conflict. Before 1949, there were no international or humanitarian rules specifically relating to the treatment of the civilian population during conflict. The Regulations annexed to the Hague Convention IV of 1907 did not mention aid to civilians, although as early as 1899 some provisions were made regarding the treatment of (POWs).

Since 1949, humanitarian law has specified rules and conditions that attempt to protect civilian populations from the rigours of armed conflict and social unrest. Humanitarian law is contained essentially in six international treaties. These are the four Geneva Conventions of 1949 and their Additional Protocols of 1977. 188 states are signatories to the Geneva Conventions. 110 states are a party to Protocol 1 with 100 states being a party to Protocol II.[24] In the spirit of natural law and international law, the laws of armed conflict are not isolated from universal codes of morality or humanity. Peacekeeping missions are fielded from the heart of this sense of moral obligation to humanity.[25]

The United Nations, like its predecessor the League of Nations, has played a major role in defining, codifying and expanding the realm of international law in this area. The International Law Commission (ILC), established by the General Assembly in 1947, was the primary institution responsible for developing international laws. The ICJ reinforces legal norms through its judgments. The commission and assembly have influenced international law in several important domains. These domains include the laws of conflict, law of the sea, treaty law and human rights law. The work of the UN on developing and codifying the laws of war has built on the previous accomplishments of the Hague Conferences, the League of Nations and the Kellog-Briand Pact (Pact of Paris).

---

24 Denise Plattner, 'Assistance to the Civilian Population: The Development and Present State of International Humanitarian Law,' *International Review of the Red Cross* (1992): pp. 249–50.

25 Antje Mahys, 'War and Peace: Of Law, Lawlessness, and Sovereignty' (paper presented at the Joint Chiefs of Staff Conference on Professional Ethics XIX, Washington, D.C., 30–31 January, 1997).

The UN's first concern after World War II was the punishment of war criminals. As a result, the General Assembly directed the International Law Commission (ILC) to formulate the principles of international law recognised at Nuremberg. It required the ILC to prepare a draft code of offences against the peace and security of mankind. In 1950, the commission submitted its formulation of the Nuremberg principles. These covered crimes against peace, war crimes and crimes against humanity.

The following year, the commission presented its draft articles to the General Assembly. These enumerated crimes against international law, including any act of aggression, threat of or preparation for aggression, annexation of territory and genocide. Although the General Assembly did not adopt these reports, the commission's work in formulating the Nuremberg principles significantly influenced the development of human rights law. The UN also took up the complex problem of defining aggression: a task attempted unsuccessfully by the League of Nations.

Both the International Law Commission and the General Assembly undertook complex and prolonged negotiations with member states, which eventually resulted in agreement in 1974. The definition of aggression, passed without dissent at that time, includes unprovoked military attacks and sending armed mercenaries against another state. Aggression was also defined as allowing one's territory to be used for perpetrating an act of aggression against another state.

The General Assembly adopted a series of resolutions, in 1987, to strengthen legal norms in favour of the peaceful resolution of disputes and against the use of force. The UN also has worked to advance the law of treaties and laws regulating relations between states. In 1989 the assembly passed a resolution declaring 1990–99 the UN Decade of International Law. This was dedicated to promoting acceptance and respect for the principles and institutions of international law.

## The Experience of Humanitarian Law Post 1945

The scale of military and civilian deaths, casualties and human suffering achieved monstrous proportions during World War II. Aerial bombing was indiscriminate, and deliberate targeting of massed civilian populations (by all sides) resulted in many civilian casualties. The deliberate and systematic planning for the extermination of religious and racial groups further contributed to human suffering and death.

The appalling treatment of POWs and the frequent and deliberate abuses of any basic notion of humanitarian law by occupying forces, especially but not exclusively throughout Eastern Europe, the Far East and the USSR, are testimony to the savagery of the human condition. They also point to the inadequacy of humanitarian laws that were intended to moderate such behaviour.[26] The ICRC attempted to secure humane treatment for the victims of war, but its effectiveness is to this day largely dependent on the consent of the warring factions. The ICRC has no legal right to visit POWs

---

26 Robertson, *Crimes against Humanity. The Struggle for Global Justice.*

or concentration camps. With access denied, the ICRC, is unable to monitor the conditions inside these camps and prisons.

In 1949, four Geneva Conventions (comprising of 417 articles) were adopted in an effort to address past deficiencies of humanitarian law. These are now the central part of the International Humanitarian Law of Armed Conflict.[27] These Articles relate specifically to the treatment of POWs, the care of the sick and wounded military forces, and the treatment of civilians in war. The four conventions also, for the first time, provided a system of obligatory punishments for breaches of the Articles.

The updated and amended Articles of the Conventions have been proven to be largely ineffective because the international community appears incapable of enforcing compliance to the provisions.[28] For example, the International Criminal Tribunal for the former Yugoslavia (ICTY) was established in 1993 by the UN Security Council. In 1994, the UN set up a second international tribunal to try perpetrators of the Rwandan genocide. The Yugoslav tribunal issued twenty-one public indictments against fifty-six people from all three ethnic factions in Bosnia and it is continuing to investigate crimes committed in Kosovo.

After a series of arrests and surrenders during 1998, the Yugoslav tribunal has 25 accused in custody and it is currently holding three trials involving eight defendants. Five defendants have been convicted and sentenced. Radovan Karadzic and Ratko Mladic, the former Bosnian Serb civilian and military leaders respectively, are under indictment and in hiding.[29]

The International Criminal Tribunal for Rwanda found Jean-Paul Akayesu guilty, in September 1998, of genocide and crimes against humanity. This was the first-ever judgement by an international court for the crime of genocide. Akayesu, the former mayor of Taba, was indicted on 15 counts of genocide, crimes against humanity. He was found to have violated Article 3 Common to the Geneva Conventions and additional Protocol II. Akayesu was found guilty of genocide, direct and public incitement to commit genocide and crimes against humanity. His crimes against humanity included extermination, murder, torture, rape and other 'inhumane' acts.[30] [31]

Thousands of others directly involved in similar atrocities have not been indicted for any crimes in Rwanda. Until the international community insists on accountability for conduct in war, no humanitarian convention or protocol will be effective. Even in conflicts where the rules of humanitarian law could apply (the

---

27  Gerald Draper, 'Humanitarianism in the Modern Law of Armed Conflicts,' in *Armed Conflict and the New Law : Aspects of the 1977 Geneva Protocols and the 1981 Weapons Convention*, ed. Michael A. Meyer and Geoffrey Francis Andrew Best (London: British Institute of International and Comparative Law, 1989), p. 14.

28  Ibid., ed. M Meyer, pp. 12–16.

29  'A Challenge to Impunity,' *The Economist*, 5 December 1998.

30  'Press Release, Arusha,' (International Criminal Tribunal for Rwanda, 1998).

31 'Case No: Ictr-96-4-I. The Prosecutor of the Tribunal against Jean Paul Akayesu,' (Arusha: International Criminal Tribunal for Rwanda, 1996).

Korean War, the Vietnam War, the Falklands War and the Gulf War/s) the fragility of the Geneva Conventions was constantly tested. The Geneva Conventions are not structured to address the more recent types of internal or guerrilla style of conflict. Customary law is totally inadequate as some sort of over riding principle when formal conventions do not work.

During 1971–74 a number of Government officials and experts worked to assist the ICRC to draft two Protocols for submission to the United Nations. The two Protocols were intended to supplement the Conventions of 1949 and to update the law of hostilities from 1907. Protocol I was designed to update the laws of conflict (laws of the Hague), and international humanitarian law (laws of Geneva) into one document. Protocol II was designed to protect the victims of internal conflicts. Both Protocols link the law of armed conflict and international protection of human rights.

The combination of the Hague Rules of 1907 (laws governing how war should be conducted), the four Geneva Conventions of 1949 and the two Protocols of 1977 (laws which outlined the principles of humanitarian behaviour during conflict) has resulted in today's version of the law of armed conflict. The difficulties of applying and enforcing humanitarian law were demonstrated during the hostilities in Bosnia Herzegovina in 1992. This is where simply determining what is and what is not an international conflict confounded the international community.

Commander Fenwick, a member of the Commission on the Legal and Policy Issues Relating to the Commission of Experts, pointed out to the UN and the European Community that Bosnia Herzegovina was not an independent state until 6 April 1992. He recommended that conflict occurring before this date should be classified as 'internal' conflict. 'Activities' occurring between 6 April 1992 and 19 May 1992 were considered to be international armed conflicts. Those occurring after 19 May 1992 then reverted to being thought of as internal armed conflicts.

As borders and societies disintegrated in the Balkans the commission was playing an impossible, theoretical catch-up game trying to determine who had sovereignty, for how long and over what. The result was stymied inaction because the commission of experts could not determine whether the Balkan's conflict was or was not an international conflict. According to Fenwick's assessment sometimes it was and sometimes it was not.

Most of the allegations of war crimes during this particular period arouse from one group of Bosnians against another. Protocol II contains laws referring to non-international armed conflicts but it makes no reference to the Conventions, breaches of the Protocol or the law of conflict. It also makes no provision for punishment. This meant that until very recently there was no international tribunal to prosecute those accused of war crimes.

Humanitarian law is gradually defining protocols that apply to all citizens regardless of their statehood. This is important because there is a range of criminal activities that are being defined external to individual states' legal systems. Humanitarian law applies to everyone, including those who profess ignorance about the existence of such laws and those who reject such laws. Two common examples of human activity deemed unacceptable to a civil society are genocide and the more specific term, war crimes.[32] The application of both terms to international law is as follows.

## Genocide

Genocide is the deliberate and systematic destruction of a racial, religious, political or ethnic group. The term evolved after events in Europe during 1933–45 called for a legal concept to describe the deliberate destruction of large groups. Despite many historical incidents of genocide, there had been no attempt until after World War II to construct a legal framework through which the international community could deal with cases of mass extermination of peoples.

In 1946, under the impact of revelations at the Nuremberg and other war-crimes trials, the General Assembly of the UN affirmed that genocide is a crime under international law. The UN also affirmed that those who carry out such crimes are to be subjected to severe punishments. In 1948, the UN General Assembly approved the Convention on the Prevention and Punishment of the Crime of Genocide. This convention became effective in 1951. Under this Convention, genocide is a crime whether it is committed in time of peace or during conflict. This distinguishes it from crimes against humanity, as defined by the International Military Tribunal at Nuremberg.

The Nuremberg ruling contended that these particular acts are committed in connection with crimes against peace or war crimes. According to this convention, genocide is an act that intends to destroy, in whole or in part, a national, ethnical, racial or religious group. Killing members of the group, causing serious bodily or mental harm to members of the group, and deliberately inflicting on the group conditions of life calculated to bring about its physical destruction is genocide. Imposing measures intended to prevent births within the group or forcibly transferring children of the group to another group are all acts of genocide according to the convention.[33]

Conspiracy, incitement and complicity in genocide are also punishable by law. Perpetrators of such crimes may be punished whether they are constitutionally responsible rulers, public officials or private individuals. They may be tried by a competent tribunal of the state in which the act was committed or by an international penal tribunal.

Most importantly, one of the results of the convention has been the establishment of the principle that genocide, even if perpetrated by a government in its own territory, is not just an internal matter. It is also legally a matter of international

---

32 'A Challenge to Impunity.' Human Rights lawyers and legal scholars claim that both war crimes and crimes against humanity enjoy 'universal jurisdiction', meaning that, in theory, any country has the right to try any perpetrator, no matter where the crime was committed or by whom.

33 Stacy Sullivan of the Institute for War and Peace Reporting, 'Milosevic and Genocide: Has the Prosecution Made the Case?.'

concern. Any state may call upon the UN to intervene and to take such action for the prevention and suppression of acts of genocide. The real question remains as to whether anything will really be done about holding belligerents accountable for their actions.

*War Crimes*

The term 'war crime' has no definite meaning. It is commonly thought of as a violation of the laws of conflict committed by a combatant or even a civilian. In 1945, the charter of the Nuremberg tribunal gave the Nuremberg court jurisdiction to try crimes against the peace (the waging of a war of aggression), war crimes (a violation of the laws and customs of war), and crimes against humanity (the killing and ill-treatment of civilians).

In particular, the tribunal confirmed that individuals could be held responsible not only for actual war crimes but also for any breach of international law. Crimes against international law were deemed to be committed by men or women, not by abstract entities. Only by punishing individuals who commit such crimes could the provisions of international law be enforced.

Twenty-two persons were charged for war crimes at Nuremberg and twenty-five people were charged for the same offence at the Tokyo tribunal. Many more were tried by other tribunals established by Allied governments in territory they occupied at the conclusion of World War II. These tribunals had a profound effect on the development of international law.

The UN affirmed the Nuremberg principles in 1946. In 1948, the UN prepared a Convention on the Prevention and Punishment of the Crime of Genocide. In 1968, it offered for signature a convention that removed the statute of limitations from war crimes and crimes against humanity. The four Geneva Conventions of 1949 took a different approach to trying those responsible for breaches to the laws of conflict. Each convention lists a number of grave breaches, which include wilful killing, torture or inhuman treatment and the causing of great suffering or serious injury to body or health.

States party to the conventions undertook to enact legislation to try those suspected of grave breaches. Britain enacted the Geneva Conventions Act of 1957, making it a criminal offence for any person to commit a grave breach of the conventions anywhere in the world. The first Protocol of 1977 adds to the list of grave breaches. A grave breach is; making the civilian population or individual civilians the object of attack, launching an indiscriminate attack affecting the civilian population, and the perfidious use of the distinctive emblem of the Red Cross. The transfer of protected persons from occupied territory is also a grave breach according to the Protocol.

The evolution of humanitarian law has resulted in a bewildering array of protocols and conventions. Some humanitarian laws are written, some are accepted as valid despite the lack of formal ratification, some states accept a few or all of the conventions, other states reject them totally. Despite the many problems in drafting, interpreting and applying such laws in the post WW II period, they have achieved a measure of success in reducing some of the savagery of conflict. Increasingly, the international community is identifying with the humanitarian consequences of modern conflicts.

No longer is the outcome of conflict primarily focused on the destruction of property or the annihilation of armies. The scale of destruction and the killing efficiency of modern weaponry mean that many civilians and non-combatants are killed, injured or displaced in today's conflicts. Total war, involving all those within a conflict area, is a reality and a humanitarian disaster.

## Human Rights and the Law

Humanitarian law has evolved since WW II as a protector of common humanity during conflict. Most humanitarian law is conventional law that has, over time, become enshrined in various legal documents and protocols. Humanitarian law attempts to protect basic human rights through detailed and practical rules. This differs from human rights law that sets out a series of general rights, which all persons are assumed to have.

Increasingly, the international community is reacting to conflict situations when basic human rights appear to have been violated. Humankind has at least two fundamental challenges in the application of this notion of human rights. Firstly, there is the challenge of defining what human rights actually means in the practical world. There is also the problem of defining what it means as a concept in law.

The second major challenge for the international community is to recognise that human rights have a legal status at least equal to national law. This is very difficult, perhaps even impossible, but unless this is done, there will always be opportunity for belligerents to follow the ancient Roman example of pointing out the imperfections of conventional law as some sort of obtuse justification for humanitarian abuse.[34]

Human rights must be enshrined into international law. The problem is that this is a complex, convoluted process that is still not nearly complete 50 years after the signing of the Universal Declaration of Human Rights.[35] During this period, millions of people have been killed, abused and disenfranchised without any real

---

34 Margaret, 'Natural Rights.'

35 Amnesty International, '50 Years of the Universal Declaration of Human Rights and 50 Years of Human Rights Abuses', Pol 10/04/98,' (Amnesty International:The International Secretariat News Service, 1998). Amnesty International observed in this report that fifty years on from the adoption of the Universal Declaration of Human Rights (UDHR), the victims of human rights violations have yet to see the world without cruelty and injustice promised by governments in 1948. The report - covering human rights abuses in 141 countries during 1997 - details atrocities committed by governments and armed opposition groups including unlawful killings, torture, 'disappearances' and the jailing of prisoners of conscience. 'For most people around the world, the rights in the UDHR are little more than a paper promise.' said Pierre Sané, Secretary General of Amnesty International.

recourse to legal mechanisms that would uphold their fundamental rights as human beings.

The term human rights conjures up images of clearly spelt out definitions of the rights of humans enshrined in some sort of legal framework. The Virginia Declaration of Rights of 1776 and the US Declaration of Independence of 1776 are a few examples of attempts by the international community to legally enshrine the notion of fundamental rights for human beings into law. The Declaration Of The Rights Of Man And Of Citizens (1789) and the more general Universal Declaration of Human Rights are other examples.

The problem is that many of these so-called rights are far from being clearly spelt out within an acceptable legal framework. There are a number of complex factors involved in turning a perceived right into international law. Geoffrey Robertson, the Australian human rights lawyer, points out that this entire process is more of an act of faith than anything else.[36]   Equally challenging is the attempt to make international law binding not only on states who ratify and formally endorse them but also on states who disagree with the law. Over the last quarter of this century, the international community has attempted to formalise the promises outlined in the Universal Declaration of Human Rights into international law. This process is continuing, at a glacial pace, to this day.

One reason human rights are still not recognised as being part of international law is that the states voting in favour of the Universal Declaration in 1948 never anticipated that they were assuming any obligation for enforcement. There is also the eternal conflict between a state's rights (recognised by international law) to conduct its own affairs free from external interference verses individual human rights (mostly not recognised by international law), which has never been satisfactorily resolved.[37] When push comes to shove, state rights usually wins.

This is not just because the individual state has a vested interest to protect its own sovereignty. It is because all states have a vested interest in maintaining the sanctity of statehood for everyone else as well. If external states challenged a sovereign state, which apparently was not treating its citizens according to some agreed upon standard of behaviour, then potentially all states could be challenged the same way. This threatens the entire concept of sovereignty and state hood.

In 1948, the General Assembly directed the Human Rights Commission to draft a treaty that upon ratification would oblige states to guarantee human rights to their citizens as part of their domestic laws. Throughout the cold-war period the commission laboured away trying to come up with a workable treaty to satisfy the European and American states who favoured civil and political rights, and the communist countries who insisted that social and economic rights must have priority.

Nearly twenty years later, in 1966, the Commission finally tabled two Covenants in an attempt to satisfy the requirements of both liberalists and socialists. The

---

36 Robertson, *Crimes against Humanity. The Struggle for Global Justice.*

37 Key Centre for Ethics, 'Globalising the Rule of Law'.

more important of the two Covenants, from a human rights point of view, is the International Covenant on Civil and Political Rights (the Civil Covenant). This covenant guaranteed certain liberty rights enunciated in the Universal Declaration between citizen and state. A liberty right is a clear obligation by the state to provide its citizens with the basic necessities for life.

The other Covenant proclaimed communal or fraternity rights. These were generally perceived as unenforceable aspirations, such as policy goals involving trade and commerce. Communal rights were to be encouraged but not imposed upon a sovereign state by any external court. A court might adjudicate on infringements involving matters of human liberty but it could not also include judgements involving trade or commercial matters. It could not, for example, impose trade sanctions against a state in response to finding that human rights had been violated.

Sanctions in international law and politics are measures of coercion to induce a recalcitrant party to conform to a norm of international behaviour. Assuming a threat to peace exists or that an act of aggression has actually taken place, four types of sanctions are available. These are; economic embargoes, arms embargoes, the severing of communications, and international criminal prosecution.

The most commonly applied form of sanctions is economic and trade embargoes, and cessation of development assistance. Often the first response to military aggression or other threats to international peace and security is to limit the target country's access to weapons by means of an arms embargo and by reducing military assistance programs. The sanction of international criminal prosecution was 'invented' in 1993 where the UN Security Council established an international penal court to try individuals responsible for war crimes in the former Yugoslavia.

In 1976, only 35 states agreed to ratify the two Covenants to the Declaration. The US did not ratify the Covenants until 1992. As of 1999, states which refused to sign the Covenants were; Singapore, Saudi Arabia, Malaysia, Bangladesh, Indonesia, Cuba, Myanmar, Pakistan and Turkey. Very few states have signed the Optional Protocol to the Civil Covenant. This protocol provides a mechanism in law by which individual victims of human rights abuses may complain to an international body such as the Human Rights Committee situated in Geneva.

By mid 1976, most states that had at least some empathy with the development of human rights as a concept in law were becoming increasingly sensitised to the large scale, deliberate human rights abuses occurring in many places around the world. The fact that the two Covenants exist at all, 30 years after they were originally envisaged, has more to do with on-again/off-again international reaction to the appalling brutalities and human atrocities that have occurred during this period rather than as a result of any coherent strategy of development in international law.

The Universal Declaration of Human Rights is now truly universal in the sense that almost every country is a member of its declaratory body, the UN. More than 140 countries have ratified the two Covenants. Although meaning different things to different states, ratification of a treaty is important in legal terms. Some countries (France and Spain) must, according to their own laws, automatically incorporate a treaty as part of their national laws immediately on ratification. Ratification is a very serious act with immediate legal implications for these countries.

In other countries (for example, most other Commonwealth countries) the ratification of a treaty has no real effect until the elected parliament subsequently passes legislation to incorporate the legal intent of the treaty into domestic law. In the U.S., the President may sign a treaty but ratification must first be approved by two thirds of the American Senate. The President may then proclaim a treaty, which will then override inconsistent state or federal laws.

Concepts of human rights are still often not enshrined in law but this does not make basic human rights morally any less valid. Civilised society devalues the notion of fundamental rights for human kind when it relies solely on a passage in law to say *'...thou must not torture other human beings'*. It is morally inadequate to shrug our collective shoulders and regretfully say that we are not legally entitled to act because we cannot come up with an appropriate legal mechanism.

Law or no law, violation of basic human rights is morally wrong. Non-action or ineffective action to address humanitarian concerns specifically devalues, indeed violates, the notion of human rights. Individuals or nations are inconsistent if they say that they highly value human rights, but then ignore the violation of such rights. Human rights must be incorporated into international law. Until they are, the rights of individuals must have ascendancy over the rights of that artificial political construct – the state.

## Laws of Armed Conflict

The current definitions of the laws of armed conflict have evolved since World War II subject to the vagaries of legal opinion. Despite their Eurocentricity and generally Westphalian orientation, most in the international community has accepted these laws as recognisable and reasonable legal constraints on behaviour during conflict. The primary intent of laws of armed conflict is not to stop or make illegal conflict. They are intended to place restrictions and restraints on how warfare is conducted to reduce the savagery of conflict. These laws have a number of basic functions. They attempt to establish legal boundaries within which armed conflicts are fought and they provide some legal safeguards for the victims of conflict.[38]

The laws of armed conflict are extremely important to interventionists intending to use force to stop human rights abuses. They are important because the international community will eventually judge the legitimacy of intervention based on a positive humanitarian outcome and whether this outcome was as a result of interventionists complying with international law. A positive humanitarian outcome does not mean saving the abused at the cost of causing *unnecessary* suffering or death to anyone.

The laws of armed conflict are sometimes known as the international humanitarian laws of armed conflict or the laws of war. These laws were the first sections of

---

38 Gretchen Kewley, *Humanitarian Law in Armed Conflicts* (Melbourne: VCTA Publishing, 1984), p. vi.

international law to be translated from natural law to govern how hostilities between opponents are conducted and how the weapons of conflict are used.[39]   The laws of armed conflict evolved from early codes of behaviour in warfare (such as the Chivalric Code), humanitarian law and international law. The laws of armed conflict were originally intended to be operable during times of conflict as opposed to the regimes of human rights.

Human rights were originally thought of to be applicable only during peacetime.[40] Increasingly, humanitarian law, international law, the laws of armed conflict and human rights are overlapping. The original distinctions between them are blurring. The laws of armed conflict are not only written laws as they include codes of convention, protocol and principle.[41]   For example, the traditional objective of conflict (recognised in international law) is to destroy or to significantly weaken the military strength of an opponent.  Convention dictates that it is not acceptable for an entire nation is to be obliterated in order to achieve this goal.

The challenge for the current laws of armed conflict is that modern ethnic conflicts, tribal wars, religious wars and civil insurrections may not have as their primary objective the aim of destroying or weakening the military strength of their opponents.  Their primary aim may be to eliminate civilians who are ethnically different or to expel those who have different beliefs and cultures.  Military engagement may actually be a side effect of such policies.

International law has great difficulty in addressing such conflicts because they often do not conform to conventional forms of conflict according to accepted legal definitions.  International law usually requires a formal declaration of war in order for it to recognise that a state of war actually exists between two waring parties. These days most heads of state no longer bother declaring war on each other.  At no time did Slobodan Milosevic declare war on non-Serbs in Bosnia Herzegovina nor did he declare that a state of war existed between the Serbs and the Kosovo Liberation Army.

During modern ethnic or tribal conflicts there is often no formal head-of-state; just waring factions, tribes or religious groups.  Despite these difficulties, the laws of armed conflict (the original term laws of war has largely been dropped because of its restrictive connotations) cover a wide range of human behaviour.  These laws apply to all conflict, formally declared or not, and they are recognised by international legal tribunals.  In this aspect the laws of armed conflict differ significantly from international and humanitarian law.

There are a number of fundamental humanitarian principles on which the international humanitarian laws of armed conflict are based.  These are directed primarily, but not exclusively, against the aggressor.  Infliction of harm is to be in proportion to the requirement for military advantage, military targets and not civilian

---

39  Ibid., p. vii.

40  Ibid., p. xiv.

41  Hartle, *Moral Issues in Military Decision Making.*

targets are to be the primary objectives, the means of injuring an opponent is not unlimited, and weapons causing cruel and unnecessary suffering are not to be used.

Those who oppose war and all it stands for will question that there are any real or imagined restraints placed on the brutal business of warfare. However, the reality is that restraint between protagonists usually does occur. Absolute extremes of mass human behaviour during warfare are not historically unknown, but they are very rare. There must be something other that practicalities and logistics driving such restraint.

If there were no restraints at all, and assuming that there is no practical benefit in treating the vanquished humanely, victors would never give any quarter, all prisoners would be executed, all civilians and non-combatants not directly contributing to the victor's war effort would be eliminated and the opposition's civil infrastructure would be utterly destroyed. This does not occur in most conflicts.

Protagonists often feed, clothe and shelter tens of thousands of prisoners despite there being little practical reason for doing so. Subdued populations are usually not eliminated despite the very real risk that they will ferment further unrest or conduct a resistance campaign. A final victory of one side over another other usually means that POWs are sent home, civil infrastructures are rebuilt and new alliances formed. Sometimes the victors contribute substantially to the rebuilding process.

Even if conflict is conducted with minimal ethical restraint, the absolute elimination of the opposition's infrastructure and civil society simply wastes valuable resources, which could be reused or modified for the victor's advantage. The sheer logistics of carrying out scorched earth policies on a large scale would be formidable. From a realist perspective, it is not in the victor's best interests to execute all POWs after a battle, or to eliminate all civilians they come in contact with, because this would greatly increase the resistance of the opposition. There is no point in surrendering to an enemy if you will be killed anyway. You will not give in and you will fight on even if the odds are hopeless. Endless resistance means endless conflict, which would eventually wear down even the most determined aggressor.

As fortunes in war ebb and flow a protagonist could be victorious one day and suffer a devastating defeat the next. This means that the victors of battles will, in all probability, some day be at the mercy of those who were once the vanquished. It makes practical sense to treat opponents decently and humanely if one expects to be decently and humanely treated in return.

The most dangerous, and usually the most lethal, conflicts are those where one side has a significant tactical advantage over another side, or where the cause of the conflict is based on some long standing ethnic, cultural or religious difference. Restraint, in these cases, tends to vary depending on how secure in victory (also how free from retribution the aggressor feels) or how righteous the victors consider their cause to be.

A dichotomy exists between the idea that conflict must be restrained and the reality of the savagery of warfare, but conflict could be much more destructive and the suffering much more extreme if absolutely no restraints (ethical or otherwise) existed on how it was conducted. The attempt by the international community to restrain the nature of warfare by legal means is matched by militarists who strive to overcome the opponent through the direct use of force.

Sir Hersch Lauterpach stated the magnitude of the problem. '...the very idea of a legal regulation to a condition of mere force has appeared to many incongruous to the point of absurdity.'[42] Despite this apparent absurdity the true character of the laws of armed conflict is in their intent. That is, the laws of armed conflict are intended as being humanitarian in the literal sense of the word. The regulation of hostilities is not their essential purpose or primary intent.[43]

There is a danger in considering the laws of conflict as being the yardstick that determines whether or not international intervention should take place. For example, if the laws of conflict are violated then intervention must be warranted. But this is neither the function nor the intent of such laws. They are a damage control strategy intended only to limit the brutality of conflict by placing some constraints on how conflict is conducted. Enforcement of international law must aim to stop the killing and unlawful deprivation. It must not just provide some boundaries to the extent of violence.

The attraction of using such laws as the platform for humanitarian intervention is that they are clear legal codifications of convention. As such they form a pillar for international jurists and international courts. The problem is that the laws of armed conflict do not, and never will, cover all the legal contingencies of human behaviour during conflict. No law or convention can hope to achieve this ideal.

The most the laws of armed conflict can hope to achieve is to limit human suffering caused by conflict. Military intervention must aim to do much more than just limit human suffering. It should aim to stop conflict in its tracks by addressing human rights concerns directly rather than responding simply because a particular humanitarian law or a law of conflict has been violated.

## Conclusion

One needs to accept that there is a conjunction between how conflict is conducted and morality if humanitarian law is to be at all effective. To many there is an inherent contradiction between acts of organised (and non-organised) conflict and any humanitarian operation that is intended to reduce the loss of life or suffering in conflict. Realists say that the fundamental purpose of legitimate, state sanctioned warfare is to apply the most effective type of direct force to overpower an opponent with a minimum of casualties, time and logistics expenditure on both sides of the conflict. They propose that the idea of an ethical military trying to adhere to some humanitarian law is nonsense.

According to this reasoning, attempts to limit or constrain the activities of war, either by rules or regulations or by ethical restraints, merely extends the requirement

---

42 Draper, *op. cit*, p. 3.

43 H. Lauterpacht, The Revision of the Law of War. The British 1952 Year Book of International Law, Vol., 29, pp. 381–382.

for conflict to continue which ultimately causes even greater death and suffering. Realists would argue that humanitarian law, which recognises the legitimacy of war, inappropriately seeks to impose obligations on states and individuals to how conflict is conducted. If war is a legitimate activity recognised in law why place constraints on how it is conducted?   Indeed, during warfare, anything goes.

This type of convoluted logic about the nature of organised conflict confuses the rationale of having conventions and rules that limit the conduct of such conflict. It is irrelevant whether humanitarian law recognises the legitimacy of war or not. Humanitarian law is intended to regulate how warfare is conducted for humanitarian reasons. The legitimacy or otherwise of conflict is a separate issue.

Such views highlight a fundamental flaw in humanitarian law. The flaw is that by recognising the legitimacy of conflict, humanitarian law can only ever be a band-aid solution to human conflict. Ultimately the international community must aim to outlaw conflict itself. The laws of armed conflict and humanitarian laws attempt to minimise harm and suffering to non-combatants and to all those not directly involved in the fighting. Legal constraints currently placed on those directly involved in the fighting are intended to apply some ethical and legal boundaries to the awfulness of war.

# Chapter 4

# Objections to the Ethical Principles and Applications

## Introduction

This chapter addresses three categories of objection to the use of coercive force for humanitarian reasons. They are; practical feasibility, moral acceptability and political viability. These three categories are not totally exclusive but most objections will fall into one or more of them. One could provide all sorts of arguments as to why humanitarian intervention might, under some circumstances, be a moral requirement but people are generally not swayed by ethical arguments alone. The logistical and strategic outcomes of humanitarian intervention must ensure that lives and resources are not needlessly wasted in pursuing unattainable objectives. Practical feasibility is a basic requirement for military success. The discussion below addresses the technical challenges of carrying out forcible humanitarian intervention in order to fulfil the humanitarian requirements and objectives.

Interventionists and potential interventionists must consider the overall practical feasibility of intervention. Where does international responsibility end and interference in a state's internal affairs start, and where does international law fit into such humanitarian crusades? Many will argue that the use of external force against a sovereign state violates accepted legal norms and conventions. Concern over possible interventionist casualties and the economic costs of intervention are important objections. Even if intervention could be seen to be a moral requirement, and it is technically feasible to undertake such an operation, people will still question the rationality of sending their sons and daughters into a potentially lethal conflict environment to try to fix somebody else's mess. The costs in materiel and personnel for forcible humanitarian intervention will be substantial.

The moral acceptability of using force to try to resolve international conflicts is problematic. If a civil and caring society professes concern about human rights then it is difficult to argue that some sort of obligation does not exist to do something effective to support such rights. The problem is that when non-violent strategies have been tried and the mass killings simply go on, what then? There are three possible options; muddle on as before, walk away, or stop the killing by force.

The question of whether the use of force is politically viable is very important. Even a clear moral imperative that could realistically be backed up by the use of military force will degenerate into procrastination and inaction if the international community cannot construct a rational political framework for a response to extreme human rights abuse. Humanitarian responsibility, the active pursuit of justice, disarming belligerents, repatriating displaced persons and rebuilding civil infrastructures are all essential elements of such a political construct. Any suggestion that we should send our citizens to some far flung corner of the globe on a military crusade to save the oppressed gets short shrift in real-life domestic and political arenas. There is very little political mileage in such suggestions.

This chapter does not attempt to develop the theoretical or philosophical arguments regarding the international community's use of directed force to address extreme human rights abuses. This was done in Chapter One and it was further developed within a conceptual framework in Chapter Two, *Plausible Interventionist Strategies.* Here, I am providing a more pragmatic response to the objections about the use of coercive force during humanitarian intervention.

### *The Role of the Military during Humanitarian Intervention Revisited*

The role of the peacemaker during humanitarian intervention is to immediately stop the killing and the severe deprivations of those being abused when alternative, non-violent means are ineffective. Military intervention must be undertaken when the killing and deliberate atrocities just continue on regardless of international pleas for them to stop. Military intervention is not about solving the myriad of complex ethnic, cultural, ideological and religious problems in the world's hot spots. The conflicting parties in the end must be prepared to address their own problems and differences. Politicians, negotiators, international lawyers, diplomats, NGOs and concerned individuals all have a contribution to make in this process.

Most forcible international humanitarian intervention has to date been instigated and managed by western military powers. These are the sometime international community's foot soldiers. However, they are not moral guardians, they are not police forces, they are not directly concerned about issues of justice, and they are not political negotiators or mediators. Western military forces are specifically trained and equipped to apply force and to react to the application of force on themselves or on those they are mandated to protect.

Military action *must not proceed* unless the international community is prepared immediately to address questions of justice regarding the perpetrators of extreme violence, to repatriate refugees and to set up civilian legal and policing systems. Also critical is the re-establish of essential civil services and the ongoing provision of humanitarian aid. The use of military force will not promote humanitarian values unless the international community is prepared to undertake all these functions.

There is not one single example in recent history where forcible humanitarian intervention has not been too little or too late. This is not the fault of the interventionists who are often placed in dangerous situations. They are generally outgunned, outnumbered, poorly lead, inadequately trained and without a clear mandate or ROE to protect either themselves or those whom they hope to help. This does not mean that such intervention cannot work. It can; but firstly, there needs to be a realistic appreciation of what the military can and cannot do in humanitarian affairs. The international community must stop seeing military intervention as some sort of quick fix for deep-seated ethnic, cultural and ideological problems that have been festering for centuries. The following are a range of common objections to the use of direct force for humanitarian purposes.

## Using Force Does Not Improve Humanitarian Outcomes

An underlying assumption made by those who support the concept of unilateral forcible humanitarian intervention is that in some cases it may be the only way to halt massive human rights violations. The problem is that the record of post-cold war intervention does not lend much support to the overall proposition that the use of force will promote humanitarian values.

The most common argument against the use of military force for humanitarian reasons is that it does not do what it sets out to do. That is, it cannot alleviate an already desperate humanitarian situation: in fact it will probably make it worse. Others say that force itself does not work. To dismiss the use of force on the basis that it can only make things worse for oppressed peoples means that allied entry into World War II to stop the spread of fascism in Germany, Italy and elsewhere should not have occurred. Allied entry into WW II was not primarily for humanitarian reasons, but this does not mean that humanitarian issues did not exist or that they did not become important. Very few people will seriously argue that Nazi attempts to exterminate the Jews should not have been stopped. Stopping Nazis exterminating Jews could not have occurred without force.

There are four key players in humanitarian affairs. These are; the onlookers, potential or active interventionists, those being abused, and those doing the abusing. Any assessment of whether the use of force may enhance humanitarian outcomes must consider all four positions. If morality has a place in such assessments (I argue that it must have a place) then the primary focus must be on the immediate plight of the oppressed. Attention must be focussed on the oppressed because they are doing most of the dying and the suffering.

Currently the onlookers, and occasionally the interventionists, have the loudest voices regarding what they think about the humanitarian value of the use of force. The interventionists have the added difficulty of trying to stay alive themselves. The problem with this fundamental equation is that those being tortured, hacked to death, raped, deliberately set on fire, and dismembered or decapitated are generally not listened to regarding what they think of the use of force to enhance humanitarian outcomes and values.

The focus should be on the abused and on ramifications to the wider human community if such crimes are not stopped. Statements such as 'The use of force cannot (or can) promote humanitarian values' are generalised in nature. A generalised response is that sometimes force may promote humanitarian values and sometimes it will not. If there is a real chance that force will promote such values, and other options either do not work or will not work, then the use of force should occur. If it is likely that the use of force will not alleviate the suffering of the abused, or that an even greater humanitarian disaster will result from the use of force, then it must not be used.

The International Federation of the Red Cross and Red Crescent Societies, World Disasters Report 1997 argues that humanitarian action is controlled by the principles of neutrality, impartiality, and independence. Humanitarian action is apolitical and, by definition, excludes the use of military force. The military, claims the report, cannot qualify as humanitarian because every soldier, whether backed by a nation, regional organisation or the UN, comes connected to political governance.[1]

This is a very common view of the perceived role of humanitarian organisations compared to the role of the military. The thinking is that even if the military is used for humanitarian purposes it just cannot be considered to be a 'humanitarian endeavour' simply because of its capacity to use force and its inherent political agenda.

The problem is with some of the fundamental assumptions behind this approach. Firstly, humanitarian action may not be neutral, impartial or independent at all if a particular humanitarian disaster is so dreadful that only direct intervention by the international community can stop it. Even the UN can hardly be called neutral, impartial or independent if the selective few on the Security Council pass resolution after resolution demanding an end to conflict and abuse then eventually (maybe) mandating peacekeepers or peace enforcers (often asking states near to the conflict area to contribute troops) to directly intervene. Those on the receiving end of such a disaster do not care about the supposed neutrality, impartiality or independence of interventionists providing the abuse stops and the perpetrators are brought to justice.

Secondly, there is the question about the assumed political agenda behind the military. Political agendas are not inherently good or bad (as the report seems to imply) it depends on what the agenda is. If the political agenda is to encourage and convince potential interventionists to provide immediate humanitarian relief to help those in desperate need how is this inappropriate? Dismissing political agendas in this way ignores many of the realities of how the world community functions, and it smacks of moral puritanism.

In the end the report probably makes its most significant observation by admitting that, 'Military intervention and humanitarian action can coexist. Military intervention can increase the likelihood of success of humanitarian action.'[2]

---

1 International Federation of Red Cross and Red Crescent Societies, 'Can Military Intervention and Humanitarian Action Coexist? World Disasters Report 1997, Section 1, Chapter 2,' (International Federation of Red Cross and Red Crescent Societies).

2 Ibid.

**There is no Guarantee of Military Success**

There is not, nor will there ever be, an iron clad guarantee that military intervention will be successful either militarily or from a humanitarian perspective. As previously stated, there is also no guarantee that diplomacy, mediation, economic sanctions, threats and pleas by the UN or waving banners and placards in the streets will be successful either.[3] The lack of such guarantees does not mean that diplomacy or mediation should be rejected. Neither should forcible intervention be rejected on these grounds.

If the argument revolves primarily around the use of external force being more dangerous for the abused and for interventionists, and therefore it is less likely to succeed than non-violent means of intervention, then this line of argument must be challenged. It is true that the use of force is dangerous, but this does not automatically mean that it is less likely to succeed. What makes any sort of intervention succeed is a willingness to totally commit to end the killing and the violence as soon as possible. Military intervention can do this providing all sides understand that retribution for extreme human rights abuses will be swift, robust and immediate.

Botched diplomacy and ineffectual mediation are usually not seriously analysed as being direct contributors to significant numbers of deaths during humanitarian crises. As time ticks away around mediation tables, and yet another round of talks begins, the atrocities continue. It is naive to think that just because diplomacy and mediation is going on, determined belligerents will suspend their genocidal activities. History repeatedly shows that this simply does not occur.

It is technically feasible for military intervention to be successful and to have good humanitarian outcomes providing such an engagement is conducted with speed, vigour and determination. It is crucial that intervention is militarily realistic and achievable in the first place.[4] If one or more of these elements is absent then military intervention will cause more suffering and death than it tries to stop. Under these circumstances intervention will not be successful and it must not proceed.

Interventionists must maximise and concentrate their use of force to be militarily successful. They must have the resources and the will to assert military superiority over an opponent. An opponent or the opponents must be disarmed after conflict. These are simple military maxims as identified during the early 1800s by the military strategist Carl Von Clausewitz and others.[5] If interventionists apply less than the maximum use of concentrated force against an opponent this provides a military advantage to the opposition with predictable outcomes. The predictable outcome is a protracted and bloody military campaign.

---

3    Alan Winkler, 'Just Sanctions,' *Human Rights Quarterly* (1999): pp. 133–35. Also see J Gordon, 'A Peaceful, Silent, Deadly Remedy: The Ethics of Economic Sanctions,' *Ethics and International Affairs*, no. 13 (1999): pp. 128–33.

4    Elliot Abrams, 'Just War. Just Means?,' *National Review* 51, no. 12 (1999): p. 17.

5    Carl von Clausewiz, 'On War,' ed. Michael Howard and Peter Paret (Princeton, New Jersey: Princeton University Press, 1984), pp. 75–76.

The 1999 NATO air campaign against Yugoslavia did not apply the maximum use of concentrated force against Serb troops in Kosovo. It resulted in a military campaign of eleven weeks rather than the few weeks it should have taken. As a result of this strategy many Kosovars were either killed or displaced.

*Sooner is Better than Later*

The timing of military intervention is vital to success. Military engagement, whether for humanitarian purposes or for any other reason, is much more successful before opponents are fully dug in, before they have time to lay high explosives around critical civil infrastructure, and before they are able to round up and use their victims as human shields. Sooner is better than later because military success comes from striking first and striking hard.

Just-war concepts support the idea that force should only be used as a last resort option, but this limits the effectiveness of military operations because it gives an opponent crucial time to prepare for an assault. Waiting until other humanitarian policies and strategies are exhausted and have failed often forfeits the opportunity to use force effectively. The timing of a military response to counter severe human rights abuses is an emotive issue.

Most people prefer to use non-violent means to resolve conflict and to apply all other strategies before the direct use of force is even contemplated (if it is contemplated at all). The stark military reality is that if a determined use of coercive force is only used as a last resort the outcome will most likely be many casualties on all sides.

During the Gulf crisis of 1990, the Bush administration concluded that if the coalition had waited a few months more before intervening there would have no longer be a Kuwait left to save. The Gulf War was a war over access to oil resources and the defence of Kuwait not a humanitarian rescue mission but the military imperatives for an early strike were the same. The timing of a military response is crucial. The following are some examples of where sooner would have been better than later.

In Rwanda, in a matter of weeks during April 1994, Hutus killed over 1 million defenceless Tutsis. For several months prior to this humanitarian disaster the UN (and at least some in the international community) were aware that a catastrophe was going to befall this tiny African state. According to the Guardian, President Bill Clinton's administration was aware that Rwanda was being engulfed by genocide in April 1994 but buried the information to justify its inaction. This evidence was presented according to classified documents being made available in 2004.

Intelligence reports show the U.S. Administration had been aware of a 'final solution' to eliminate all Tutsis before the killing had reached its peak.[6]     Hutu

---

6    Rory Carroll, 'U.S. Chose to Ignore Rwandan Genocide: Classified Papers Show Clinton Was Aware of 'Final Solution' to Eliminate Tutsis,' *Guardian Unlimited*, 31 March 2004.

death squads took three months from April 6 to carry out their murderous intent against the Tutsis and moderate Hutus and, the Guardian argues that at each stage accurate, detailed reports were reaching Washington's top policymakers. Nothing short of physically separating the conflicting sides would stop such a tragedy from occurring.[7]   Uwe Friesecke, who prepared the report for the Defense Team in the Ntagerura Case (International Criminal Tribunal for Rwanda) states that the US, British, French and Belgian governments were fully aware of the carnage going on during the massacres in Rwanda.[8]

After much futile and prolonged deliberation by the UN (nobody wanted to take on the responsibility of military intervention in Rwanda) the French government sent its own interventionist forces into Rwanda in Operation Turquoise.[9]   In May 1994, the UN finally authorised the tiny UN force (UNAMIR) in Rwanda to protect civilians.  Unfortunately there were too few troops available to actually carryout this mandate.  It was too late anyway to save the more than one million Rwandans who had been killed the month before.  Military intervention was not only far too late, it was intervention in name only by 2,330 poorly armed and ill prepared UN peacekeepers.[10]   The UN withdrew UNAMIR personnel from Rwanda in May 1996.[11]

Another catastrophe, similar to what had occurred in Rwanda, then loomed in the neighbouring state of Burundi.  This time, in an attempt to avoid the interventionist fiasco of the Rwandan crisis, the UN called for states to volunteer to intervene in this humanitarian disaster.  None volunteered and no peacekeepers were sent resulting in at least 50,000 further deaths.

The sooner is better than later rationale may be applied to East Timor in 1999.  In 1975, East Timor was invaded by Indonesia resulting in massacres and famine that killed over 250,000 people: nearly one third of the population.[12]   Twenty-four years later, in August 1999, after many more deaths and human rights abuses, the President of Indonesia B. J. Habibie announced that East Timor could participate in a vote for independence.  Maps 6 and 7 show the region of East Timor.

International observers, including Amnesty International, HRW, and others predicted that without a peacekeeping force to ensure security immediately prior to, during, and especially after the election, there was a very high likelihood of even

---

7    Richard Connaughton, 'Wider Peacekeeping – How Wide of the Mark,' *British Army Review* (1985): p. 63.

8    Uwe Friesecke, 'Strategic Considerations of the Rwandan Catastrophe of 1994,' in *a report by Uwe Friesecke, Prepared for the Defense Team In the Ntagerura Case, International Criminal Tribunal for Rwanda* (Arusha, Tanzania: 2002).

9    Groenewold, Porter, and Mâedecins sans frontiáeres (Association), *World in Crisis. The Politics of Survival at the End of the Twentieth Century.*

10   Christopher Bellamy, *Knights in White Armour* (Sydney: Random House Aust, 1997), p. 107.

11   UN Press Release, 'Note to Correspondents: Rwanda Mission Provided Assistance Beyond Mandate,' (United Nations, 1996).

12   'Terror in Timor,' *The Economist*, 30 Oct 1999 – 5 Nov 1999.

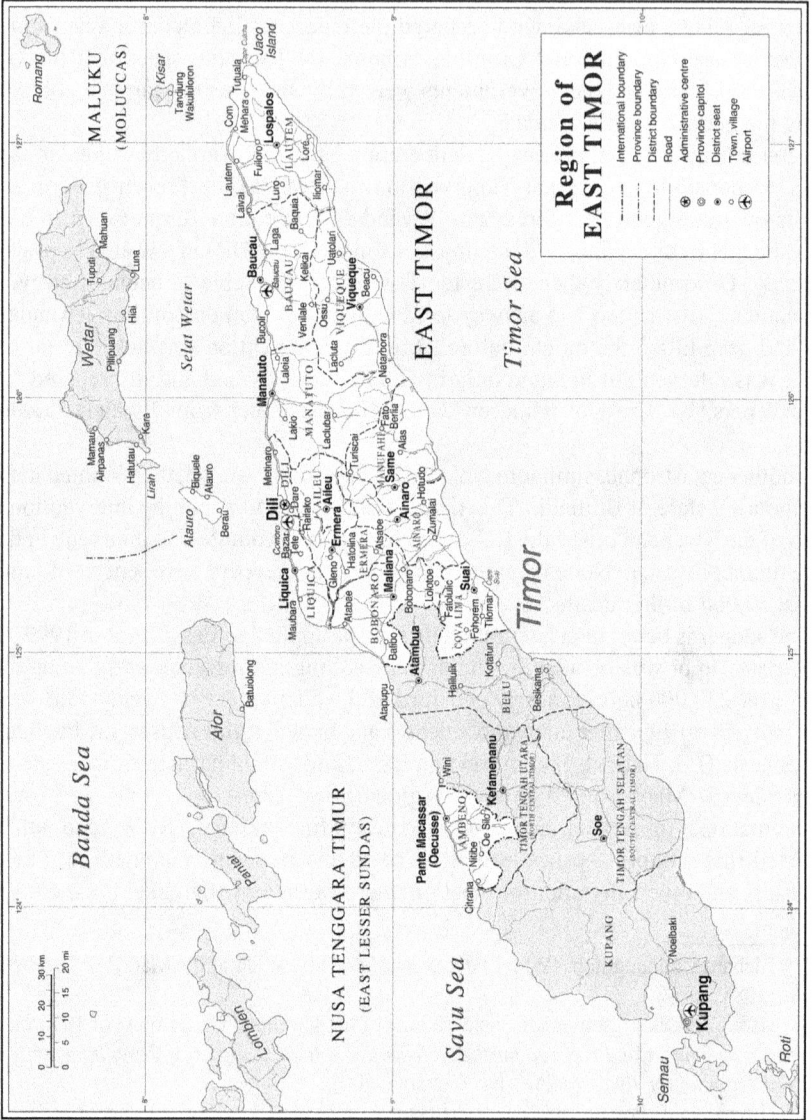

**Map 4.6  East Timor**

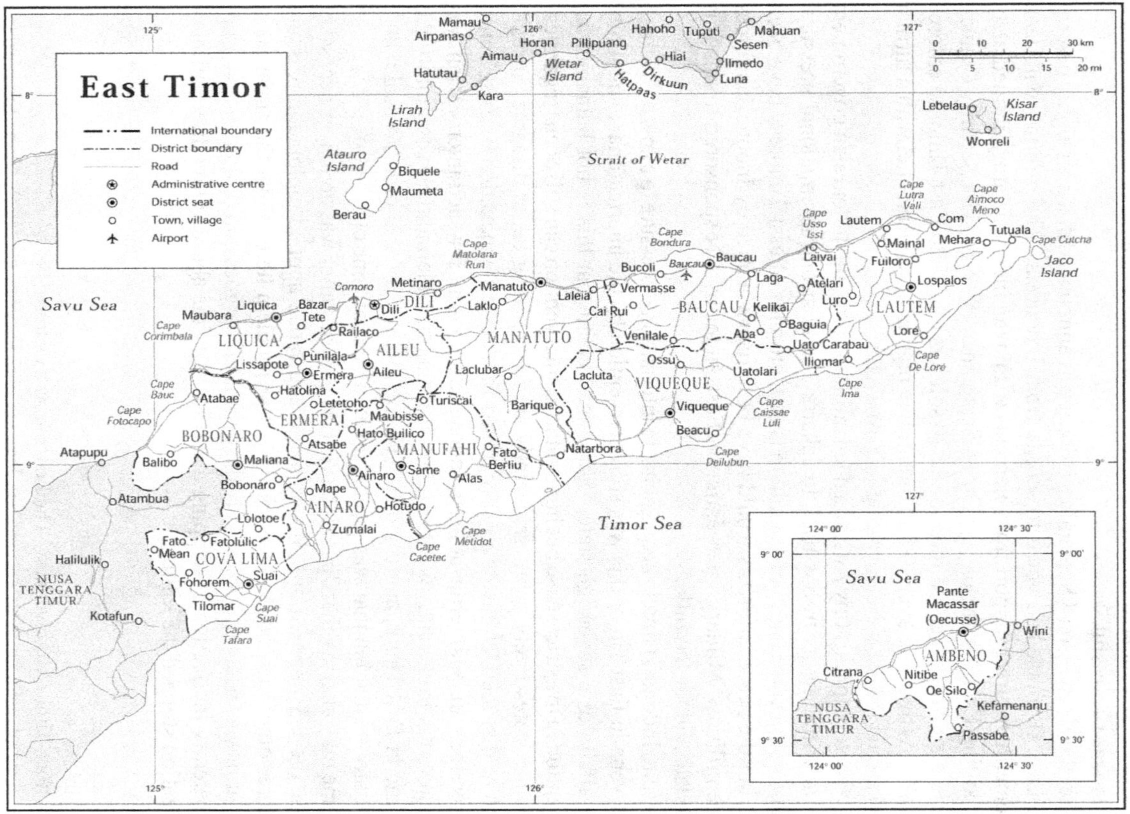

**Map 4.7 East Timor Map Enlarged**

greater violence than in the past.[13]     Prior to the UN sponsored election, military sources from within East Timor repeatedly predicted a bloodbath in East Timor if the vote for independence was successful.[14]     Anti-independence forces within East Timor openly intimidated the local population with the threat of torture and death if the vote was successful.[15]

After the election, on 4 September 1999, it was announced that over eighty percent of the East Timorese had voted to secede from Indonesia.  The militias, with tacit and sometimes direct support from elements within the Indonesia army, immediately began killing East Timorese.[16] [17]     On 15 September 1999, the UN Security Council authorised an Australian-led force of 8,000 soldiers to go into East Timor to enforce the peace.  At this time over 20,000 Indonesian regular army personnel with a further 25,000 armed militia were operating in East Timor.

Fortunately for this tiny Australian led military force, the Indonesian government began to withdraw its troops back to Jakarta due to strong international pressure.  Had this not occurred not only would tens of thousands of east Timorese have been killed, but the peace enforcers would have been overwhelmed by Indonesian forces and the militias.  Military intervention in East Timor by UN sponsored troops was far too late and far too little.

Despite Indonesia finally acquiescing to international pressure to allow a UN force to intervene in East Timor this was still intervention by the international community in the affairs of a sovereign state.  Some may claim that this is not humanitarian intervention in the strict sense but humanitarian intervention can still occur regardless of whether states freely agree, reluctantly are forced to agree, or disagree outright.  The point that the UN has never recognised Indonesia's annexation of East Timor and therefore, in legal terms at least, Indonesia's consent for such intervention was not required is irrelevant.  What is relevant is that the international community did intervene in East Timor, and it did so with the force of arms in order to deal with a humanitarian situation that was rapidly spinning out of control.

Some may also say that direct intervention in East Timor was no longer necessary because the US imposed an arms embargo and Japan applied diplomatic pressure therefore 'other methods were working'.  The problem here is that the situation in East Timor was becoming a blood bath so arms embargoes and diplomatic pressure were patently ineffective in stopping the killing and the abuse.  Only direct military intervention stopped the killing.

---

13  Ibid.

14  'East Timor Misadventure,' The Economist, 2 October 1999.

15  'Friend or Foe in East Timor,' *The Economist*, 25 September 1999.  Many Indonesians genuinely wonder why those East Timorese living in the '27th province' were so ungrateful, especially after all the central government has done for them in the 24 years since the army moved into the former Portuguese colony.

16  *'East Timor Misadventure.'*

17  FOUR CORNERS Television Program, 'The Vanishing,' (Australia: Australian Broadcasting Commission, 1999).

*Military Advantage*

The relationship between attack and defence is a vital one for interventionists to consider. Attackers are always at a military disadvantage because they need greater numbers, more resources and stronger resolve than defenders if they hope to be successful. It is easier to hold ground than to take it. Interventionists considering military engagement may need to apply technological superiority (if they have it) against their opponents to make for up numerical and tactical disadvantages. Most importantly they must use their limited numbers or technology in such a way as to overwhelm their opponent's weak points.

This does not mean interdiction using only guided missiles and remote control technology. It is possible to have some military successes by simply bombing opponents back to the Stone Age, but troops on the ground, and many of them, are needed to ensure the humanitarian outcomes of these military engagements. There are no guarantees that military intervention will be militarily successful, or that it will be successful as a humanitarian endeavour, because conflict is a constant state of fluidity and chaos. Good military planning tries to limit the conflict variables so that some sort of predictable outcomes are possible, but there is absolutely no guarantee that this will occur.

This does not mean that military action cannot be used successfully to intervene in humanitarian matters. Where there is a high likelihood of military success and a subsequent improvement in the humanitarian circumstance, military force can and should be used. Providing there is no significant strategic advantage or disadvantage present a strong large military force will always beat a strong small military force, and a well-equipped and trained force will defeat a poorly equipped and trained force. A force endorsed by strong domestic support will be victorious compared to a force with weak domestic support, and a tactically superior force will defeat a tactically inferior force.

There may be serious strategic disadvantages facing potential interventionists. For example, superior numbers of opposing military forces which cannot be offset by home team technological advantage, populations to be immediately slaughtered the instant interventionists move in, human shields placed in front of opponent's military structures and so on. In these cases there is no military or moral point in sacrificing interventionists lives and the lives of the abused by intervening. Other means (previously briefly outlined) must immediately be found and applied to address situations where the use of military force is simply not possible without significant loss of life on all sides.

From a humanitarian point of view such military engagement must not be undertaken because it will not be successful. It will cause many more deaths to those already at serious risk. The military has no business in such an environment and if it had a choice it would not contemplate military engagement under these conditions.

## Interventionists are Likely to Suffer Casualties

An important objection to the use of coercive force in humanitarian situations is that such action may cause interventionist casualties. The reality is that one must expect casualties to interventionists who are in lethal combat zones. For interventionist planners to somehow aim for, then actually expect, zero casualties when undertaking humanitarian intervention is unrealistic. Concentrating on casualty aversion to the exclusion of the achievement of military or humanitarian objectives severely restricts the effective use of coercive force to address man-made humanitarian crises.

Since World War II, the Korean War and the Vietnam War, Western military planners have increasingly concentrated on risk aversion as a deliberate political and military strategy.[18] A significant problem for potential interventionists is to determine acceptable levels of risk. How many casualties should interventionist forces be prepared to accept? There is no simple answer to this question because a number of factors will influence what is and what is not considered acceptable regarding own side casualty numbers. For example, if intervention has a realistic chance of stopping humanitarian abuses then a higher level of interventionist casualties may be acceptable.

Other factors also come into play. If an interventionist's national interest is at directly stake then this may alter what is and what is not considered to be an acceptable casualty rate. There is a more willing acceptance of casualties during conflict if there is a high level of domestic support for intervention. In the West, this level of support tends to drop significantly once the body bags start coming home.

Response strategies to humanitarian crises have decreased as concern over own-side casualties increases. Either nothing is done militarily for fear of casualties or interventionists try to conduct war by remote control relying on the doubtful accuracy of precision weapons. Only 25 percent of such weapons actually hit their intended targets during Gulf War I. Both these positions cause significant problems for people suffering severe human rights abuse. People will keep on dying and being abused if the international response is limited to diplomatic protestations and threats of economic sanctions. On the other hand, if intervention consists of war by remote control, not only are the munitions used inaccurate but without ground forces to confront a widely dispersed enemy those being abused are at increased risk.

The military perceives conflict casualties very differently to the public or the politicians. In democratic societies, politicians must weigh up the risks to their political futures if war casualties are seen by their constituents to be 'excessive'.[19] As demonstrated during both Gulf Wars, the Western voter's enthusiasm for military adventurism quickly wanes as the home side body count increases. The military is more concerned about the logistics of battle losses and how this would impact on military objectives. Excessive human attrition during conflict may lose the war

---

18  Karl Eikenberry, 'Take No Casualties,' *Parameters* (1996): pp. 109–18.

19  Ibid.: p. 110. Eikenberry claims that it is impossible for a statesman to openly discuss in quantifiable terms what he deems a tolerable level of casualties to be.

despite winning the battle. Battle casualties must be carefully weighed against the need to overcome opposition, to hold ground, to respond to counterattack and to continue the conflict in the future.

Then there is the overall problem of risk assessment. Possible interventionist casualty numbers is a prime consideration for politicians who are trying to decide whether or not to intervene in a humanitarian disaster situation in the first place. A final decision usually comes down to how many casualties interventionist's would be prepared to accept rather than how many people are being abused in a conflict area.

The desire to limit casualties during conflict is not new but, increasingly, Western society appears unwilling or unable to accept even relatively low levels of home side casualties during military operations. The United States of America, arguably the world's most powerful military force, is beginning to include specific goals of casualty limitation as a cornerstone of its military doctrine. This type of doctrine places significant constraints on military planning at the strategic and at the tactical level. It either encourages the application of military force by remote control or it forces the military into inaction.

The military's altruistic ethos is in danger of being replaced by the notion that self-preservation has primacy over mission accomplishment. Brigadier General Terry Schwalier, whose promotion to Major General was stopped following the bombing of the Khobar Towers in Saudi Arabia during the Gulf War, was punished not because he failed to accomplish his mission of enforcing the no-fly zone in Southern Iraq, but because he allegedly failed to take sufficient steps to protect his forces.[20] An obsession with casualty aversion also sends the message to oppressive regimes around the globe that they need not fear accountability because those who could act will probably fail to act because they fear taking casualties. Oppressors are often quite willing to accept high casualty numbers of their own people in order to achieve their goals. During both Gulf Wars, Saddam Hussein was counting on the various anti-Iraqi coalitions' aversion to casualties.

## Intervention is 'Illegal'

To say that military intervention for humanitarian purposes is illegal assumes that a law (probably an international law) has been broken or is being violated. The fundamental question relating to the legality or otherwise of military intervention for humanitarian purposes is as follows: 'What right, according to international law, does the international community have to intervene across a sovereign state's borders to halt violations of human rights?'

---

20 Charles Dunlap, 'Organizational Change and the New Technologies of War,' *Joint Services Conference on Professional Ethics* (1997): p. 8.

Tom Farer claims that the answer, in purely legal terms, is none.[21]  But this is not to say that such intervention is therefore considered to be illegitimate.  Legality and legitimacy (depending on how it is measured) are two very different issues because an action may be illegal yet considered to be morally legitimate.  Arguments about the legality or otherwise of intervention for humanitarian purposes revolve around what the legal benchmark for intervention is, who determines this benchmark, and who supports the benchmark.

Is the international legal benchmark the UN, is it unilateral action by a state which believes itself under threat, is it a limited multilateral action (for example, the Coalition of the Willing action in Iraq), or is it all just about self defence and contests over sovereignty and the national interest?  All or a combination of these have at various times been used to legally justify intervention in the affairs of another state.  Some would say that the UN and the UN charter is the legal benchmark but if the UN is unable or unwilling to act and for example, tens perhaps hundreds of thousands of lives are at immediate risk then there is at least a powerful moral argument that intervention should proceed anyway.  Who will do the actual intervening is another consideration.

This will not sit well with the legal purists who, for example, favour UN authority over everything else but this is precisely what some in the international community have done, and continue to do, to address real or perceived threats to sovereignty or the national interest.  The Coalition of the Willing was unable to obtain a UN mandate to intervene in Iraq – the basis for intervention moved from some initial claims about a need for regime change, then to stop WMDs from falling into the hands of terrorists, then to the push for Iraq to have some democracy – but the Coalition intervened (or invaded depending on what side of the fence you are on) anyway.  The legality and legitimacy or otherwise of this action will be debated long into the future.

The principle of non-intervention for anything other than the defence of sovereignty is central to what most people understand to be international law.  Article 2(4) of the UN Charter identifies the legal and moral force of state boundaries.  Considerable opposition exists to any form of intervention at all.  Since there are no provisions within the UN charter for peacekeeping operations, the legal basis for each operation is the mandate given to it.[22]

The sovereignty of statehood is a cornerstone of international law and non-intervention expresses a correlative duty to respect sovereignty.[23]  This means that humanitarian concerns usually take a back seat to the rights and legitimate interests of

---

21  Tom J. Farer, 'An Inquiry into the Legitimacy of Humanitarian Intervention,' in *Law and Force in the New International Order*, ed. Lori F. Damrosch and David Scheffer (Boulder: Westview Press, 1991), p. 200.

22  Jett, *Why Peacekeeping Fails*.

23  Robert Murray Lyman, 'The Possibilities for 'Humanitarian War' by the International Community in Bosnia-Herzegovina between 1992 and 1995: Occasional Paper No 27,' (Camberley: The Strategic and Combat Studies Institute., 1997).

states. Most people concerned about human rights will disagree with the fundamental idea that states should have rights before the rights of individuals. Even if states had some rights in law these must, at least according to some humanitarians, be subservient to the rights of its citizens.

An important legal legacy of the Nuremberg trials was that for the first time individuals had a right to be treated with a minimum of civility by their own governments. This meant that all governments had a correlative duty to uphold such a right. Military intervention for humanitarian purposes has a legal basis if its intent is to uphold such a right.

Early post cold-war era interventions (India in Bangladesh 1971, Tanzania against the excesses of Adi Amin in Uganda 1979, and Vietnam against Pol Pot in Cambodia 1979) which resulted in significant humanitarian benefits were not justified by intervention on humanitarian grounds. These actions were justified on the grounds of self-defence. Even on these grounds, all these actions were condemned by the international community because they broke the rule on cross border aggression.[24]

There are no legal statutes that establish the right of intervention for humanitarian purposes only, and few modern precedents exist. The intervention in East Timor is perhaps the exception. Yet, absolute prohibitions against humanitarian intervention do not exist either. What is important is how states and world leaders who ultimately assume responsibility for authorising military action in the first place interpret the various legal definitions of sovereignty, non-intervention and intervention.

International law (depending on the benchmark question) allows a legal right to intervene in the affairs of a sovereign state if non-intervention poses a threat to international peace and security. Such a right legally justifies humanitarian intervention in Somalia, in Rwanda, the safe-havens for the Kurds and in the Balkans.[25] There are two central reasons why the legal status of the protection of human rights is weak in international law. Firstly, the mass of treaties, conventions and protocols which relate to human rights deal not with rights but with vague ideas about 'duty' and moral value. Secondly, there are grave doubts about the implementation of such rights in law. The basic assumption being that a law means a rule that is actually capable of enforcement through institutions created for that purpose. There is no recognised international policeman to enforce international law. If a rule cannot be enforced then it has minimal status as a law.

Robert Lyman argues that the principle legal hurdle to humanitarian intervention is articulated in Michael Walzer's 'legalist paradigm'.[26] That is, there exists an international society of independent states, which has established a law that substantiates the rights of its members. These rights are rights of territorial integrity and political sovereignty. An act of force or even the threat to use force against the state or its citizens constitutes aggression and is a criminal act.

---

24 Hedley Bull, *Intervention in World Politics* (Oxford: Clarendon Press, 1984), p. 97.

25 Lyman, 'The Possibilities for 'Humanitarian War' by the International Community in Bosnia-Herzegovina between 1992 and 1995: Occasional Paper No 27.'

26 Ibid.

The problem with this approach is that it assumes that those who are the rulers of states are moral and rational, and that they use the so-called sanctity of statehood for the benefit of their own citizens. Allan Buchanan argues that the moral legitimacy of states cannot simply be assumed. Even if, he says, we assume that peace and justice are the ultimate moral goals for political institutions generally (as liberal normative political theories seem to do), we may question whether these goals are best served, or served effectively at all, by a system of states. If the assumption is that states are legitimate legal and moral entities, as most people clearly do, then surely states should exist in the first place for the benefit of their citizens. Citizens do not exist for the benefit of states.[27]

The other problem with the approach as previously outlined is that it conveniently subsumes individual rights into the morass of state rights, and claims that the sanctity of statehood is actually based as an expression of the rights of its citizens. This is convoluted thinking. Whatever sanctity a state is legally assumed to have, it is really only for the welfare of its citizens that such a position exists in the first place. Humanitarians will argue that states should not have rights, people should.[28]

Cold-war mentality assumed that intervention could never really be solely for humanitarian purposes (there must be an ulterior motive) therefore, intervention should be banned because it would upset the delicate balance of mutual respect between states. Such a ban on humanitarian intervention has resulted in millions of citizens being abused without formal recourse to legal protection under international law.

The legalist paradigm concept has been revised or extended to specify circumstances in which humanitarian intervention could be legitimised. These are; when the state has virtually ceased to exist (Somalia); when the state engages in genocide or the mass expulsion of minorities and it conducts a deliberate reign of terror (Iraq under Saddam Hussein); and when a state is in a constant state of civil war in which no side has a reasonable chance of winning (Bosnia Herzegovina).

Others accept the inherent weakness of the international law of human rights, yet they caution that this weakness does not do away with the idea of a general obligation to relieve human misery and suffering. Some, for example Kalevi Holsti, go further.

> In the United Nations, collective intervention in the internal affairs of member states seems to have become a legitimate method of coping with widespread domestic chaos that promises to involve external powers exclusively.[29]

During the NATO air campaign in Kosovo in 1999, NATO's decision to intervene using armed force did not have as clear a legal endorsement as its governments

---

27 Allen Buchanan, 'Recognitional Legitimacy and the State System,' *Philosophy and Public Affairs* 28, no. 1 (1999): pp. 46–78.

28 Charles R Beitz, *Political Theory and International Relations* (New Jersey: Princeton University Press, 1999), pp. 69–71.

29 Kalevi Holsti, *International Politics: A Framework for Analysis* (Englewood Cliffs: Prentice-Hall, 1988), pp. 267–68.

might have wished. Despite these limitations, it was far from being an unambiguous violation of international law either. According to Adam Roberts there were two main legal arguments used to support the NATO action in Kosovo.[30] One was based on UN Security Council resolutions and the other on an application of general international law.

UN Resolution 1199 of 23 September 1998 demanded that Yugoslavia cease all action by the security forces affecting the civilian population. It directly referred to possible further action if measures demanded in the resolution were not taken. Resolution 1203 of 24 October 1998 demanded that the Serbs comply with a number of key provisions of the accords concluded in Belgrade on 15 and 16 October. These Resolutions also verified that the NATO Alliance had a direct standing and interest in the Kosovo issue.

Therefore, even if the UN Security Council was not able to follow these resolutions into Kosovo with a specific authority to use force, the Resolutions still provided a legal basis for military action by NATO. On 26 March 1999, two days after the bombing began, Russia sponsored a draft UN resolution calling for 'an immediate cessation of the use of force against the Federal Republic of Yugoslavia'. Russia's stance was supported by two non-member states, India and Belarus. Only three member states (Russia, China and Namibia) voted in favour of this draft resolution, twelve voted against.

During the debate for the resolution, Slovenia made the key point that the Security Council does not have a legal monopoly on decision-making regarding the use of force. It has 'the primary, but not exclusive, responsibility for maintaining international peace and security'.[31] This debate confirmed that the NATO action was not considered manifestly illegal. Prior to military intervention in Kosovo, several NATO governments presented the argument that military intervention against another state could be justified in cases of overwhelming humanitarian necessity according to general international law.

The central basis for such an argument is contained in the formal conventions of international law that, in conjunction with the UN Charter or Security Council resolutions, provides a legal platform for military intervention. Increasingly, the international community is intervening in the affairs of sovereign states when the killing and the abuse have become so extreme and so awful that these acts are deemed to be crimes against humanity. The sanctity of statehood argument must be balanced against the moral requirement for the international community to stop serious human rights abuses carried out by states against their own citizens.

Sovereignty is not an absolute good, as many of its supporters claim. It is a legal definition of a right that is contingent on the protection of citizens within

---

30 Adam Roberts, 'Nato's Humanitarian War over Kosovo,' *Survival* 41, no. 3 (1999): pp. 102–23.

31 United Nations, 'Security Council – 4 3989th Meeting (Am) Un Press Release Sc/6659,' (New York: 1999).

such a state.[32]   If these citizens are grossly abused, then there is a legal basis for an external power or powers, under the auspices of the United Nations, to step in to stop the killing.  Human interest must replace national interest as the driving force of human endeavour.  State borders are social and political constructs that can change according to ideological, cultural or political requirements.  Human interest is immutable.  Whatever moral good the entity of statehood is assumed to possess, it must yield to the superior imperatives of the rights of humanity.

### Non-Violent Intervention 'Works Better'

I shall not strictly try to define what people believe the phrase 'works better' means because this will vary according to the views and beliefs of those who make such a claim.  Similar to the assertion that the use of force cannot promote humanitarian values, this is an implied objection.  There is no empirical evidence to suggest that non-violent intervention works better than anything else in the resolution of international conflicts.  There is empirical evidence to suggest that genocide and other serious crimes against humanity have increased dramatically during the twentieth century.  This is despite the fact that the majority of these conflicts were addressed (where they were addressed at all) by non-violent means.

Trade embargos, mediation, conflict resolution strategies, peace monitoring, UN Resolutions demanding that the killing stops and so on are non-violent means of humanitarian intervention.  Later I shall discuss the Contingency Approach to non-coercive intervention, but first I will address the view that non-violence just works better than the use of force.  Military intervention cannot be effective from a humanitarian perspective if we wait until 100,000 (or 10) people have been slaughtered before we intervene.  We may be able to save some others from being killed but we will not be able to save any of the 100,000.  Neither non-violent means nor violent means could be deemed to work better after many people have died.  The fact is that nothing worked to save those who are dead.

The timing of any interventionist strategy is critical so when people say that non-violence works better it is important to define what time frame we are talking about. I have previously argued that non-violent conflict resolution strategies are essential humanitarian tools that should be used up to the point when people are about to die. At this crucial point in time the use of force must be used to stop the killing from occurring in the first place.

Many will say that it is impossible to make such a judgement.  How can one reasonably assess that people are about to die?  How many people are we talking about, and what if some people do die but military intervention will result in many more dying?  There are no definitive answers to any of these questions, but this does not mean that non-violence works better simply because the potentiality of using

---

32 John Simmons, 'Justification and Legitimacy,' *Ethics and International Affairs* 109, no. 4 (1999): pp. 739–71.

force in humanitarian affairs is unpredictable or dangerous or that it has not always proven to be successful.

The reality is that if people start to die, or have already died, non-violence is not working, never mind not working better than anything else. The same could be said about the use of force. Both are not working if people die. A strategy which according to some works better than the use of coercive force is non-coercive intervention.

*Non-coercive Intervention - The Contingency Approach Model*

Ronald Fisher and Loraleigh Keashly outline a Contingency Model of Third Party Consultation. According to the contingency approach to mediation methodology it is possible to precisely model a response to conflict through the use of mediation and other conflict management techniques.[33] Mediation attempts to turn a dyadic conflict into a triadic relationship by the non-coercive intervention of a third party. Supporters of the contingency approach to mediation argue that third party intervention must 'match the characteristics of the conflict'.

They make a strong distinction between different types of intervention, and they differentiate between the various modes of consultation and mediation carried out by the intermediary. Fisher and Keashly propose that conflict is a dynamic process that can be broken down into distinct stages of; discussion, polarisation, segregation and destruction. Between these stages there is communication, perception and conflict-management techniques.

Within the different stages of conflict are varying objective and subjective elements that in turn influence, and are influenced by, the progression of conflict. For example, the subjectivity of certain cultural, ethnic or religious views become more prevalent as the conflict progresses to the detriment of a more objective strategic or political perspective. They suggest that there is a clear-cut distinction between mediation and consultation, and that there has been an unfortunate blurring of the boundaries between the two. This often results in frustration and failure.[34]

The main problem with the contingency approach model is that it does not correspond to what actually happens during humanitarian crises. Discerning different types of non-coercive intervention may be useful when constructing response models, but belligerents will not follow the rules so carefully laid out for them. Belligerents will be ruthlessly carrying out genocide, calling for cease-fires, complaining about bias when the international community supports the other side, resupplying and preparing for new offensives, and attending peace conferences probably all at once.

---

33 Ronald Fisher and Loraleigh Keashly, 'The Potential Complementarity of Mediation and Consultation within a Contingency Model of Third Party Consultation,' *Journal of Peace Research* 28, no. 1 (1991): pp. 29 – 42.

34 Jacob Bercovitch, *Resolving International Conflicts* (London: Lynne Rienner Publisher, 1996), p. 173.

It may be possible to continue mediation even as the atrocities occur. But to what purpose? The purpose of mediation should not just be to mediate or to simply claim that mediation as an ongoing process is continuing. The purpose of mediation must be to quickly, if not immediately, stop the killing and deprivations. If the killings just continue on there is no purpose to mediation.

Clearly defined stages of discussion, polarisation, segregation and destruction are useful processes in the theoretical world of mediation modelling. The problem is that real world inter-racial, religious and ideological upheavals do not follow such neat sequential categorisations. Discussion and polarisation probably occurred decades ago. Many such hatreds are sustained by myth building alone. Discussion in this context has little relevance in a mediation model today.

An external mediator would be hard pressed using discussion alone to convince determined belligerents, such as the Serbs, that their thousand year dream of a Greater Serbia in the Balkan's is unrealistic and irrational in today's world. The Serbs consider that such a goal is perfectly rational – it is also realistic with adequate ruthlessness on their part and a confused international community only occasionally paying attention. There is usually no discussion in these sorts of long standing feuds. Polarisation is deeply entrenched and spread across racial, ethnic or ideological lines.

Segregation is also not a pre-determined outcome, although it often appears to outsiders that clear-cut delineations along cultural or religious lines exist. For example, during the 1992–96 conflict in the Balkans, the Bosnian Government was also at war at various times with the Bosnian Croats. These two groups were sometime-allies against the Serbs. Alliances and segregation, which initially appears to the outsider to be ethnic, religious or ideologically based, frequently change depending on circumstance and opportunity.

A significant problem with the many contingency approaches to mediation models is that the ROE and their accompanying list of 'things to do' and 'things to look out' for is in their lack of sophistication in addressing serious humanitarian crises. Many of them just do not work because the belligerents will not follow the rules, or they become so complex and unwieldy as to make them unworkable for mediators and potential interventionists.

The supporters of this modelling process fundamental defence seems to be, 'Do not blame the contingency model if it does not work...blame the application of an inappropriate model to the wrong contingency'. Whatever contingency model for mediation is used it cannot work whilst the bombs and bullets are flying. It cannot work when people are being killed and seriously abused on a daily basis. Individuals, former statesmen, single countries, groups of countries and international organisations have all attempted some form of mediation during the conflict in the former Yugoslavia without success. Mediation, as a primary interventionist strategy, cannot be successful until the guns fall silent first.

My concern about attempting mediation under these impossible circumstances is not only that it will not work but that it is used as a '...at least we are doing something' response by the international community. This leaves those who are suffering serious human rights abuse where they started – being abused. In areas of extreme humanitarian need where gross human rights atrocities are committed many conventional interventionist strategies fail because they are more suited to mollify the sensibilities of potential interveners than to seriously and effectively address gross abuses of human rights.

*Other Conventional Non-Violent Response Strategies*

Conventional non-violent response strategies include; the imposition of international trade embargoes, peace conferences, declaration of cease-fires, withdrawal of diplomatic privileges, and shuttle diplomacy. Most of these types of strategies do not stop the killing and the atrocities in the short term or even the longer term. This does not mean that mediation and diplomatic efforts at conflict resolution are not valid and important medium to long-term strategies in international disputes. It means that non-violence may not always be the only answer to a difficult humanitarian situation.

Most supporters of non-violent strategies fail to understand that many of the conflicts between different ethnic, tribal, religious, or ideological groups are not rational according to the accepted norms of civilised behaviour. They have great difficulty in accepting that many protagonists have a deep seated, quite irrational hatred against their opponents which has very little to do with the potentially fixable day to day problems between them.

How is it rational for Serbs to hate and to fear their Muslim neighbours for a military defeat at the Battle of Kosovo where a Serbian king was killed centuries ago? What rationality was there in the essentially Hutu Burundian army slaughtering 10,000 Tutsis in reprisal for guerrilla attacks in 1963? Why did the Hutus kill a further 250,000 Tutsis in 1972; and, in three months in 1994, slaughter with the use of machetes and hoes, over 1 million Tutsis?

Non-violent interventionists persist in the mistaken belief that if only such protagonists could sit around a conference table to thrash out their differences then serious international conflicts can be resolved. The reality is that, although mediation and consultation may be occurring, the warring parties usually either ignore such efforts outright or they simply pay lip service to suggestions of how to resolve their differences – and the killing continues. Attempts at mediation and consultation in these long standing tribal and ethnic wars have little effect. The mass killings simply go on.

Most conventional interventionist strategies are only as effective as the willingness of warring parties to respond to external diplomatic efforts to modify their behaviour. If those perpetrating gross violations of human rights do not care about international opinion, then the international community needs more than diplomacy, good will and hope to halt the killing.

**Who's Going to Pay For It?**

The cost of UN peacekeeping reached a high of nearly $US 4 billion in 1993 and it has dropped significantly since then – $US 1.4 billion in 1996, $US 1.3 billion in 1997, and less than $US 900 million for 1998.[35] The question often arises regarding who should pay for all this peacemaking and peacekeeping. One needs only to look at global military spending; and how the diversion of a tiny proportion of these funds could make a substantial and lasting difference to humanitarian efforts. The problem is not that adequate funds do not exist to support the UN and its peace endeavours, but that such funds and resources are inequitable distributed.

Globally, states spend more than 12 percent (peaking at 1.26 trillion U.S. dollars in 1986) of all outlays to support the world's military systems?[36] In 1995/96 total military spending was estimated to be around $750 billion. Dr. Oscar Arias, in his December 1995 address to the UN Year 2000 Campaign to Redirect World Military Spending, pointed out that in developing nations 900 million people are unable to read and write yet military spending far exceeds spending on education.[37]

Military spending overall is more than double the amount spent on health, yet one billion people never see a health professional and two million children die each year of preventable infectious diseases. Developed countries alone account for 82 percent of global military spending, and they are responsible for 90 percent of arms transfers to the developing countries.[38] In 1997, the U.S. alone spent $US270 billion on its military. Humankind places spending on the military well before social development. The U.S. Fiscal Year 2004 budget request included $782 billion for discretionary spending (the money the President and Congress must decide and act to spend each year). $399 billion of discretionary spending is for the Pentagon. The 'National Defense' category of the federal budget for FY04 accounts for over half (51.0 percent) of all discretionary spending.[39]

Governments of developing countries spend over $US 25 billion every year on arms while their people go hungry. Four percent of the developing world's annual military budget could support programs that would increase literacy levels by fifty percent, educate women to the same level as men and provide universal primary education. Eight percent of the developing countries' annual military expenditures could finance voluntary family planning packages that, according to some calculations, would stabilise the world's populations by the year 2015.

Twelve percent of developing countries' annual military expenditures would pay for the cost of basic health care for the world's entire population, provide immunisation for all children, eliminate severe malnutrition and provide safe drinking water for

---

35 Jett, *Why Peacekeeping Fails*.

36 Arias, Friedman, and Rossiter, 'Less Spending, More Security: A Practical Plan to Reduce World Military Spending'.

37 Ibid.

38 Ibid.

39 Christopher Hellman, 'Cdi Fiscal Year 2004 Budget,' (Washington: CENTER FOR DEFENSE INFORMATION, 2004).

all.[40] A tiny portion of these military resources redirected to support humanitarian efforts would pay for peacemaking and peacekeeping.

### Force Should Only be Used in the National Interest

The view that we should not be meddling in the affairs of other states unless there is a direct benefit or identifiable threat to our own state's national interest traces its roots at least back to the pessimistic realism of Machiavelli in the 15th century. It repudiates even earlier Western perceptions of Judeo-Christian biblical morality, Hellenic idealism and the teachings of medieval churchmen such as Thomas Aquinas. Machiavelli argued that you may have splendid moral goals but without sufficient power and the willingness to use it you will accomplish nothing. Power rather than morality was, and is today, the crux of national-interest thinking.

Medieval religious teachings proposed that human behaviour in the here-and-now was accountable in the afterlife. Humans had souls, therefore they could be held accountable to exacting standards of behaviour. States, on the other hand were artificial constructs. They have life only in this world. If a state is destroyed it has no afterlife. Therefore, states may take harsh measures to protect themselves and ensure their survival. States were seen to be amoral and a state can do things humans cannot.

This rationalisation of the place of humankind and the state in world affairs resulted in religious leaders, such as Thomas Aquinas, proposing theories of *Jus ad Bellum* – Just-cause – and *Jus in Bello* – Just-means during conflict. They argued that military action (which includes military intervention) was sometimes morally justifiable providing a range of criteria regarding aggression and response to aggression were met. Both these concepts are discussed in Chapter One, *Ethical Reasoning and Moral Principles.*

In the early 1800s, Carl von Clausewitz, the Prussian military strategist, contributed to national-interest thinking when he proposed that all state behaviour is motivated by its need to survive and prosper. He argued that to safeguard state interests the state must rationally decide to go to war. He said that there must be no other reason for going to war. War is an instrument of policy and is simply a continuation of political intercourse, with the addition of other means.[41] Hans Morgenthau (1904–1980), the father of Western Realism, combined the nationalistic views of Machiavelli and Clausewitz. He told Americans that they must arm then oppose first the Axis Powers and then the Soviet Union. This was not to be done out of any abstract love of liberty and justice but because the United State's most fundamental national interests were threatened.

Morgenthau was roundly criticised and denounced by some academics who preferred Woodrow Wilson's more idealistic world order approach. Wilson proposed

---

40 Arias, Friedman, and Rossiter, 'Less Spending, More Security: A Practical Plan to Reduce World Military Spending'. p. 10.

41 Clausewiz, 'On War.'

that peaceful, co-operative behaviour should be the international norm.[42]  They resisted what they perceived as Germanic amorality, (Morgenthau was a German émigré) the idea that individual state interests should dominate international affairs. Morgenthau believed that he had an objective standard for the measurement of foreign policies that claimed to be for the national interest.  He defined interest as power.  That is, if the state acts to preserve and enhance its power then this was deemed to be a matter of national interest.[43]

The attraction in defining national interest in this way is that state foreign policy may then be judged on some sort of rational and empirical basis without the vexing question of values muddying the waters.  It does not matter whether the national values are Christianity, Islam or moon worshipping.  The only rational judgement needs to be whether or not state power is being enhanced.  Supporters of national-interest thinking are essentially realists who will question the relevance of morality in state affairs in the first place, particularly when the state is under direct threat from external powers.  The realist position was discussed in Chapter One *Ethical Reasoning and Moral Principles.*

Realists, who do not reject outright the place of morality in human behaviour, will argue that nothing could be more 'moral' than the interests of the state.  Even seemingly immoral ends could be employed to support such overriding interests.  There is a very fine line between what is considered immoral in such cases and what is considered a military or political necessity.  For example, Emmett Barcalow claims that almost everyone agrees that it is immoral to intentionally attack defenceless non-combatants. Although such behaviour still occurs in war time, when it occurs, virtually every nation condemns it.  However, he says, there is sharp disagreement about whether it is morally acceptable to attack military targets if such attacks will inevitably and foreseeably lead to numerous casualties among non-combatants.  In such cases the goal is not to kill the non-combatants but to destroy targets of military value; the non-combatant casualties are an unavoidable by-product, often referred to as 'collateral damage'.[44]

Those who say that force should only be used in the national interest generally argue either that the plight of other citizens in other states is not a moral issue anyway or that, if the concept of human moral obligation was not totally ruled out, stated citizens have a moral obligation to look after their own people first and foremost.

There is a range of possible responses to this fundamental position.  Proponents of new world order thinking will say that state interests are being subsumed by global interests and that human connectivity is rapidly increasing in the modern age.[45]

---

42  Woodrow Wilson despised as amoral or even immoral approaches that used power, national interest, and recourse to violence as normal components of international relations. He passionately believed that America had a higher calling than that.

43  Hans Morgenthau, *Politics among Nations*, 6th ed. (Chicago: University of Chicago Press, 1984), p. 5.

44  Barcalow, *Moral Philosophy. Theory and Issues.*

45  Anthony McGrew, 'Conceptualising Global Politics,' in *Global Politics : Globalization and the Nation-State*, ed. Anthony G. McGrew and Paul G Lewis (Cambridge: Polity Press, 1992), p. 3.

International travel, global communications and information flows are breaking down the tyrannies of distance and ignorance. Therefore, individual states can no longer assume anonymity in how they conduct their affairs nor can they, according to John Merriam, rightly claim that human rights abuses within the borders of a sovereign state are solely the 'internal' affair of that state. He argues that this is because of the increasing importance of human rights in international law. This last point is very debatable but the legitimacy of how states conduct their affairs is on the global agenda despite the overall very selective approach to human rights by the international community. [46] Isolationism is out, globalism is in.

They say that world wide economic pressures increasingly determine national wealth. Environmental issues such as pollution of our atmosphere and our oceans, global warming, deforestation and the holes in the ozone layer are issues that impact on *all* of humankind.[47] So, a total preoccupation with matters deemed only to be important if somebody's version of the national interest is directly threatened is at odds with the increasing connectivity of all human endeavour. The national interest is dependent on the interests of those beyond the nation being advanced.

They will probably say that the use of external military force is sometimes necessary in international affairs not because of some ethical imperative but because the use of force may be the only way to stop rogue states from creating chaos and disruption in defiance of this new world order.[48] There is a direct and mutual benefit for all states to be living and working in harmony together. Those who would deliberately disrupt such processes must be stopped for the greater utility of all.

Moralists who attempt to counter the powerful national interest arguments have a number of challenges to overcome. This is because firstly, rationalists will simply reject the notion the morality has anything to do with the behaviour of states in conflict in the first place. Secondly, by pushing the line that states should consider military intervention against other states on humanitarian grounds alone, one must still confront the morality of condoning the use of force.

Another problem for opponents to the national interest view is in pinning down exactly what somebody else's perception of the national interest actually is. For example, Hans Morgenthau proposes two levels of national interest, one that is 'logically required' and in that sense necessary, and one that is variable and determined by circumstance. He claims the relative permanency of the 'hard core' national interest stems from three factors: the nature of the interests to be protected, the political environment within which the interests operate, and the rational necessities which limits the choice of ends and means by all actors on the stage of

46 John Merriam, 'Kosovo and the Law of Humanitarian Intervention,' *Case Western Reserve Journal of International Law* 33, no. 1 (2001): pp. 111–40.

47 John Vogler, 'Regimes and the Global Commons: Space Atmosphere and Oceans,' in *Global Politics: Globalization and the Nation-State*, ed. Anthony G. McGrew and Paul G. Lewis (Cambridge: Polity Press, 1992), pp. 119–21.

48 John Vogler, 'Regimes and the Global Commons: Space Atmosphere and Oceans,' in *Global Politics*, ed. A McGrew and P Lewis (Cambridge: Polity Press, 1992), pp. 128–29.

foreign policy.[49]  Unfortunately, such vagaries do little to pin down what the national interest for a state really is.

Perhaps it is may be clearer just to refer to the national interest as being either vital or secondary.  The vital concerns the very existence of the state whereas the secondary (some use the term marginal) are somewhat removed from immediate border security issues and represent no threat to sovereignty.[50]   Others, talk about national interest issues being temporary or permanent, specific or general, and complementary or conflicting, or some combination of these.[51] [52]   Most attempts to define the essence of the national interest degenerate into theoretical musings that have little meaning in the real world, yet this term is used extensively (as is the term national security) by our leaders who try to add a level of great gravity to the supposed seriousness of a particular event or issue.  Trying to define the national interest is no more or less problematic than defining what morality is.

One could try to argue that forcible humanitarian intervention is necessary because conflict in another state is somehow not good for regional trade issues, or that there is a danger of the conflict spreading and involving other states.  But there are serious problems with this approach.  Firstly, and most importantly, if one argues that humanity has a moral conscience then to simply put this aside for the sake of justifying intervention for some other reason rejects the view that human beings have any real moral obligation to care for each other in the first place.  Either there is a moral imperative for humanitarian intervention or there is not.  Moralists must not degrade their position just because it is difficult to convince non-believers that such a moral position exists.

Most of humanity is torn between not interfering in another state's genocidal activities because of the very real risk of death or injury to family or friends, and the awful realisation that every minute of inaction means that more atrocities are occurring.  For the sake of a suffering and dying humanity, it is (morally speaking) not good enough to be stunned into indecision.  Only observers to atrocities have the luxury of moral indecision.  Those suffering and dying in the tens of thousands have no such moral dilemmas to worry about.

To argue that military intervention may be necessary in these cases because some regional trade agreements are being threatened means that morals and ethical behaviour are essentially pretty irrelevant after all.  All we really need to worry about is whether or not our economy moves up one percentage point.  This is a morally inadequate response.

---

49  Hans Morgenthau, *Politics of the Twentieth Century* (Chicago: University of Chicago Press, 1971), p. 216.

50  John Hillen, 'American Military Intervention: A User's Guide,' *The Heritage Foundation: The Backgrounder* (1996): p. 8.

51  Arnold Wolfers, *Alliance Policy in the Cold War* (Baltimore: John Hopkins University Press, 1959), p. 191.

52  '1995 Annual Defense Report: Part 2 Challenges for the New Security Environment. Report of the Us Secretary of Defence to the President and the Congress,' (Washington: United States Department of Defence, 1995).

Secondly, the problem with trying to convince people to intervene in another state's affairs because of some real or imagined threat to their national interest is that the next time such conflict occurs (and there will always be a next time) such artificial imperatives to intervene may not be present. Regional trade may not be disrupted, the conflict may be totally confined with a particular state and non-moral imperatives to intervene may simply not exist.

The reality of contemporary civil conflict is that massive human suffering is usually involved, but this rarely poses a direct threat to the strategic interests of most other states. Most of these conflicts are intrastate rather than interstate affairs. The aim must be to stop the dying and the suffering because it is morally wrong not to do so. This is important because otherwise the imperative for action is severely limited to whether or not some contrived national interest is at risk.

One should not try to present a case for intervention on the basis that some national interest is always somehow at risk when rogue states abuse their citizens. This abrogates a moral responsibility to address moral issues. Military intervention for humanitarian purposes is required because it is morally wrong to allow fellow human beings to suffer and die when we have the capability to effectively stop the slaughter. If interventionists are criticised for using lethal force in order to uphold a moral position then it becomes a matter of acting decisively to address the greater of two evils.

It is morally confronting that lethal force is sometimes the only effective method of stopping extreme human rights abuses, but it is even more morally confronting to deliberately allow atrocities to continue when one is capable of stopping it. This is particularly the case if potentially few interventionists' lives are at risk or the financial costs of intervention are relatively small. If a significant number of interventionist lives are at risk, or the financial costs of intervention are large, there is still a case for intervention on moral grounds providing the final outcome of such intervention stops the mass killings and alleviates the suffering of the majority of people. To do otherwise is morally wrong.

## Using Force is Morally Wrong

A moral objection to the use of force is not only about practical issues such as whether alternatives to force work better or if peace-building, peace-enhancement/encouragement initiatives should be used in lieu of force. It is also about whether the use of force itself is morally acceptable. Those who believe that using force is morally wrong abhor violence. Conversely this does not necessarily mean that those who use force love violence. The assertion is often made that people who are prepared to use force have a propensity for violence. I will deal with this assumption later in this section.

The objection that using force is morally wrong is difficult to counter in isolation. It does not matter how one attempts to rationalise the use of force all arguments would be neutralised by a simple statement of belief that using force is wrong. This is further complicated by a belief that strategies other than force somehow must have better humanitarian outcomes just because force is not used. I have previously argued that the use of force is not intrinsically morally wrong or right. It depends on why and how such force is used, and it depends on whether human welfare and utility is enhanced by such activity.

The objection that using force is always morally wrong ignores the moral ramifications of not using force when force, and force alone, could reasonably be expected to stop serious abuse. I do not ignore such ramifications, indeed I have argued that it is morally unacceptable to allow belligerents to continue with their atrocities against helpless human beings. The fundamental idea that only non-violent means are morally appropriate to address humanitarian issues ignores outcomes.

How can non-violent humanitarian intervention be morally acceptable when it cannot stop the abuse? Persisting with ineffectual strategies to combat some of the worst humanitarian abuses occurring around the globe today is morally wrong. Any meaningful objection to the use of force must consider the ramifications of not using force where other alternatives do not or will not work.

Most people will express abhorrence about the use of force but the uncomfortable reality is that sometimes force is the only response that determined belligerents understand and will respond to. Opponents to the use of force will say that all non-violent measures cannot possibly have been tried. That is, if non-violent measures were properly initiated and implemented with adequate support systems, the right approach taken, things tried for long enough, and so on surely there would be no need to use force.

In the end the response to the claim that using force is morally wrong under all circumstances comes down to presenting enough appalling examples of extreme human rights abuses to convince people that at least a moral obligation to directly act does exist at some point in time. Then one would need to show that all non-violent means have been tried and failed, and that intervention will not cause more problems than it tries to solve. For some people only then may the use of directed force be considered to be a morally viable option.

### Everyone's Appalled

A significant part of the moral objection to the use of force includes a philosophy of non-violence or pacifism. The term 'pacifism' has fallen into disfavour because it implies passivity when faced with aggression.[53] A philosophy of non-violence on the other hand, as espoused by Mahatma Gandhi and Martin Luther King, Jr., emphasised that one must be active in seeking to prevent violence, to resolve conflicts without violence and to confront injustices.[54]

---

53 Joshua Goldstein, *International Relations*, 2nd ed. (Washington, DC: Harper Collins, 1996), p. 132.

54 Ibid., p. 133.

For consistency in this section, I do not use the term pacifism in its most literal or narrow sense. When I say pacifism I mean a fundamental philosophy of non-violence. Committed pacifists believe that conflict and violence are immoral, inhumane, unjust, impractical and wasteful. My primary focus is on the pacifist idea that the use of force is immoral. Pacifism is about a fundamental personal revulsion regarding the use of force and it is based on a unilateral commitment to refrain from using any forms of violence to achieve desired outcomes. Pacifists disagree with realists who claim that war and conflict is non-moral. They say that this is where ethics must be applied. They believe that physical conflict is morally wrong.

I argued in Chapter One that pacifism is actually incoherent because it is self-contradictory in its fundamental intent. For example, how can one claim that all human life is precious and special, but then not defend a life if one is physically capable of doing so? Abhorrence about the morality of using force is not restricted to pacifism. This is important because debates over whether or not the use of force is morally wrong or right often degenerates into a 'hawks' and 'doves' standoff. The hawks are seen as the aggressors and warmongers: the doves as peace loving, anti-war supporters.

Many people are morally appalled at the use of force, particularly lethal force. This does not mean that they would not be prepared to (and do) use force because a particular circumstance has dictated that not using physical force will result either in their own death or in the deaths and suffering of large numbers of fellow human beings. There is very little difference between being morally appalled at what one must do in conflict and considering the act itself to be morally appalling. This causes significant psychological trauma for people who are unable to reconcile the need to use force and the outcomes of such an act. [55]

One cannot just automatically assume that *all* moral objection against the use of force is just about personal values of non-violence, anti-war, anti-aggression; or that force itself is simply immoral, inhuman, and so on. This is because many people firmly believe that force is intrinsically wrong, yet they do not agree at all with the idea that only non-violent means should be used against determined and intractable belligerents. To them, the use of force may be abhorrent but if this was the only way to stop atrocities from occurring then it would be even more abhorrent not to use force.

This may appear contradictory. How can one say that using force is morally wrong, yet at the same time reject the fundamental values of non-violence? The answer is that human behaviour is not confined to either/or moral choices. Many people do not consider that the use of force is morally wrong under all, or even many, circumstances but this does not mean that they spend their lives trying to kill other human beings. These people will probably have few moral qualms about reacting violently if their family is threatened or perhaps if they find themselves as interventionists at the other end of the globe trying to stop some belligerent

---

55 Grossman, *On Killing*.

conducting atrocities on other human beings. Again, this does not mean that they have no moral restraints to killing other human beings.

Most people who have been directly involved in life threatening conflict are not war mongers who believe that it is morally acceptable to use force under any circumstance. The reality is that by circumstance or design they find themselves in a conflict situation and they do what they must to survive in a lethal environment. In the case of military intervention for humanitarian purposes, they do what they must in order to stop the genocide and the suffering from continuing endlessly on.

Conversely, many people who claim to be ardent pacifists relent and accept the need for military intervention when faced with the stark realities of a deliberate regime of terror, torture, and mass slaughter in places such as Rwanda, Somalia, or Bosnia Herzegovina.[56] This does not mean that they have rejected their fundamental opposition to violence. It means that they have accepted the fact that not acting immediately (in *this* place, at *this* time) to stop the killing will result in an even greater disaster than the use of force in the first place.

Many people are appalled at the need, and the actuality, of using directed force. They would say that using force is immoral under most circumstances, but some of them would not hesitate to stop a Hitler or Idi Amin if they thought that they could. If any workable alternative to the use of force stops the disembowelling of pregnant mothers in the Congo, or the dousing with petrol and setting alight of groups of Kosovars by the Serbs then it must be used. But if no workable alternative to the use of force is available, and the suffering and the killing simply continue on, then it would be immoral not to use force. The international community claims outrage at the conduct of belligerents, so it has at least some moral responsibility to protect those being abused.

Protecting one's self or one's immediate family from unprovoked attack involves the more palatable concept of 'self defence' compared to protecting someone whom one does not know personally. Again, this does not mean that one is a lover of violence just because one is prepared to defend one's self. I think that I would have few moral qualms in defending myself if I am attacked and I fear for my life. My immediate instinct would be for survival and I would physically respond accordingly. Very little philosophical conjecture would be running through my head at the time of the attack.

I do not know how I would feel after the attack. If I have somehow managed to defend my own life by killing my attacker, I would probably have some momentary remorse about my actions. I am sure that I would be thankful to be still alive. Perhaps I would suffer endless anguish over the taking of another human life. I may be thinking about the attacker's family, whether or not I should have been walking the dark streets at this late hour, or whether I should have tried to flee not fight. What I would not do is prowl the streets looking for someone to kill because I find out that

---

56 Mackinnon, *Ethics. Theory and Contemporary Issues.*

I am capable of killing another human being (and doing so without a full measure of remorse) if I was attacked.

A similar rationale may be applied to international man-made crises. Our impetus for action is not immediately for self defence or defence of family, but for the protection of people suffering extreme human rights abuse. To argue that the use of force is absolutely wrong under all circumstances, no form of violence is ever justified and violence is always morally wrong is an extreme position. There are times when the deliberate use of force is not only morally the right thing to do but it would be morally wrong not to use force to stop an even greater evil from occurring.

Using force during humanitarian intervention is not morally wrong providing the intent is to alleviate serious and consistent human suffering, and providing intervention does not cause more suffering than it tries to relieve. Where other non-violent options are not available or will not work to stop the killing then the option to use force must be considered. 'Will not stop the killing' is a judgement call but such assessments, difficult and fraught with danger though they are, must in the end be made. If by a rational and reasonable assessment it can be determined those other strategies are just not working, and realistically have no or very little chance of ever working, then forcible intervention is another option.

# Chapter 5

# Ethnic Conflict in the Balkans 1992–1999
# A Case Study

## Introduction

The 1992-96 ethnic wars in Bosnia Herzegovina and the conflict in Kosovo during 1999 are frequently cited in this book as examples of where external military intervention for humanitarian reasons may have been warranted. This chapter outlines the significant events during these conflicts that prompted international outrage over extreme human rights violations.

This chapter does not offer arguments for or against military intervention for humanitarian purposes: this was done in the previous chapters. However, it does attempt to make a judgement about the timing and the effectiveness of UN and NATO action in the Balkans. I argue that humanitarian intervention by the international community in Bosnia Herzegovina and in Kosovo was too little, too late and poorly executed. This action indirectly (some say directly) caused the deaths of tens of thousands of people and the displacement of hundreds of thousands more.

What follows is an observation of events in the Balkan's, leading up to and including the Kosovo conflict, in order to support the various arguments put forward in this book. The central argument is that external military intervention is sometimes the only way to stop a determined belligerent from a deliberate campaign of atrocity. The use of such force must be swift and overwhelming. This was not the case in the Balkans.

## The 1992 –1996 Balkans War

The war in Bosnia Herzegovina had its genesis in 1968, when Yugoslavia began to unravel after the government crackdown on the student movement in Zagreb. The students aligned themselves with the Yugoslav New Left who, supported by the intellectual fringe and spurred on by enormous popular appeal, had a vision of a trans-ethnic democratic socialist model. The various republican components, in particular the power elites in Zagreb, responded to this challenge with an ideological counteroffensive, Croatian nationalism. Political and ideological changes undermined and devalued the Yugoslav dominant class promoting fierce ethnic separatism between the various Yugoslav states for the next twenty years. All social and political conflict was transposed into a nationalist idiom. Map 8 is a map of

Croatia and Map 9 shows the former Yugoslavia prior to the separation by Slovenia and Croatia. Map 10 is a map of Yugoslavia after the separation.

The republics of Croatia and Slovenia declared, on 26 and 27 September 1990 respectively, that their legislation overruled Yugoslav federal law. On 25 June 1991, they proclaimed themselves to be independent states. The Croats elected a non-Communist government with the former general Franjo Tudjman as president. The new government immediately became embroiled in a bitter six month conflict with Yugoslav Serbian troops and Serb sympathisers within Croatia. The Serb enclave of Krajina was a hot bed of discontent regarding the secession from Serbia. Simmering animosities between Serbs and Croatians surfaced repeatedly.

The Serb dominated Yugoslav government in Belgrade violently reacted to these secessionist activities and the Yugoslav military (essentially a Serbian military force) attacked the provincial Slovenian militia. The Yugoslav army instigated its military action in Croatia to 'protect' the 600,000 Bosnian Serbs living in the Serbian enclaves of Croatia.[1]   This led to two brief civil wars between Croatian and Slovenian separatist forces and local Croatian and Slovenian Serbs backed by Serbia. The conflict in Slovenia ended quickly with the Slovenians successful in their nationalistic ambitions. The war in Croatia dragged on with one third of the country under the control of the Bosnian Serbs by the end of 1991.

The European Union (EU) and the Conference on Security and Cooperation in Europe (CSCE) moved to address the crisis under Article 52 of the UN Charter.[2] These organisations had been involved for some time in trying to reach a consensus with the Balkan states on a foreign and military policy. Unfortunately, Europe had no agreed means of carrying out a common security policy, much less an agreed foreign policy.

---

1   Mark Weller, 'The International Response to the Dissolution of the Socialist Republic of Yugoslavia,' *American Journal of International Law* 86, no. 3 (1992): pp. 570–74.

2   Article 52 of the United Nations Charter.
   • Nothing in the present Charter precludes the existence of regional arrangements or agencies for dealing with such matters relating to the maintenance of international peace and security as are appropriate for regional action provided that such arrangements or agencies and their activities are consistent with the Purposes and Principles of the United Nations.
   • The Members of the United Nations entering into such arrangements or constituting such agencies shall make every effort to achieve pacific settlement of local disputes through such regional arrangements or by such regional agencies before referring them to the Security Council.
   • The Security Council shall encourage the development of pacific settlement of local disputes through such regional arrangements or by such regional agencies either on the initiative of the states concerned or by reference from the Security Council. This Article in no way impairs the application of Articles 34 and 35.'

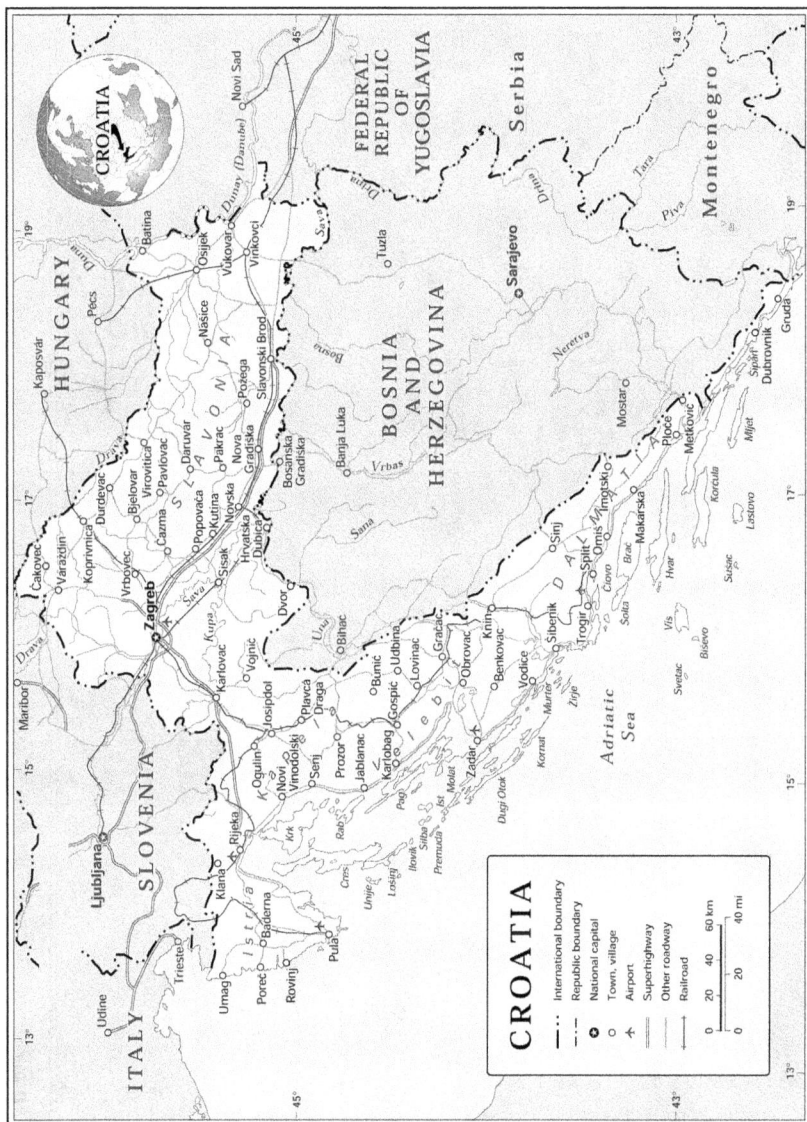

**Map 5.8  Croatia**

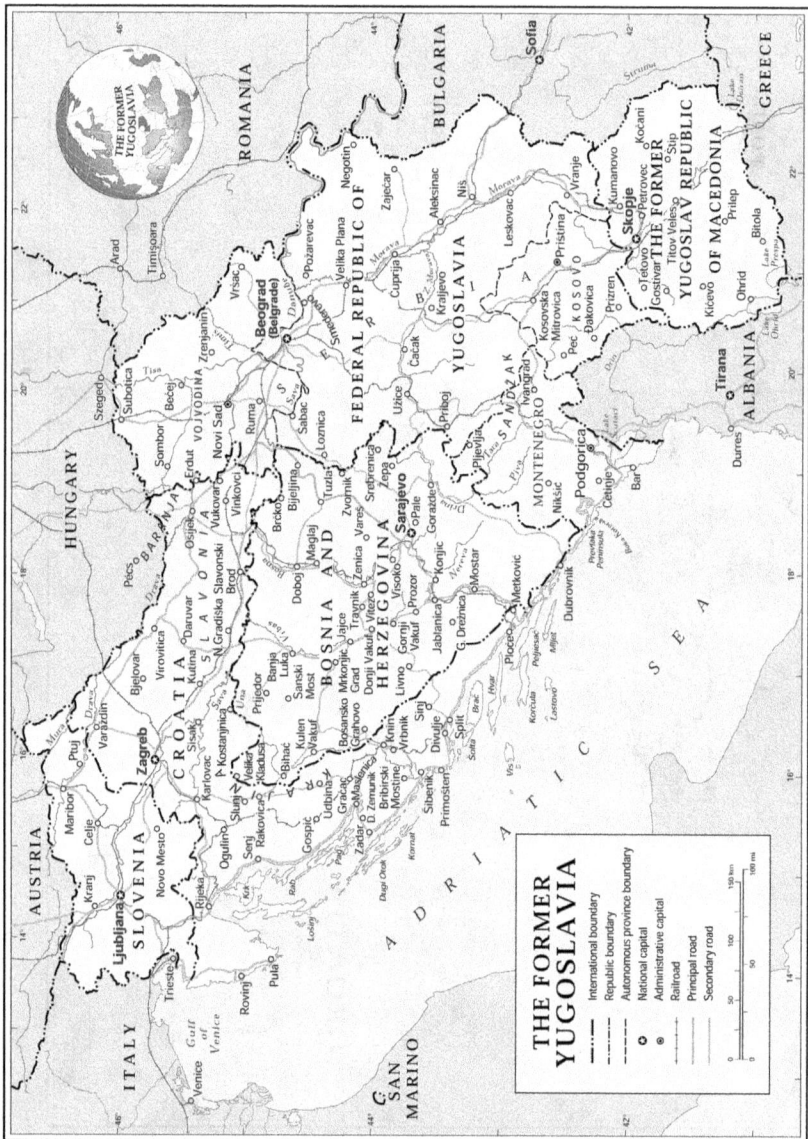

**Map 5.9  The Former Yugoslavia Today**

**Map 5.10 Yugoslavia Today**

Confusion within the EU and the CSCE about how to address the conflict led the UN to take over the peacekeeping forces on the ground in Yugoslavia. The UN Secretary-General, Javier Perez de Cuellar, appointed Cyrus Vance as his Special Representative responsible for securing a cease-fire. EC participation continued through Lord Carrington who was responsible for a negotiated political solution on the conflict.[3]

On 21 February 1992, 14,000 UN peacekeepers were deployed in the Bosnian Serb dominated enclaves in Croatia. Sarajevo was the centre of UN operations. This UN action froze the territorial status quo leaving over a quarter of Croatia, including Krajina, in Serb hands. The majority of Croats had by this time been 'cleansed' from the Serbian enclaves by the Serbs. The UN Security Council implementation of Resolution 713 under Article 52.2 of the UN Charter expressed support for the EU and the CSCE peace efforts.[4]

It was hoped that this support would provide a legal and practical framework for settling the crisis. The many EU/CSCE sponsored ceasefires were widely ignored by all sides and Serbian ethnic cleansing activities within the predominantly Bosnian Serbian areas of Bosnia Herzegovina continued almost unabated. This was despite repeated UN resolutions demanding a halt to aggression in the region and the presence of the peacekeepers on the ground.

The haste in which the European Community (Germany in particular) recognised the breakaway states exacerbated separatist ambitions and contributed significantly to the region plunging into civil war. The Bosnian Serbs bitterly complained in 1991 that the Western powers had no legal or moral authority to disenfranchise the Bosnian Serbs in this way.[5]  Robert Lyman argues that the Serbs felt themselves disenfranchised by the EU/UN who they believed recognised not a new multi-ethnic Bosnian state but an exclusively Muslim backed Bosnian government.[6]  They also complained that the EU threatened military intervention if the Bosnian Serbs reacted against this Muslim political coup.[7]

The Serbian leader, Slobodan Milosevic viewed the separatist efforts of Slovenia and Croatia as further degeneration of the Serb vision of a Greater Serbia. He also saw this to be an opportunity to rid Croatia of its Muslim population. The Yugoslav army and the Bosnian Serbs combined their forces to implement the policy of 'ethnic cleansing' in Bosnia Herzegovina. Despite repeated UN pleas, then demands, to stop the violence and the imposition of an arms embargo against all of Yugoslavia

---

3   Weller, 'The International Response to the Dissolution of the Socialist Republic of Yugoslavia.'

4   Article 52 of the United Nations Charter.

5   Gordon Bardos, 'No Innocents in Bosnia or Serbia,' *St. Louis Post-Dispatch*, 18 March 1993.

6   Robert Lyman, *Possibilities for 'Humanitarian War' by the International Community in Bosnia-Herzegovina, 1992–1995* (London: The Strategic and Combat Studies Institute – British Army Review, 1997), p. 19.

7   Ibid.

in September of 1991, the war against the poorly armed Muslims continued with increasing ferocity.

Nationalism and republican ethnocentrism pushed Yugoslavia to the edge but the final push came from the outside. The power play of Germany's Helmut Kohl in formally recognising the breakaway republics of Slovenia and Croatia quashed any glimmer of hope for a negotiated settlement between the breakaway republics and the power elites in Yugoslavia. His actions lent some credence to heated accusations by the Serb leadership that Germany and the other Great Powers in the region were bent upon establishing a monocentric system in Europe.

Western European powers were ambivalent about, if not quietly opposed to, the preservation of the territorial integrity of Yugoslavia.[8] Their own vision of an ever expanding greater Europe subsuming the Slavic states was at odds with an ideologically and culturally isolationist Yugoslavia. The continual bickering of the Great Powers over a vision of a Greater Europe was not based on a desire for peacemaking and integration. It was a fundamental desire for expansion in a region that was previously non-aligned.

The drive for republicanism in the Yugoslav states, fuelled from within each enclave and from outside by Western European Powers who had their own expansionist agendas, resulted in the establishment of internal borders. This partitioning immediately transformed each ethnic group living outside its kindred republic into a minority group within a foreign state. Overnight, the 1.5 million Serbs living in Bosnian enclaves were deprived of the protection of a federal system. Rightly or wrongly, they felt themselves vulnerable to Muslim hegemony.

On 1 March 1992, Bosnia Herzegovina held a independence referendum. This referendum resulted in over 60 percent of non-Serbian Bosnians voting for independence from the Yugoslavian Federation. Bosnian Serbs within Bosnia Herzegovina boycotted the voting. The results of the referendum, which favoured secession, was an important factor which led the EU to recognise Bosnia Herzegovina as an independent state on 6 April 1992.

The UN and the EU subsequently stated that internal boundaries within the Yugoslav Federation were not to be changed by force or without the consent of the parties concerned.[9] UN acknowledgment of an independent Bosnia Herzegovina was prompted, in part, by Bosnian Serb military action that ignored the EU and CSCE ceasefires. Resolution 752 of 15 March 1992 stated that,

...all forms of interference from outside, as well as attempts to change the ethnic composition of the population, must cease immediately and those units of the Yugoslav Peoples Army and elements of the Croatian Army be withdrawn, or be subject to the authority of the Government of Bosnia Herzegovina.[10]

---

8   Radmila Nakarada, 'Critical Thought and the Lessons of War,' in *The Collapse of Yugoslavia: Protraction or End of the Agony*, ed. D Kovacevic (Belgrade: IES, 1991), p. 96.

9   J Dempsey, 'Ec Tries to Keep War out of Bosnia,' *The Financial Times*, 21 February 1992.

10   United Nations, 'United Nations Security Council Document, 752/Res/(1992).'

This Resolution recognised the independent authority of the Government of Bosnia Herzegovina. In response Bosnian Serb gunners began their siege of Sarajevo by directing heavy mortar and artillery fire directly into heavily populated civilian areas within the city. The independence of Bosnia Herzegovina was further supported by UN Resolution 755 of 20 May 1992. This resolution admitted Bosnia Herzegovina to membership of the UN. Resolutions 753 and 754 also admitted Croatia and Slovenia to membership of the UN.[11]

The admission of Bosnia Herzegovina, Croatia and Slovenia to the UN, and the UN's recognition of the independence of the Government of Bosnia Herzegovina against strategic incursions by the Yugoslav and Croatian military, internationalised the conflict in the Balkans. This was no longer (some say it had never been) a simple internal squabble between aspiring breakaway states within the federation of Yugoslavia. Despite repeated warnings and Resolutions passed by the UN, which held Serbia responsible for the continuation of hostilities in the region, the Serbs ignored pressure from the EU, the UN and the international community generally.

Rather than conflict in the region diminishing, it quickly increased. An important factor, which influenced an increase in hostilities, was the Yugoslav Army relinquishing control of 100,000 troops in Bosnia Herzegovina on 5 May 1992. This established an autonomous BSA that continued cleansing Bosnia Herzegovina of unwanted ethnic populations.

### Resolution After Resolution

The UN continued to pass one Resolution after another against Serb aggression. Resolution 757 held Serbia directly responsible for continuing the hostilities. Resolution 770 on 13 August 1992 re-iterated the need for a non-military political solution in the region and it authorised peacekeeping forces to support the delivery of humanitarian aid to Bosnia Herzegovina. The UN identified the Bosnian Serbs as the primary aggressors. The UN resolutions provided legal authority for peacekeepers to deliver aid, but they were totally ineffectual in halting Serb atrocities against the Muslim population. The Bosnian Serbs dismissed notions of culpability and in many cases did not allow humanitarian aid to be delivered.

Without a backup of force to ensure even minimal compliance, the EU/UN Resolutions could not halt Bosnian Serb aggression and they could not assist in the flow of aid to where it was desperately needed. The continued involvement of the EC in the drafting of the Resolutions and in negotiations on the ground also gave the impression that the international community at large was incapable of effectively addressing the humanitarian crises enfolding in the Balkans. The UN in particular, lacked direction and the political will to completely take over diplomatic efforts. It also failed to positively back up its rhetoric with enforcement.

---

11 United Nations, 'United Nations Security Council Documents, 753/Res/(1992) and 754/Res/(1992).'

Vague and unenforceable directives continued to emanate from EC/UN negotiators throughout the remainder of 1992. The agenda at the London Peace Conference on 26 August 1992 was to negotiate a political settlement to the dispute, ensure the flow of humanitarian aid continued, and to support the ceasefires. The problem was that there was no political settlement to negotiate. The flow of humanitarian aid was a trickle that was either stopped completely or diverted by the Bosnian Serbs for their own use. There were no ceasefires to support because there were no ceasefires. The frequent violations of the many EC/UN sponsored ceasefires by all sides nullified any attempts to halt the war in Bosnia Herzegovina.

*No-fly Zones, Safe-areas, and Protected Enclaves.*

On 10 November 1992 the UN passed Resolution 786, which designated a no-fly zone over Bosnia, and on 16 November 1992 the UN authorised a naval blockade of Serbia and Montenegro.[12]   Clearly, the negotiations by the EU and the UN teams with the parties involved in the Balkans conflict were not working. More positive action was desperately needed.

Critics pointed out that enforcement action, as proposed by a no-fly protection zone, would only be applied to Bosnian Serbian forces. This one sided action was seen as violating the overall intent of UN operations which were supposed to be impartial and neutral. [13] [14]   The on-again/off-again nature of the international community's attempts at setting up protected enclaves and so called no-fly zones provided critics with the argument that the UN was aiding and abetting ethnic cleansing. For example, the last Bosnian Government stronghold of Srebrenica was under serious threat from Serb forces up until the Serb massacres took place in April 1993.

In the months and weeks before it was overrun, the UN attempted to evacuate the Bosnian Muslims from the town. The idea that populations should be moved from safe area to safe area lends credence to the UN ethnic cleansing argument because all the Bosnian Serbs needed to do was to directly threaten or attack a safe area to herd the UN and the local population to another location. This effectively cleansed the area of an unwanted population.

In the end the UN was not successful at relocating the inhabitants of Srebrenica, and when Serb forces overran the town many civilians were killed.[15]   This was despite the presence of UN peacekeepers on the ground in and around Srebrenica. The U.S. vehemently opposed UN proclamations of safe-areas. President Clinton

12  United Nations, 'United Nations Security Council Document, 786/Res/(1992).'

13  Hilaire McCoubrey, *The Blue Helmets: Legal Regulations of United Nations Military Operations* (Vermont: Dartmouth Publishing Company, 1996), p. 94.

14  Boutros Boutros-Ghali, *An Agenda for Peace 1995*, 2nd ed. (New York: United Nations, 1995), p. 30.

15  Jan Honig and Norbet Both, *Srebrenica: Record of a War Crime* (New York: Penguin Books, 1997), pp. 62–73.

called the enclaves shooting galleries and at first refused to let American troops join the UN forces to patrol them. The European allies were unwilling to lift the arms embargo against the Bosnian Muslims, they refused NATO authority to bomb Serbian military targets, and they were willing to let Bosnian Serbs keep most or all of the territory they had seized. Reluctantly the US agreed to the declaration of a limited number of safe-areas.

## The Vance-Owen Plan

The EU and the UN continued with diplomatic efforts to reconcile the warring factions. The Vance-Owen plan of early January 1993 envisaged territorial sub-divisions within Bosnia Herzegovina. The idea was to divide the state into 9 or 10 autonomous areas, each with one of the three ethnic groups in a majority. These would then be joined together by a Bosnian federation of some sort.

The territorial divisions were to be defined by the area protagonists occupied when a cease-fire came into effect. Somehow this status quo would then be formally transferred into territorial boundaries and a federation of Bosnia Herzegovina declared. The sheer unworkability of such a plan makes it difficult to see how it was conceived in the first place except to view it as an act of desperation.

In essence, the Vance-Owen plan ratified ethnic enclaves. The plan ignored the fact that these 9 or 10 areas still contained a volatile mix of ethnic minorities, many of whom had already been forced to and from the various enclaves up until the beginning of 1993. The Bosnian Serbs simply rejected the idea of sub-dividing traditional territories because they would have been left with only 43 percent of the land, and they would have to relinquish up to a quarter of Bosnia Herzegovina to Muslim control.

The concept of a loose Balkan federation with 10 autonomous states was just plain unworkable, but this did not stop the EC and the UN supporting such a proposal.[16]    Politically, the plan was doomed from the outset. The US was against the EC/UN Vance-Owen initiative because of the impossible logistics of implementing a workable cease-fire or maintaining peace long enough to establish a quasi-federation of 10 autonomous states under Bosnian control. The US also thought the Vance-Owen plan actually rewarded ethnic cleansing policies rife in the region by confirming areas already ethnically purged of unwanted groups as being autonomous territories.

The U.S. instead wanted to lift the arms embargo against the Bosnian Muslims so that they could protect themselves against Bosnian Serb attacks, but this was rejected by the EU and the UN. The EU and the UN proposed a compromise by the declaration of more so-called safe-areas in exchange for the US dropping its insistence on arming the Bosnians. On 6 May 1993, after another Bosnian Serb massacre of Muslims in Srebrenica, the UN Security Council passed Resolution 824

---

16 'Peace at Last, at Least for Now,' *The Economist*, 25 November 1995.

which again declared Srebrenica as a safe-area, with the addition of Sarajevo, Tuzla, Zepa, Gorazade, and Bihac to the growing list of protected zones. This resolution once again threatened force to compel a peace within the safe-areas.

In response to Resolution 824, the Bosnian Serbs stepped up with their assault on Zepa and initiated new military action against Gorazade. The EU/UN once again did not carry out their threat to use force to counter Serb aggression. The numerous EU and UN sponsored declarations and ceasefires seriously lacked credibility. They were generally dismissed as being irrelevant by the belligerents involved in the conflict.[17]

After the collapse of the Vance-Owen Plan it appeared that the EU was about to give up in Bosnia Herzegovina. The UN peacekeepers, UNPROFOR, were in an impossible position. They could not maintain the safe-areas and protected zones. The transportation and delivery of humanitarian aid was subject to the whims of the various militias blocking access to the safe-areas, and they could not retaliate against attack because; '...this posed a serious danger to UN impartiality and credibility.'[18]

After the collapse of the Vance-Owen Plan, the Serbian and Croatian leaders Slobodan Milosevic and Franjo Tudjman agreed between themselves to carve up Bosnia Herzegovina into three areas, regardless of UN initiatives and ceasefires. Faced with this ultimatum, The EU chief negotiator, Lord Owen, suggested to the ethnic-Muslim Bosnian Government that they should accept the Serb-Croat proposal. This was despite the fact that this division of territory would render any future Muslim enclave within Bosnia Herzegovina economically, strategically and politically unviable.

Such an arrangement would mean that the proposed enclaves would be completely dependent on their enemies even for access to the outside world. In September 1993, during talks aboard The British warship HMS Invincible, the President of Bosnia Herzegovina, Mr Izetbegovic vetoed the deal. Bosnian Serbs and Croats stopped going through the motions of cooperating with the UN officials in Yugoslavia once the possibility of Western military intervention vanished in May 1993.

The Bosnian Serbs even demanded tolls from UN vehicles entering Bosnia from Serbia. A letter from the Bosnian Serbs announced that aid convoys heading toward Muslim-held territory would now have to pay for using Bosnian Serb-controlled roads. The Bosnian Serbs' charges included; armoured personnel carriers $500, tracked vehicles $700, tractors $350, buses $240 and automobiles $140.[19] Bosnian Serbian leaders added that the UN observer's jeeps would be billed an extra $200 a month while in Bosnia Herzegovina. The UN hotly responded that it would not pay the tolls.

---

17 Michael Tanner, 'Gorazade Begs for Help to End Bosnian Siege,' *The Independent*, 15 June 1993.

18 Russell Block, 'Life or Death Dilemma for Un Troops,' 12 June 1993.

19 Un May Evacuate Bosnian Muslims Serb Forces Are Blocking Aid; 'Safe Area Is Too Dangerous,' *St. Louis Post-Dispatch*, 3 July 1993.

Another EU/UN sponsored peace conference, this time in Geneva on 1 September 1993, failed to resolve any of the issues intended to halt the conflict in Bosnia Herzegovina. This peace conference had hoped to achieve a political settlement based on a three-way ethnic split of Bosnia but the Bosnian Serbs simply continued to arbitrarily change ethnic boundaries by force. They used the negotiations in Geneva as a delaying tactic to establish their control more completely in the region.

The Bosnian Government, swayed by Muslim hardliners, also was not enthusiastic on the Geneva talks resolving the conflict. Instead they hoped the UN and NATO would carry out air strikes against the Bosnian Serbs. They waited for nearly three years for such action to take place.

## The Situation in Bosnia Herzegovina Deteriorates Further

By early 1994, the humanitarian situation throughout Bosnia Herzegovina was becoming desperate. Large-scale genocide and the practices of ethnic cleansing continued unabated. The UN itself came under fire and had to contend with kidnappings and casualties of humanitarian aid workers.

Closing Tuzla airport meant that no aid at all could be transported to the various safe-areas. Both Serbs and Croats continuously breached the no-fly zones. Reports and pictures of the Bosnian Serb's siege of Sarajevo were transmitted out of Bosnia Herzegovina via the world's news services. Still the UN opposed NATO air strikes. Boutros Ghali said that, '…there were not enough UN Peacekeepers on the ground to carry through an effective military operation in the aftermath of NATO air strikes.'[20] He was also concerned that air strikes would lead to a breakdown of the political negotiation process.

The fact that the political negotiation process was in complete disarray did not persuade the UN to use military force to relieve Sarajevo, transfer aid to where it was desperately required or to enforce the no-fly zones. The political situation in the Balkan's was in stalemate but the killings and deprivations continued unabated and with increasing ferocity. The morale of UN officials involved with Bosnia Herzegovina had hit rock bottom and the UN operation was in serious danger of collapsing totally. 'We are in a quagmire,' said a senior UN official. 'We did everything wrong from the start.'[21] The problem was that they could see no way out of the quagmire.

Above all, with their current mandate, there was no way to stop the Serb-Croat partition of Bosnia Herzegovina nor was there any way to stop the ethnic cleansing of hundreds of thousands more people. The Bosnian Serbs had closed Sarajevo's airport, cut off the city's utilities, blocked aid convoys, seized heavy weapons from the UN and they stepped up their shelling of Muslim cities, particularly Sarajevo.

---

20 David Ottaway, 'Boutros-Ghali Opposes Bosnia Air Strikes,' *The International Herald Tribune*, 20 January 1994.

21 'A World More Scared Than Scaring,' *The Economist*, 17 April 1993: pp. 47–48.

*NATO Fires Its First Shots*

On 5 February 1994, a mortar shell was targeted directly by the Bosnian Serbs into a crowded marketplace in Sarajevo. The deliberate firing of mortars and other heavy siege weaponry into massed civilian population areas was not unusual and not infrequent. Over 60 people were killed and some 200 seriously injured during this attack. This time NATO not the UN responded by giving the Bosnian Serbs an ultimatum. Withdraw the heavy guns from around Sarajevo by 20 February 1994 or face air strikes.

On the day the deadline expired, Russian peacekeepers arrived in Sarajevo and convinced the Bosnian Serbs to temporarily pull back their heavy weapons. The withdrawal of the Bosnian Serb heavy weapons was a tiny victory for the increasingly desperate humanitarian situation evolving within the confines of Sarajevo. The reality was that the Serbs simply used these occasional interruptions to their assault as an opportunity to resupply and to rotate their troops from the front line.

The first shots fired by NATO occurred on the 28 February 1994 when U.S. F-16 fighter aircraft enforcing the no-fly zones destroyed four Bosnian Serb aircraft. France and Britain spurred on by the U.S. declared that any future attacks on UN safe-areas would result in retaliatory air strikes. NATO conducted two more air strikes against the Bosnian Serbs advancing on Gorazade. They issued further ultimatums for the Bosnian Serbs to stop firing and to pull back. Neither the air strikes nor repeated ultimatums succeeded in halting the Serb advances.

Throughout 1994, NATO operations were severely hampered by a complicated dual UN/NATO command and control structure. Each step of a tactical response to Bosnian Serb aggression required authorisation by a number of UN officials before NATO command could assume control of an operation. This resulted in delay and procrastination over what possible tactics NATO could, or should, undertake in response to violations within the no-fly zones.

In the spring of 1994, the five-nation Contact Group again attempted to broker a settlement between the Yugoslav federation, the Bosnian government and the Bosnian Serbs. The Contact Group proposed three principles as a basis for reconciliation.[22] Firstly, Bosnia Herzegovina would remain a single state. Secondly, that state would consist of the Federation and a Bosnian Serb entity. Thirdly, these two entities would be linked by mutually agreed constitutional principles. These principles would also spell out relationships with Serbia and Croatia proper.

In July 1994, the five-nation Contact Group proposed a 51/49 percent territorial compromise between the federation and the Bosnian Serbs. The Bosnian, Croatian and Serbian governments all accepted the Contact Group's proposal in principle. The Bosnian Serbs repeatedly rejected the entire proposal. Meanwhile, Milosevic announced that he was withdrawing support for the Bosnian Serbs. This declaration was more a political maneuver by the Serbs in Yugoslavia than a real breakthrough. The Bosnian Serbs already had complete autonomy from Serbia since 5 May 1992.

---

22  US Department of State, ' Us Department of State Dispatch: Fact Sheet,' (1995).

In September 1994, Bosnian government forces scored their biggest military victory in the war so far by taking the area around Bihac in northwest Bosnia Herzegovina. The Bosnian Muslims managed to hold the area for only one week until a fierce Bosnian Serb counterattack pushed them back. 50 NATO warplanes attacked a Bosnian Serb airfield conducting support operations for the counterattacking troops but this failed to halt the Serb counteroffensive.

The Bosnian Serbs then took hostage 55 Canadian peacekeepers as insurance against further NATO air strikes. NATO tried to force a release of the hostages by bombing a Serb munitions dump in Pale. The Bosnian Serbs immediately retaliated by taking a further 350 UN personnel hostage. Britain and France reacted to the hostage taking by dispatching a rapid-reaction military force to protect the UN contingents in Bosnia Herzegovina.

In late 1994, former U.S. president Jimmy Carter became involved in mediation attempts in the region. After a number of meetings between the Bosnian government, Croats and Bosnian Serbs, he managed to broker a Christmas cease-fire. The five-month nationwide truce took effect from 20th December 1994. Except for Bihac, which continued with the fighting, most other regions reduced or stopped hostilities.

This uneasy truce lasted until 8 April 1995 when a U.S. aid aircraft was hit by gunfire in Sarajevo. This resulted in all UN aid flights to the city being cancelled. Soon after the attack on the U.S. aircraft, the Croats launched a major offensive against the Bosnian Serbs. The Bosnian Serbs retaliated to these attacks by shelling the civilian areas of Zagreb causing many Croatian casualties.

The UN again ordered the Bosnian Serbs to return the heavy weapons to UN control and to remove all heavy weapons from around the hills overlooking Sarajevo. On the 25 May 1995, after the Bosnian Serbs ignored the UN demands, NATO warplanes attacked a Serb munitions depot. The Bosnian Serbs immediately responded by shelling the civilian safe-areas, including Tuzla killing 71 civilians and injuring more than 150.

Hostilities escalated from mid 1995. The Bosnian Serbs still dismissed UN calls for a cessation to the hostilities, release of hostages, protection of safe-areas and so on. Instead, more UN hostages were taken and more safe-areas came under sustained shelling and mortar attacks. The UN hostage taking by the Bosnian Serbs, then their subsequent release, continued throughout June 1995. The last UN hostages were released on 14 June 1995.

## The Fall of Srebrenica and Knin

On 11 July 1995, the Bosnian Serb General Mladic again seized the UN designated safe area of Srebrenica. According to Red Cross estimates, the Serbs immediately killed at least 8,000 Muslim males. A further 15,000 Muslim males were marched through Bosnian Serb held territory to Tuzla. Only 4,000 finally arrived. Some 20,000 women, children and elderly Muslims were forcibly expelled to Tuzla, bringing with them stories of Bosnian Serb atrocities being conducted against the

Muslims. Fighting and reports of further atrocities in and around many of the UN designated safe-areas intensified in subsequent weeks.

The U.S. ambassador to the UN revealed aerial spy photographs that allegedly showed mass graves of executed Bosnian Muslims. Human Rights investigators uncovered at least four mass gravesites around Knin. This time the Muslims and Serbs were both accused of atrocities. The massed gravesites at Knin were filled with Serb and Muslim dead after Croatian Muslims launched a massive assault on the Serbs in Knin on 4 August 1995 – shelling UN peacekeepers, aid workers and civilians in the process.

Most of the previously Serb dominated areas in and around Srebrenica and Knin were captured in about four days. Tens of thousands of Serb civilians fled their homes with over 180,000 people streaming towards Bosnia Herzegovina. This column of Serb refugees was repeatedly attacked by mobs of Croats wielding clubs, bricks and stones. The Bosnian Serbs, meanwhile, continued unabated with their shelling of Sarajevo.

*The Catalyst for Change*

In late August 1995, an event occurred which changed the international community's response to the situation in Bosnia Herzegovina. The event was a mortar attack on yet another marketplace in Sarajevo that killed at least 68 people and seriously wounded hundreds.

This attack, which was not dissimilar to thousands of others carried out in the safe-areas, finally acted as a catalyst for a change to the UN approach to the war in Bosnia Herzegovina. The change occurred, in part, because of the immediate and detailed reporting of the event by the world's news services. The graphic pictures of the dead and dying lying in large pools of blood stirred Western public opinion against the Bosnian Serbs in favour of forceful military retaliation.

There were a number of reasons why the UN finally sanctioned all-out air strikes against the Serbs. The Bosnian Serb's persistent disregard and outright public contempt of the UN threatened the UN's position within the international community itself. The international community saw NATO and its allies, particularly the U.S., Britain and France, as lacking relevance and credibility by their inaction in the conflict. As the UN had originally authorised NATO and the EC to try to solve the Bosnian crisis under Article 52.2, continuing not to do so questioned the integrity and the commitment of the international community at large.

NATO retaliated against the continued shelling of the safe-areas, but this time they did so with massive force. On 30 August 1995, NATO flew 3,400 sorties against Bosnian Serb gun emplacements and troop concentrations around Sarajevo. They did not stop their attacks until the heavy weapons around the city were either destroyed or fully withdrawn.[23]  At the same time a combined Bosnian government and Croat offensive pushed the Bosnian Serbs back to Western Bosnia Herzegovina.

With discreet support from the U.S., the Croatian leader Franjo Tudjman unleashed a blitzkrieg on the Bosnian Serbs of Krajina.  The Bosnian Serbs were completely over run in three days and several hundred thousand fled the region. Slobodan Milosevic left his former allies to their fate.  Richard Holbrooke (President Clinton's adviser and negotiator in the Balkans) negotiated a cease-fire between all the warring parties in Bosnia Herzegovina on 12 October 1995.  On 1 November 1995, he convened the Dayton Accord peace talks. [24]

Immediate widespread hostilities between Croats, Bosnian Serbs and Muslims effectively ceased on 21 November 1995.  The Balkan leaders initialled the peace accord that allocated 51 percent of Bosnia Herzegovina to a Muslim-Croat Federation and 49 percent to the Bosnian Serbs.  The Dayton Agreement, signed by Bosnian President Izetbegovic, Croatian President Tudjman, and Serbian President Milosevic, divides Bosnia Herzegovina between the Muslim/Croat Federation and the Bosnian Serbs while maintaining Bosnia's current borders.  IFOR, the 60,000 troop NATO led IFOR, served in Bosnia Herzegovina during 1995 and 1996 to monitor and implement the Dayton Accord.

IFOR was to create a stable environment for civil reconstruction to proceed. This military force was deployed to enforce peace, not to fight a war.[25]   Map 11 shows the Dayton Agreement line within Bosnia Herzegovina. The main objective of the Implementation Forces was to ensure compliance with the military aspects of the General Framework Agreement for Peace.  IFOR was then replaced by the smaller NATO led Stabilisation Force (SFOR).[26]

UN involvement was limited to a representative of the Security Council who was responsible for civilian implementation of the accord, monitoring the implementation of the accord, facilitating any problems arising in connection with civilian implementation, and coordinating activities of the civilian organizations and agencies within Bosnia Herzegovina.  Despite the success of Dayton Accord in halting the conflict in Bosnia Herzegovina, a lasting peace settlement in the Balkans was as elusive as ever.  Slobodan Milosevic and his Yugoslav military and police now turned their attention to Kosovo.

---

23  B Nelan, 'The Balkans: More Talking, More Bombing Despite Diplomatic Progress,' *Time Magazine*, 18 September 1995: p. 76.

24  'Bosnia and Herzegovina Country Report on Human Rights,' (US Department of State, Bureau of Democracy, Human Rights and Labour, 1997).

25    William Aiken, 'Bosnia-Herzegovina and Croatia an Environmental Health Perspective,' *Journal of Environmental Health* 59 (1996): pp. 6–11.

26  Central Intelligence Agency, *Cia World Fact Book, 1997* (Washington DC: CIA, 1997).

CROATIA

Velika Kladusa Stn.
Cazin Stn.
Novi Grad Stn.
Gradiska Stn.
Prijedor Stn.
Derventa Stn.
Modrica Stn.
Orasje Stn.
Loncari Sub-Stn.
2 Stns. and 2 Sub-Stns.
Pelagicavo Stn.
Prnjavor Stn.
Bihać RHQ
2 Stns.
Banja-Luka RHQ
Brčko RHQ
Sanski Most Stn.
Doboj RHQ
Bijela Stn.
Gornji Rahic Stn.
Gracanica Stn.
Bijelina Stn.
Janja Sub-Stn.
Kotor Varos Stn.
Teslic Stn.
Lopare Stn.
SERBIA (FRY)
Kljuc Stn.
Tuzla RHQ
Sapna Stn.
Mrkonic Grad Stn.
Zavidovici Stn.
Zvornik Stn.
Drvar Stn.
Jajce Stn.
Travnik Stn.
Zenica Stn.
Vlasenica Stn.
Bugojno Stn.
Breza Stn.
Kiseljak Stn.
Vogosca Stn.
HQ UNMIBH
CROATIA
Livno Stn.
Novo Sarajevo Stn.
Sarajevo RHQ
Rogatica Stn.
Prozor Stn.
Ilidza Stn.
Pale Stn.
Tomislavgrad Stn.
Kula Stn.
Visegrad Stn.
Jablanica Stn.
Konjic Stn.
Gorazde Stn.
Foca Stn.
Sirokibrijeg Stn.
Mostar RHQ
Nevesinje Stn.
FEDERAL REPUBLIC OF YUGOSLAVIA
Capljina Stn.
Stolac Stn.
Trebinje Stn.
MONTENEGRO (FRY)
ADRIATIC SEA
ALBANIA

**UNMIBH**

**IPTF and Civil Affairs Locations**

as of June 1999

——— Dayton Agreement line
—·—·— International boundary
—··—··— Republic boundary
¤ Co-location of IPTF and Civil Affairs
○ IPTF location

BOSNIA AND HERZEGOVINA

0 10 20 30 40 50 60 70 80 km
0 10 20 30 40 50 mi

**Map 5.11:  Dayton Agreement Line Within Bosnia Herzegovina**

**Events Leading Up to the 1997–1999 Civil War in Kosovo**

Kosovo is the ancestral Serb heartland and the focus of much national Serb folklore. Medieval Serb heroes revered by modern day Serbs fought and lost against the Ottoman Turks in the battle for Kosovo in 1389. The legendary Serb hero, Prince Lazar was defeated and killed during this battle. His death marked the end of the medieval Serb nation and the beginning of brutal Turkish oppression for the next 500 years.[27]

The largest ethnic group within Kosovo today is the ethnic Albanians. The Zagreb census of 1987 calculated that the Kosovar population consisted of 77 percent Albanians, 13 percent Serbs, and 4 percent Bosnians. The high Albanian birth rate of around 30 per 1,000 (compared to the Serb birth rate of around 4 per 1,000 in Kosovo) meant that the relative numbers of the Albanian population increased significantly from 1981 to 1999. Many Serbs considered it unthinkable that their historic heartland should be overrun by ever increasing numbers of Muslim interlopers.

Comparatively few Serbs lived in Kosovo but still the idea of Muslim Albanians swamping the province affronted many Serbians. Of equal concern to the Serbs was Kosovo's repeated attempt to secede from Yugoslavia proper. Serbs were particularly offended by the revised Yugoslav constitution of 1974, which granted limited autonomy to Kosovo.[28] In practice this level of autonomy only meant that Kosovo could institute Albanian-language schools, observe Islamic holy days and send its own representative to sit on the collective federal presidency. Serbs saw even this small concession to the Kosovars as a betrayal to their vision of a Greater Serbia.

The new Yugoslav constitution in 1974 declared Kosovo to be a semi-autonomous province within Serbia. This suited neither the Kosovars who wanted full independence nor Yugoslavia who considered Kosovo to be its cultural heartland. In 1989, the Serbian President Slobodan Milosevic stripped Kosovo of its autonomy and dissolved Kosovo's fledgling government.

The Kosovar Albanians strenuously opposed the move back to complete domination by Belgrade. In response, Yugoslavia sent in the troops in 1990 to maintain law and order. These actions did not stop Kosovo's push for independence. In 1991, separatists proclaimed Kosovo a republic and elected Ibrahim Rugova, an advocate of a peaceful path to independence, as President. Neighbouring Albania immediately recognised the Republic of Kosovo.

In 1996, the pro-independence Kosovo Liberation Army (KLA) claimed responsibility for the bombing of a number of police targets. These attacks, and subsequent reprisals by the Yugoslav militia, increased in frequency and ferocity

---

27 Duésan Batakovic, The Kosovo Chronicles, Part One: History and Ideology, Kosovo and Metohia. A Historical Survey (Beograd: Plato, 1992), pp. 25–66.

28 Veliki geografski atlas Jugoslavije (Large Geographical Atlas of Yugoslavia) Zagreb, ' Map Zagreb,1987 Census,' (1987).

throughout 1997 and 1998. The vastly superior Serbian forces attempted to crush the pro-independence movement in Kosovo.

By mid 1998, the western press and other media increasingly began to focus on the escalation of violence by Serb military and police units against the Kosovar Albanians. Western news reports were filled with graphic pictures of Serb tanks belching black diesel smoke across the green countryside of Kosovo, and Serb tanks firing directly and indiscriminately into burning villages.

Once again the international community was seen to be standing by, as it repeatedly demanded all sides to halt the violence. According to the Clinton administration, the harm to the people of Kosovo was inevitable and entirely the fault of the Serbs. Yugoslav President Slobodan Milosevic, the administration said, had long planned to evict all Albanians from Kosovo as part of his ethnic cleansing program to ensure perpetual Serb control of the province.

There is some doubt about the accuracy of western assertions that Milosevic's spring offensive against non-Serbs in Kosovo was long intended and carefully planned. After all, Belgrade had total control over Kosovo for at least ten years without attempting to oust all non-Serbs from the province. The international community was still justifiably suspicious of any hint of a new offensive instigated by Belgrade.

Open conflict between the Serbian military, Serb police and Kosovar Albanian forces resulted in the deaths of over 1,500 Kosovar Albanians and forced 400,000 people from their homes. The international community became increasingly concerned about the escalating conflict, its humanitarian consequences and the risk of it spreading to other countries. This concern centred on the intransigence of the Serbian leader, Slobodan Milosevic. He openly stated his political aims of ethnically cleansing all non-Serbs from traditional Serb areas within Kosovo. The international community was also concerned about the increasing militancy of the separatist movement within Kosovo and the activities of the Kosovar Liberation Army (KLA).

In mid April 1998, Milosevic ordered 40,000 well-armed troops (the notorious Yugoslav 62nd and 73rd Airborne Regiments) into the rebel areas of Kosovo. Belgrade defended its crackdown in Kosovo by claiming that Albania was supplying arms to the rebel Kosovars. UN Security Council Resolution 1199 once again expressed deep concern about the excessive use of force by Serbian security forces and the Yugoslav army.[29] It called for an immediate cease-fire by all parties.

Western military analysts based in Belgrade doubted there was any grand Albanian conspiracy to supply guns to the Kosovars. They suspected that the Yugoslav Army's demonstration of allegedly captured arms caches to be weapons they brought with them.[30] Albania denied that it was supporting the rebels and claimed Serbs were

---

29 United Nations, 'United Nations Security Council Document, S/Res/1199 (1998),' (1998).

30 M Calabresi, 'Kosovo Smolders,' *Time Magazine*, 11 May 1998.

conducting incursions across its borders. Tirana called for NATO intervention to stop further violations of its airspace and territory by the Serbs.

The Contact Group (the U.S., Britain, France, Germany, Italy, and Russia) charged by the UN to monitor the Balkan's peace repeatedly issued threats of sanctions and reprisals against the Serbs if Milosevic did not end his crackdown in Kosovo. Milosevic responded to the threats by swamping his state-run media with stories of torture and murder of Serbs by the Kosovars. The Contact Group offered international mediation to settle the separatist struggle. In response, Milosevic immediately ordered up a plebiscite in Serbia that firmly rejected external meddling in Serbian affairs.

In early May 1998, the U.S. threatened to pull out of the Contact Group if the group did not stiffen penalties against the Serbs. The situation in Kosovo rushed once more into the familiar territory of an all out ethnic war. The Kosovar rebels had also grown dangerously belligerent and uncompromising. 'The Serbs have been trampling all over us for years,' said a young tough at a Smonica checkpoint. 'Not any more. We are not Bosnian Muslims and we will not allow ourselves to get butchered.'[31] That cockiness combined with Serb intransigence and Western inaction was a recipe for a wider war.

In July and August of 1998, the KLA seized control of 40 percent of Kosovo before being routed by an overwhelming Serb counter offensive. The Serb offensive was not only a rout of the KLA but large numbers of Albanian Kosovar civilians were killed or brutalised. The UN Security Council proclaimed yet another resolution for an immediate ceasefire, this time after 22 Albanians were found massacred in Kosovo.

In late 1998, Serb forces launched a massive military offensive against the KLA. The UN responded by repeatedly threatening '…a stern response' by NATO if the Serbs did not desist from what many in the west considered to be an overreaction against isolated KLA activities. A temporary ceasefire was arranged between the waring factions but only after NATO aircraft began reconnaissance flights into Kosovo and Yugoslav airspace. NATO allies sponsored by the UN authorized air strikes against Serb military targets in October 1998. This authorisation resulted in Milosevic agreeing to withdraw his troops and to allow 2,000 unarmed monitors into Kosovo to verify compliance with the ceasefire. Serb forces intent on eliminating Kosovar resistance violated this shaky ceasefire almost immediately.

The Organization for Security and Cooperation in Europe (OSCE) established a Kosovo Verification Mission (KVM) to observe the conduct of hostilities in Kosovo. They were tasked to verify whether or not all sides complied with UN demands for the fighting to stop. NATO openly began to conduct aerial surveillance over Kosovo. The establishment of the two missions was endorsed by UN Security Council Resolution 1203.[32] Several non-NATO nations that participated in the

---

31 Ibid.

32 United Nations, 'United Nations Security Council Documents, S/Res/1203 (1998),' (1998). The agreement signed in Belgrade on 15 October 1998 by the Chief of General Staff of

Partnership for Peace (PFP) arrangement also agreed to contribute to the NATO surveillance mission.

Reports of massacres and deliberate policies of genocide by Serb forces in Kosovo increased. In January 1999, a UN humanitarian aid team discovered evidence of the massacre of more than 40 people in the village of Racak. In February 1999, a second series of talks sponsored by the Contact Group were arranged between the Kosovo Albanians and the Serbs in Rambouillet, France. The Kosovars signed a peace deal calling for interim autonomy and they agreed to let 28,000 NATO troops implement the peace process. The Serb delegation refused all these conditions and walked out.

Milosevic claimed that the international community was bent on occupying Kosovo by deploying invasion ground troops. Such actions, he said, would only bolster the Kosovar separatist-terrorist organizations in their search for international sponsorship for independence from the Republic of Yugoslavia. Serbian military and police forces immediately stepped up the intensity of their operations against the ethnic Albanians in Kosovo. They moved extra troops and special police into the area supported by heavy armour and artillery.

This act was in clear defiance of the October 1998 agreement between the Kosovars, the Serbs, and the Contact Group not to escalate the fighting in Kosovo. Tens of thousands of Kosovars fled their homes in the face of this renewed Serb offensive. The OSCE despatched a team of unarmed observers to monitor the rapidly deteriorating situation in Kosovo, but by early 1999 open conflict erupted again between the KLA and Serb forces. Both sides repeatedly breached cease-fires.

NATO, led by U.S. Secretary of State Madeleine Albright summoned the warring parties to Rambouillet in France and presented to them a detailed plan for political autonomy in Kosovo under NATO auspices. Under Chapter VII of the UN Charter, the Security Council decided that a political solution to the Kosovo crisis would be based on the general principles adopted on 6 May 1999 by the Foreign Ministers of the Group of Seven industrialised countries and the Russian Federation. The general principles included an immediate and verifiable end to the atrocities, violence and repression in Kosovo, the withdrawal of Serb military, police and paramilitary forces, and deployment of effective international and security presences.

The principles insisted upon the establishment of an interim administration, the safe and free return of all refugees, a political process providing for substantial self-government, the demilitarisation of the Kosovo Liberation Army; and a comprehensive approach to the economic development of the crisis region. NATO insisted that both the Serbs and the KLA agree to the plan and threatened military reprisals if either refused. Both refused. The US again negotiated with the KLA and finally acquired its assent to the Rambouillet plan.

---

the Federal Republic of Yugoslavia and the Supreme Allied Commander, Europe, of the North Atlantic Treaty Organization (NATO) provided for the establishment of an air verification mission over Kosovo (S/1998/991, annex), complementing the OSCE Verification Mission.

The peace deal was presented in Belgrade by the President of Finland and by the Special Representative of the Russian Federation. The Serbs continued to refuse any concept of partition or autonomy for Kosovo, and they rejected out right the presence of any foreign troops in Kosovo. On 22 March 1999, U.S. special envoy Richard Holbrooke warned Milosevic that he would face air strikes unless he signed a peace agreement. Milosevic refused to sign the agreement and on 23 March NATO authorised air strikes against Yugoslavia.

By the beginning of April 1999, Serb activity in Kosovo had resulted in 226,000 refugees in Albania, 125,000 in the former Yugoslav Republic of Macedonia, and 33,000 in Montenegro.[33]   In Kosovo, the international community was faced with the reality that the UN Security Council would veto any direct military action despite yet another humanitarian catastrophe being orchestrated in the Balkans. NATO could, and did, act unilaterally.

After the Serbs refusal to comply with the Rambouillet peace proposal (by now a peace ultimatum) the U.S. and NATO waited for the withdrawal of the OSCE monitors and on 24 March 1999 started *Operation Allied Force*, the seventy-eight day bombing campaign. The Clinton administration argued that NATO could not stand by while Milosevic carried out his long-term strategy of ethnic cleansing in Kosovo and thus NATO had no choice but to respond as it did.

The NATO air campaign was not supported by ground troops. This was a serious tactical error by NATO. NATO assumed that Milosevic would immediately capitulate when NATO attacked Belgrade or that the Serb people would rise and depose Milosevic. At worst they calculated that Yugoslavia would give in to NATO demands after a few weeks. On 3 June 1999, the Government of the Federal Republic of Yugoslavia accepted the peace terms. NATO Secretary General Javier Solana announced on 10 June 1999 that he had instructed General Wesley Clark, Supreme Allied Commander Europe, to suspend NATO's air operations against Yugoslavia after confirmation that a full withdrawal of Yugoslav forces from Kosovo had begun.

## NATO Unilateral Peacemaking in Kosovo

NATO action in Kosovo raises a number of important questions regarding unilateral action by a coalition of states to address a serious human rights situation. Firstly, under what circumstances should NATO threaten or use force? Secondly, what is the legal basis of the use of such force? Thirdly, was NATO action in Kosovo successful in stopping the killing of Kosovar Albanians and in halting the ethnic cleansing activities of Slobodan Milosevic?

There are essentially two circumstances that could require a NATO military response. If there was a direct threat of attack against Alliance territory or against a single NATO state, then NATO's Article 5 commitment to collective defence comes

---

33  NATO, 'Nato's Role in Relation to the Conflict in Kosovo,' *NATO Handbook* (2004): pp. 107–31.

into play and a military response is possible.[34]   The second circumstance that may result in a NATO military response involves crises or threats that do not directly affect Alliance territory but which nonetheless, may have important national or humanitarian interests.

In Kosovo and previously in Bosnia Herzegovina the Alliance decided to use military force even though the Article 5 collective defence commitment was not directly at stake. The decision to launch a large scale bombing campaign against Yugoslavia in defence of non-Serbs in Kosovo was a defining moment for NATO because it acted not out of any threat to its collective defence but for a wider humanitarian reason.

A contentious issue relating to NATO's involvement in Kosovo is the so-called mandate question. That is, under what authority or on which legal basis may NATO threaten or use military force other than for its own collective defence?   During the early 1990's, most of the Allies believed that NATO should not act outside its explicit mandate for collective self-defence without specific authorisation from the UN or the OSCE.

Today, Alliance views differ sharply about the role and authority of the UN and other organisations in legitimising or mandating NATO action.[35]   France and to a lesser extent Germany, consider that the use of force by a single state or a collective of states should be ultimately governed by the UN Charter. Their view is that NATO may use force in self-defence or to defend a non-member state whose government requested UN assistance.

The U.S. rejects the view that NATO may only act in a wider humanitarian context with UN approval because they oppose holding NATO action hostage to the interests of non-NATO members such as Russia and China. The Kosovo conflict bought to a head what had, until very recently, been a largely theoretical argument about when a state or collection of states may act unilaterally to address a humanitarian crisis.

In Kosovo, NATO acted without a specific UN mandate to do so.   In April 1999, at the NATO Alliance's summit held in Washington DC, the NATO Allies acknowledged that the UN Security Council has the primary responsibility for the general maintenance of international peace and security.  They were notably silent on specifically who, if anyone, needs to authorise NATO action in non-Article 5 situations.[36]

---

34 The North Atlantic Treaty, Washington DC, 4th of April 1949. *Article 5.* The Parties agree that an armed attack against one or more of them in Europe or North America shall be considered an attack against them all and consequently they agree that, if such an armed attack occurs, each of them, in exercise of the right of individual or collective self-defence recognised by Article 51 of the Charter of the United Nations, will assist the Party or Parties so attacked by taking forthwith, individually and in concert with the other Parties, such action as it deems necessary, including the use of armed force, to restore and maintain the security of the North Atlantic area.

35 Ivo Daalder, 'Emerging Answers: Kosovo, Nato, & the Use of Force,' *The Brookings Review* 17, no. 3 (1999): pp. 22–24.

36 Ibid.

From a humanitarian perspective, there was a desperate need for somebody (anybody) to stop yet another genocide from happening in the Balkans. Without some sort of international action many lives were threatened. If the UN was unable or unwilling to directly address the problem then many in the international community believed that another human catastrophe was simply a matter of time.

Unilateral action by a state, collections of states, or alliances such as NATO to use military force against another sovereign state, even if for humanitarian reasons, is a highly contentious issue. Hitler's Blitzkrieg into Austria and Poland at the start of WW II was ostensibly to protect fellow countrymen in those states being threatened or abused. Serb military action in Slovenia and Bosnia Herzegovina in the early 1990s was to protect Serb police who had been attacked by separatists. In August 1999, the Russian dominated Commonwealth of Independent States (CIS) militarily intervened in Dagestan in order to protect the local government (loyal to Moscow) and Russian citizens from Islamic separatists.

Apart from trying to protect the non-Serbs in Kosovo, NATO action in Yugoslavia also established a new doctrine governing military intervention for humanitarian purposes in the post cold war era. This doctrine of humanitarian intervention has two parts. The first part is that direct military force may be used purely for humanitarian reasons rather than just for the narrower national interests sovereign states have traditionally fought over or for. [37]

The second part involves the idea that in defence of these humanitarian values military intervention in the internal affairs of sovereign states is sometimes necessary. Intervention in this case is not limited simply as a response to cross border aggression. The convoluted legal arguments regarding authorisation to carry out forceful humanitarian intervention comes down to respecting the sovereignty of states, yet being prepared to militarily intervene for humanitarian purposes in accordance with Article 42 of the UN Charter or NATO's Article 5.

The preferred option for humanitarian intervention must be for the UN to authorise military strikes against those who commit genocide, but if this is not forthcoming or if it is too late then others in the international community must be prepared to act. Not to do so condemns many people to death or extreme suffering.

The fundamental challenge facing the international community when trying to address severe humanitarian disasters is that it must realise that good intentions by themselves are not enough. Interventionist powers also need to accept the fact that rescuer's lives will be lost when they try to impose by force a set of conditions and circumstances not to the liking of determined, well armed and ruthless belligerents.

*A Botched Just-War in Kosovo*

Few would disagree that the UN, NATO and the wider international community entered the Balkans with the intent to do good. NATO's aim at the beginning of

---

37 Michael Mandelbaum, 'Nato's War against Yugoslavia: A Perfect Failure,' *Foreign Affairs* 78, no. 5 (1999): pp. 2–8.

the bombing campaign in Yugoslavia was to '...save lives...to prevent the forced displacement of the Kosovar Albanians ...and, to protect the precarious political stability of the Balkan's region...'[38] [39]

By the end of May 1999, three quarters of the way through the NATO bombing campaign, over 230,000 refugees had arrived in the former Yugoslav Republic of Macedonia, over 430,000 in Albania and some 64,000 in Montenegro. Approximately 21,500 had reached Bosnia Herzegovina and over 61,000 had been evacuated to other countries. Within Kosovo itself, an estimated 580,000 people had been rendered homeless.[40]

1.5 million people or 90 percent of the population of Kosovo had been forcibly expelled from their homes with some 225,000 Kosovar men believed to be missing.[41] At least 5,000 Kosovars had been summarily executed. The hard-won cease-fire and peace arrangements in Kosovo and in the Balkans generally were not a victory for the international community. They are the outcomes of a botched just-war, badly and irresponsibly led, firstly by the UN in Bosnia Herzegovina then by NATO in Kosovo.

Despite eventual ceasefires in both Bosnia Herzegovina and Kosovo, military intervention was not successful in stopping unnecessary deaths and suffering from occurring because it was too little, too late, and it was poorly executed. In Kosovo, NATO decided on high altitude bombing conducted over a leisurely seventy-eight day period to try to bomb Belgrade into submission.[42] Milosevic's troops and special police were relentlessly conducting atrocities on each of those seventy-eight days. Milosevic must have been reassured that no military expert believed that the war could be won by air power alone.

By the fourth week of the NATO air strikes in early 1999, more than 619,000 refugees were forcibly expelled by Serbian forces from Kosovo with the internal displacement of a further 700,000 people.[43] Almost half of the entire non-Serb population of Kosovo was either thrown out or getting ready to be thrown out of Kosovo. All non-Serb Kosovars with the exception of an estimated few thousand hiding in the hills were forcibly expelled from Kosovo by the end of the NATO air bombing campaign against Yugoslavia.

From a humanitarian perspective the NATO air campaign was a disaster. The stated reason for direct military intervention in Kosovo by NATO was that the international community was acting '...to save lives and to prevent the forced

---

38 Michael Mandelbaum, 'Nato's War against Yugoslavia: A Perfect Failure,' *Foreign Affairs* (1999): p. 35.

39 NATO, 'Nato's Role in Relation to the Conflict in Kosovo.'

40  bid.: pp. 131–34.

41 Ibid.

42 William Shawcross, *Deliver Us from Evil: Peacekeepers, Warlords and a World of Endless Conflict* (New York: Simon and Schuster, 2000), pp. 357–59.

43 International Crises Group (ICG), 'Crises Web News: War in the Balkans: Consequences of the Kosovo Conflict and Future Options for Kosovo and the Region,' (1999): pp. 1–28.

displacement of Kosovar Albanians.' [44]   NATO action did not save lives nor did it prevent the forced displacement of Kosovar Albanians.

HRW conducted a detailed investigation of civilian deaths during the Kosovar conflict. They visited ninety-one cities, towns and villages in the former Yugoslavia over a three-week period in August 1999. They inspected forty-two of the sites where civilian deaths occurred. The HRW investigation concluded that NATO committed a number of violations of international humanitarian law. They called on NATO governments to establish an independent commission to investigate these violations.[45]   HRW recommended that NATO governments should alter targeting and bombing doctrine to ensure compliance with international humanitarian law.

The HRW 79-page report revealed that U.S. commanders issued a secret executive order in May 1999 for U.S. forces to cease using cluster bombs. These indiscriminate weapons cause widespread death and suffering by releasing hundreds or thousands of bomblets from the main projectile. As many as 150 civilians died in various incidents involving the use of cluster bombs up until May 13. British forces continued using cluster bombs through out the air campaign.

The report further criticised NATO for its attacks on mobile targets without ensuring that they were military in nature and on its decision to strike some targets, such as Serb radio and television headquarters in Belgrade, which were of little or no military value. Targeting the Serbs in this way substantially increased the risk of death or injury to civilians.

Like most recent conflicts this century, civilians bore the brunt of the war deaths, injuries and atrocities conducted by the opposing factions. Kosovo death estimates alone were: allied servicemen, nil; Serb soldiers, perhaps 6,000; Serb civilians, perhaps 2,000; Kosovars, perhaps 100,000.[46]   To these must be added the wounded and the refugees: 600,000 people were displaced within Kosovo, and 800,000 driven out at gunpoint.[47]

It is not absolutely clear whether the displacement of almost 1.5 million Albanians in Kosovo was Belgrade's original aim, whether this displacement was a by-product of a strategic campaign against the KLA, or whether this was a response to NATO's air campaign.[48]   What is clear is that those who deliberately killed and who forcibly evicted over 1 million Kosovars from their homes bear personal responsibility for those acts.

President Slobodan Milosevic must take the blame for most of these deaths, injuries and deprivations but NATO and the international community also must also shoulder a significant portion of the responsibility for botching the intervention

---

44 Mandelbaum, 'Nato's War against Yugoslavia: A Perfect Failure.'

45 Human Rights Watch, 'Civilan Deaths in the Nato Air Campaign: Principle Findings,' *HRW Report* 12, no. 1 (2000).

46 'Messy War, Messy Peace,' *The Economist*, 12 June 1999.

47 George Kenney, 'Kosovo: On Ends and Means,' *The Nation* 269, no. 22 (1999): pp. 25–30.

48 George Kenney, 'Kosovo: On Ends and Means,' *The Nation* 269, no. 22: pp. 25–30.

campaign. The lack of UN leadership and the decision by NATO to try to use air power alone to bomb the Serbs into submission contributed to the humanitarian disaster in the region.

This does not mean that military intervention is not appropriate in humanitarian affairs. Sometimes it is, sometime it is not. It means that if such intervention is conducted it must be through the use of overwhelming force (air, land and sea forces if necessary) against the right type of targets. Richard Haass, a former speechwriter for Bush senior and now Director of Policy Planning in the State Department for President George W. Bush argues that the early use of force is preferable to the later use, and overwhelming force is better than gradualism.[49]

The right targets in Kosovo were Serb troops and special police militias conducting the atrocities. Not some obscure, unmanned police station or power station in downtown Belgrade.[50] Intervention must be conducted immediately after reasonable negotiations for peace have failed to halt the genocide.

NATO's spokesperson Jamey O'Shea made a number of animated proclamations to the world via live media press conferences when he enthused that, '...we [NATO] are winning...and [they] the Serbs are losing ...'. Win or lose, the reality was that the NATO campaign resulted in significant numbers of dead, tortured, wounded and missing Kosovars. Prior to the NATO intervention there were approximately 2,000 – 3,000 deaths in Kosovo. After 10 weeks of NATO action some 225,000 Kosovar men were missing and at least 5,000 Kosovars had been summarily executed.[51]

There is some dispute as to the accuracy of such casualty figures (as outlined in the previous footnote), but whether tens of thousands or hundreds of thousands of people were killed in Kosovo prior to and during the air campaign is not the central point. NATO action in Kosovo significantly increased the loss of life and misery of the ethnic Albanian people.

## What Type of Wars Were the Balkan's Conflicts?

Jane Sharp argues that the conflict in Bosnia Herzegovina was a humanitarian war where Serbs and Croats committed genocide against the multi ethnic Bosnian community. She believes that on this basis, '...the West should have intervened to demonstrate that genocide would not be tolerated.' [52]  The war, she argues, was essentially between genocidal aggressors and their victims.

---

49 John Garofano, 'The Intervention Debate: Towards a Posture of Principled Judgement,' (The Strategic Studies Institute (SSI), 2002): p. 36.

50 Human Rights Watch, 'Civilian Deaths in the Nato Air Campaign,' *HRW Report* 12 (2000): pp. 1–5.

51 'Nato's Role in Relation to the Conflict in Kosovo,'' *NATO Review* (1999): pp. 8–12.

52 Jane Sharp, 'Appeasement, Intervention and the Future of Europe,' in *Military Intervention in European Conflicts*, ed. Lawrence Freedman (Oxford: Blackwell Publishers, 1994), p. 43.

Hers is a common approach, which supports humanitarian intervention only after reducing very complex ethnic conflicts to villain and victim scenarios. This is a feature of moral minimalism, as previously discussed in Chapter One. The international community generally regards war to be a black and white issue, which in the case of Bosnia Herzegovina and in Kosovo, evolved eventually into a Serbs against the rest position.

This is the view the West embraced before finally intervening militarily through NATO air strikes in the Balkans. The need for the international community to simplify how it sees a humanitarian situation before intervening (especially in higher risk ventures) is because the international community finds it difficult, if not impossible, to act unless it can identify who the 'good guys' and 'bad guys' actually are. [53]

It could be argued that the wars in the Balkans are international social conflicts where the conflict started between communal groups within state borders, then spread to the domestic arena and became a crisis of the state.[54]   This approach supports the idea that the wars in Bosnia Herzegovina and Kosovo became internationalised when external concerns over the treatment of non-Serbs increased.

Formally naming a conflict an international/humanitarian war provides some rationality and legal justification for military intervention where complex issues of state sovereignty are involved.  This entire process is part of a defined, pre-war ritual humankind usually insists on going through prior to military engagement in the international arena.  While the international community worries over exactly who the bad and good guys are, and whether or not we are able to determine just-cause, people die and victims of serious human rights abuse continue to suffer.  The reality is that the conflict in Bosnia Herzegovina and in Kosovo was never limited to Serbs against the rest.

In Bosnia Herzegovina the Bosnian Government (essentially a Bosnian Muslim Government) was also at war, at various times, with the Bosnian Croats.  These two groups were also occasional-allies against the Serbs.  To an outsider, this situation was totally confusing when traditional enemies like Croatian and Bosnian Serb militias formed an alliance to attack the Muslim forces holding out in Maglaj in central Bosnia Herzegovina, then, after the assault, they turned and attacked each other.[55]

The wars in Bosnia Herzegovina and in Kosovo were multi layered and alliances changed depending on convenience and on other long-term historical ties not apparent to external observers.[56]   There were even reported incidents of rival Croatian forces fighting each other.  Whatever the case, it was clear the fighting was based on dictates

---

53  Walzer, 'The Politics of Rescue.'

54  Oliver Ramsbotham and Tom Woodhouse, *Humanitarian Intervention in Contemporary Conflict: A Reconceptualisation* (Cambridge: Polity Press, 1996), pp. 86–88.

55  Michael Tanner, 'Croats and Serbs Launch Joint Attack,' *The Independent*, 28 June 1993.

56  Bardos, 'No Innocents in Bosnia or Serbia.'

of local expediency. Leaders in Sarajevo, Zagreb or Belgrade had little control over what happened in the rugged Karst Mountains of Herzegovina.

The Serbs fighting in Bosnia-Herzegovina, moreover, were not invaders from Serbia proper. They originally were indigenous to Bosnia and one of the three recognized constituent nations of the state. The Serbs (who prior to the war made up approximately 33 percent of Bosnia's population) controlled approximately 60–70 percent of Bosnia. For a variety of historical reasons, the Muslims (about 44 percent of the pre-war population) were the most urbanized ethnic group in Bosnian society, with most of their population concentrated in cities and towns.

The Serbs, on the other hand, were mostly farmers who legally owned 60 percent of the land in Bosnia and Herzegovina. Thus, the land they 'occupy' was their own. The Bosnian Croats (roughly 17 percent of the population) had done much the same, yet little international pressure has been brought to bear on them. In contrast to the Bosnian Serbs, who were essentially fighting for their own land, it was mainly Croatian military units from Croatia that occupied the approximately 30 percent of Bosnia and Herzegovina where the Croats predominate. All sides in the Balkan's conflict fought a fierce battle for the sympathy of international public opinion.

It became increasingly difficult for the international community to focus on just who was the aggressor and who the victim during the conflict in Bosnia Herzegovina. Eventually the excesses of the Bosnian Serbs began to stand out amongst all the other excesses being committed in the name of nationalism and ethnic identity. The basic problem of pinning down who committed atrocities on whom remains to this day.

The Serbs fighting in Bosnia Herzegovina were not invaders from Serbia proper. They were indigenous to Bosnia Herzegovina and one of the three recognised constituent nations of the state. The Bosnian Serbs, who prior to the war made up approximately 33 percent of Bosnia's population, now control approximately 50 percent of Bosnia Herzegovina. Muslims comprise about 40 percent of the pre-war population of Bosnia Herzegovina and they are the most urbanised ethnic group in Bosnian society. Most of their population is concentrated in cities and towns. The Bosnian Croats, who were roughly 18 percent of the population, are basically farmers with large land holdings.[57]

An important aspect of the war in the Balkans is that all sides were responsible for continuing the conflict. This in no way diminishes the culpability of the Bosnian Serbs as the primary aggressors committing the greatest number of criminal acts but it must be acknowledged that Croatians and Bosnian Muslims also committed many atrocities against the Serbs.[58] This is often ignored by much of the one-sided rhetoric on the Balkans wars. It is reinforced by the West's tendency to view such conflicts in their most simplistic form. That is, the Serbs are seen to be the aggressors and

---

57  Ibid.
58  Daly, 'Arithmetic of Death That Does Not Add Up.'

the Croats, Muslims, Kosovars and so on the victims. The reality was that all sides committed atrocities in the war in Bosnia Herzegovina.[59]

Supporting the use of military force against the Serbs does not imply some sort of moral acquiescence with Muslim instituted atrocities, Muslim war aims or Muslim ethnic cleansing practices. The UN, for example, was as appalled by some of the acts of the Croatians and the Muslims against the Bosnian Serb population as it was against Serbian excesses during the conflict.[60] Some observers even attribute the Muslim-led Bosnian government of committing ferocious attacks against its own population in an effort to blame their opponents, to outrage world opinion and to force NATO to militarily intervene against the Serbs.

The need by the international community to simplify a very complex ethnic and cultural conflict situation before it is willing to act is a major failing of proponents of the New World Order in the post-cold war era. The imperative that should be driving international action in these types of human disasters is concern about the plight of fellow human beings not a fixation on political or ideological imperatives.

Just-war theory, the driving force behind most Western military interventionist strategies, is essentially unworkable in complex humanitarian crises where atrocities are committed on all sides and alliances change according to obscure rules even those directly involved in the conflict barely understand. Just-war theorists insist that a response to unprovoked aggression, a pre-emptive strike against imminent or likely aggression, and a response to the threats against the lives and well being of citizens of other states are the broad pre-requisites that morally justify the use of external force against a sovereign state.

The problem is in defining 'unprovoked aggression' and working out who the victims or the aggressors actually are in complex ethnic conflicts. In these types of conflicts all sides often engage in atrocity and counter atrocity against each other. Whether the war in Bosnia Herzegovina was technically a civil war or a humanitarian/international war is irrelevant to those suffering from humanitarian abuses in the Balkans.[61] It only matters to the state-makers within and immediately surrounding the region.

It also matters to aspiring interveners who need their legal and moral props before they act to stop atrocities from occurring. Humanitarian intervention should be for humanitarian reasons and the political relevancy of who is doing what to whom should be secondary to stopping all killing and all abuse.

---

59 Ken Booth, 'Military Intervention: Duty and Prudence', in L. Freedman. Ed., 'Military Intervention in European Conflicts,' *The Political Quarterly* (1994): p. 63.

60 Walzer, 'The Politics of Rescue.'

61 H Silajdzic, 'The Consequences of Interreligious Hatred: The Case of Bosnia and Its Lessons for World Peace' (paper presented at the Rabbi Marc H. Tanenbaum Memorial Lecture., TanenBaum Venter for Religious Understanding. New York, 14 May 1997 1997).

# Conclusion

A civilised and humane society has at least some reasonable degree of moral obligation to relieve the pain and suffering of fellow human beings who are being deliberately abused - if it is practically possible to do so. I have argued that such a moral obligation exists and I have presented a number of arguments towards defining its scope.

There is a vast difference between expressing abhorrence about the deliberate infliction of suffering and death upon the innocent, and actually doing something effective to stop such acts. We need to come up with effective strategies that take seriously the very real risk of death and injury to potential interventionists without such strategies resulting in war by remote control. Remote control warfare does not stop belligerents from conducting atrocities on the helpless and the weak. The need to take and hold territory is as relevant today as it was during Caesar's time.

The use of physical force is, under some circumstances, a morally appropriate strategy for the international community to use against determined belligerents. Military intervention by the international community in the affairs of another sovereign state is not something to be undertaken lightly but often it is the only effective way of stopping the mass killings, starvation, and tortures. Sometimes the only valid moral choice is to take direct and immediate forceful action. Should the international community be forced to militarily intervene in order to stop extreme human rights abuses, then such intervention must be swift, overwhelming and utterly determined. To do less will most likely cause a humanitarian disaster even worse than that which instigated such a response in the first place.

Crucial to any forcible interventionist strategy is the non-violent, mediation processes that must follow immediately after the belligerents have been forced to cease their activities. Concepts of human rights and international humanitarian law are important legal tools that the international community has at its disposal to hold accountable those who consider themselves to be above any law except their own.

The idea that state sovereignty should always be able provide protection to those who deliberately commit heinous crimes against humanity is increasingly being challenged by the international community. 1992 – 1999 was a significant period in the interpretation and application of international laws that prohibit extreme human rights abuses. We finally saw the practical implementation of modern international law in the establishment of the ICTY and in the setting up of the International Criminal Court (ICC) in the Hague.

The international community needs the support of legal protocols and conventions in authorising and supporting lawful intervention against states that are intent on conducting serious human rights abuses. If such legal protocols are inadequate (and many are totally inadequate) then more appropriate laws must be developed to do the task. The UN's and NATO's involvement in the Balkans during the late 1990s demonstrated that the international community ultimately did not accept the serious and ongoing human rights abuses in this region. The UN's actions and intervention in the Balkans was too little, too late, poorly organised, inadequately supported, poorly directed, and it was clearly negligent in protecting its misnamed safe-areas.

Eight core objections to the use of military force for humanitarian reasons were investigated and defused. Most of the objections are focused on the concerns of onlookers and potential interventionists over how such intervention could affect their own physical wellbeing or moral predilections. This is because the international community usually will not, or cannot, act to address serious human rights abuses unless their own concerns are addressed first.

I have argued that a much greater focus should be placed on the plight of those actually being abused rather than on the difficulties or dangers interventionists may face by directly intervening. This is not simply altruism because ultimately the way to a more peaceful world is by stopping those who deliberately set out to kill others who are culturally, ethnically, or ideologically different to themselves. Forcibly stopping belligerents who will not or cannot be stopped by other means will save lives, relieve suffering, and it will enhance utility and make for a more peaceful world.

# Bibliography

"1995 Annual Defense Report: Part 2 Challenges for the New Security Environment. Report of the Us Secretary of Defence to the President and the Congress." Washington: United States Department of Defence, 1995.

Abrams, Elliot. "Just War. Just Means?" *National Review* 51, no. 12 (1999).

Agency, Central Intelligence. *Cia World Fact Book, 1997*. Washington DC: CIA, 1997.

Aiken, William. "Bosnia-Herzegovina and Croatia an Environmental Health Perspective." *Journal of Environmental Health* 59 (1996).

Aiken, William, and Hugh LaFollette. *World Hunger and Moral Obligation*. New Jersey: Prentice-Hall Publishers, 1977.

Amnesty International. "50 Years of the Universal Declaration of Human Rights and 50 Years of Human Rights Abuses, Pol 10/04/98." Amnesty International: The International Secretariat News Service, 1998.

Amnesty International. "Rwanda: Mass Murder by Government Supporters and Troops in April and May 1994, Ai Index: Afr 47/11/94." Amnesty International: The International Secretariat News Service, 1994.

Amnesty International. "Sudan: The Human Price of Oil, 079/00, Ai Index: Afr 54/04/00." Amnesty International: The International Secretariat News Service, 2000.

Amnesty International. "Thousands at Imminent Risk of Human Rights Abuses, 144/99, Ai Index: Asa 11/08/99." Amnesty International: The International Secretariat News Service, 1999.

Anderson, Danica Borkovich. *Bosnia's Death Highway: My Personal Story of Trauma Work, Compassion Fatigue and Hope*, 2000 [cited 1 June 2005. Available from http://www.giftfromwithin.org/html/bosnia.html.

Annan, Kofi. "The Humanitarian Challenge Today." Paper presented at the Los Angeles World Affairs Council, Los Angeles, April 21 1998.

Annan, Kofi. "Two Concepts of Sovereignty. Paper Presented at the Heads of State and Governments at the Annual Session of the United Nations General Assembly." *The Economist*, 18 September 1999.

Arias, Oscar, J Friedman, and C Rossiter. "Less Spending, More Security: A Practical Plan to Reduce World Military Spending'." Paper presented at the Capitol Hill Symposium, U.S. Senate, 15 December, 1995.

Bandow, Doug. "Europe's Welfare Queens." *Cato Institute* (1999).

Barcalow, Emmett. *Moral Philosophy. Theory and Issues*. California: Wadsworth Publishing Company, 1994.

Barcalow, Emmett. *Moral Philosophy. Theory and Issues*. California: Wadsworth Publishing Company, 1994.

Bardos, Gordon. "No Innocents in Bosnia or Serbia." *St. Louis Post-Dispatch*, 18 March 1993.

Baron, Marcia. "Kanatian Ethics." In *Three Methods of Ethics*, edited by M. Baron, P. Pettit and M Slote, 7-10. Oxford: Blackwell Publishers, 1997.

Barrow, Robin. *Utilitarianism: A Contemporary Statement*. Vermont: Edward Elgar Publishing Company, 1991.

Batakovic, Duésan. *The Kosovo Chronicles, Part One: History and Ideology, Kosovo and Metohia. A Historical Survey*. Beograd: Plato, 1992.

Beitz, Charles R. *Political Theory and International Relations*. New Jersey: Princeton University Press, 1999.

Bellamy, Christopher. *Knights in White Armour*. Sydney: Random House Aust, 1997.

Benn, Piers. *Ethics. Fundamentals of Philosophy*. London: Mcgill-Queen's Universtity Press, 1998.

Bercovitch, Jacob. *Resolving International Conflicts*. London: Lynne Rienner Publisher, 1996.

Bickerton, Ian. *43 Days: The Gulf War*. Melbourne: The Text Publishing Company, 1991.

Block, Russell. "Life or Death Dilemma for Un Troops." 12 June 1993.

Booth, Ken. "Military Intervention: Duty and Prudence', in L. Freedman. Ed., 'Military Intervention in European Conflicts." *The Political Quarterly* (1994).

Borger, Julian. "Special Report Guantanamo Bay: Us Plans Permanent Guantanamo Jails." *The Guardian*, Monday January 3, 2005 2005.

"Bosnia and Herzegovina Country Report on Human Rights." US Department of State, Bureau of Democracy, Human Rights and Labour, 1997.

Bourke, Joanna. *An Intimate History of Killing : Face-to-Face Killing in Twentieth-Century Warfare*. [New York]: Basic Books, 1999.

Boutros-Ghali, Boutros. *An Agenda for Peace 1995*. 2nd ed. New York: United Nations, 1995.

Boutros-Ghali, Boutros. "An Agenda for Peace. Preventive Diplomacy, Peacemaking and Peace-Keeping." Paper presented at the Summit Meeting of the Security Council, New York, 17 June 1992.

Boutros-Ghali, Boutros. "Supplement to an Agenda for Peace: Position Paper of the Secretary-General on the Occasion of the Fiftieth Anniversary of the United Nations." New York: United Nations, 1995.

Buchanan, Allen. "Recognitional Legitimacy and the State System." *Philosophy and Public Affairs* 28, no. 1 (1999).

Bull, Hedley. *Intervention in World Politics*. Oxford: Clarendon Press, 1984.

Bureau of Democracy, Human Rights, and Labor. "Bosnia and Herzegovina Country Report on Human Rights." US Department of State, 1998.

Calabresi, M. "Kosovo Smolders." *Time Magazine*, 11 May 1998.

Carroll, Rory. "Us Chose to Ignore Rwandan Genocide: Classified Papers Show Clinton Was Aware of 'Final Solution' to Eliminate Tutsis." *Guardian Unlimited*, 31 March 2004.

"Case No: Ictr-96-4-I. The Prosecutor of the Tribunal against Jean Paul Akayesu." Arusha: International Criminal Tribunal for Rwanda, 1996.

"A Challenge to Impunity." *The Economist*, 5 December 1998.

Charvet, John. "Fundamental Equality." *Utilitas* 10, no. 3.

Christopher, P. *The Ethics of War and Peace:An Introduction to Legal and Moral Issues*. New Jersey: Prentice Hall, 1994.

Clausewiz, Carl von. "On War." edited by Michael Howard and Peter Paret, 605. Princeton, New Jersey: Princeton University Press, 1984.

Cohen, Richard. "Something Must Be Done in Bosnia." *St. Louis Post-Dispatch, Washington Post Writers Group* 1995.

Connaughton, Richard. "Wider Peacekeeping - How Wide of the Mark." *British Army Review* (1985).

Cooper, David. *Ethics. The Classic Readings*. Massachusetts: Blackwell Publishers, 1998.

Daalder, Ivo. "Emerging Answers: Kosovo, Nato, & the Use of Force." *The Brookings Review* 17, no. 3 (1999).

Daly, Emma. "Arithmetic of Death That Does Not Add Up." *The Independent*, 1 May 1996.

Deen, Thalif. "Politics: Un Laments World's Two Forgotten Emergencies." *World News, Inter Press Service*, 23 April 1998.

DeMarco, Joseph. *Moral Theory: A Contemporary Approach*. London: Jones and Bartlett Publishers, 1996.

Dempsey, J. "Ec Tries to Keep War out of Bosnia." *The Financial Times*, 21 February 1992.

Department of Foreign Affairs and Trade. "Advancing the National Interest. Foreign and Trade Policy White Paper." Canberra: Australian Government, 2003.

Draper, Gerald. "Humanitarianism in the Modern Law of Armed Conflicts." In *Armed Conflict and the New Law : Aspects of the 1977 Geneva Protocols and the 1981 Weapons Convention*, edited by Michael A. Meyer and Geoffrey Francis Andrew Best, 14. London: British Institute of International and Comparative Law, 1989.

Draper, Kai. "Self-Defence, Collective Obligation, and Non-Combatant Liability." *Social Theory and Practice* 24, no. 1 (1998).

Dunlap, Charles. "Organizational Change and the New Technologies of War." *Joint Services Conference on Professional Ethics* (1997).

Dworking, Ronald. *Taking Rights Seriously*. London: Duckworth Press, 1977.

"East Timor Misadventure." *The Economist*, 2 October 1999.

Eikenberry, Karl. "Take No Casualties." *Parameters* (1996).

Epstein, Keith. *A World of Troubles* MEDIA GENERAL NEWS SERVICE, 2005 [cited 29 April 2005]. Available from http://washdateline.mgnetwork.com/index. cfm?SiteID=wsh&PackageID=46&fuseaction=article.main&ArticleID=6501& GroupID=214.

Ernest, Evans. "The Clinton Administration and Peacemaking in Civil Conflicts." *World Affairs Policy Journal* 159, no. 119 (1996).

Farer, Tom J. "An Inquiry into the Legitimacy of Humanitarian Intervention." In

*Law and Force in the New International Order*, edited by Lori F. Damrosch and David Scheffer, 200. Boulder: Westview Press, 1991.

Fisher, Ronald, and Loraleigh Keashly. "The Potential Complementarity of Mediation and Consultation within a Contingency Model of Third Party Consultation." *Journal of Peace Research* 28, no. 1 (1991).

Fletcher, Joseph. "Give If It Helps, but Not If It Hurts." In *World Hunger and Moral Obligation*, edited by William Aiken and Hugh LaFollette, 106. New Jersey: Prentice-Hall Publishers, 1977.

Fotion, Nicholas. *Military Ethics: Looking Towards the Future*. California: Stanford University, Hoover Institution Press, 1996.

Fotion, Nicholas. "A Utilitarian Defence of Just War Theory." *Synthesis Philosophica* (1997).

Fotion, Nicholas, and Gerald Elfstrom. *Military Ethics Guidelines for Peace and War*. London: Routledge and Kegan Paul, 1996.

FOUR CORNERS Television Program. "The Vanishing." Australia: Australian Broadcasting Commission, 1999.

Frankena, William K. *Ethics*. New Jersey: En&wood Cliffs, Prentice-Hall, 1973.

Frey, Richard. *Utility and Rights*. Minneapolis: University of Minnesota Press, 1984.

"Friend or Foe in East Timor." *The Economist*, 25 September 1999.

Friesecke, Uwe. "Strategic Considerations of the Rwandan Catastrophe of 1994." In *a report by Uwe Friesecke, Prepared for the Defense Team In the Ntagerura Case, International Criminal Tribunal for Rwanda*, Arusha, Tanzania, 2002.

Garofano, John. "The Intervention Debate: Towards a Posture of Principled Judgement." The Strategic Studies Institute (SSI), 2002.

Gasser, Hans-Peter. "International Humanitarian Law and the Protection of War Victims." Geneva: International Committee of the Red Cross, 1998.

Gellman, Barton. "Storm Damage in the Gulf: U.S. Strategy Went Beyond Strictly Military Targets." *Washington Post, National Weekly ed*, 8-14 July 1991 1991.

Golder, Ben, and George Williams. "What Is 'Terrorism'?" Paper presented at the Conference: Twenty Years of Human Rights Scholarship and Ten Years of Democracy, Centre for Applied Legal Studies and the School of Law, University of the Witwatersrand,, 5-7 July 2004.

Goldstein, Joshua. *International Relations*. 2nd ed. Washington, DC: Harper Collins, 1996.

Goodin, Robert. "Utility and the Good." In *A Companion to Ethics*, edited by Peter Singer, 243-45. Oxford: Basil Blackwell Ltd, 1991.

Goppel, Anna. "Defining 'Terrorism' in the Context of International Law", Melbourne: Centre for Applied Philosophy and Public Ethics (CAPPE)w 2005.

Gordon, J. "A Peaceful, Silent, Deadly Remedy: The Ethics of Economic Sanctions." *Ethics and International Affairs*, no. 13 (1999).

Goulding, Marrack. "The Evolution of United Nations Peacekeeping." *International Affairs* 69, no. 3 (1993).

Groenewold, Julia, Eve Porter, and Mâedecins sans frontiáeres (Association). *World in Crisis. The Politics of Survival at the End of the Twentieth Century.* New York: Routledge, 1997.

Grossman, Dave. *On Killing.* New York: little Brown and Company, 1996.

"The Ground War Scenario." *The Economist*, 29 May 1999.

Haas, Richard. "Reinhold Niebuhr's Christian Pragmatism: A Principled Alternative to Consequentialism." *The Review of Politics* 61, no. 4 (1999).

Haass, Richard. "Intervention: The Use of Military Force in the Post-Cold War World." *Foreign Affairs* 73, no. 6 (1994).

Hanser, Mathew. "Killing, Letting Die and Preventing People from Being Saved." *Utilitas* 11, no. 3.

Hare, Richard. *Moral Thinking : Its Levels, Method, and Point.* Oxford: Oxford University Press, 1981.

Harrison, Ross. "Rosen's Sacrifice of Utility." *Utilitas* 10, no. 2 (1999).

Hart, H.L.A. *The Concept of Law.* Oxford: Clarendon Press, 1961.

Hartle, Anthony. *Moral Issues in Military Decision Making.* Lawrence: University of Kansas Press, 1989.

Hawkins, William. "Imposing Peace: Total Vs Limited Wars, and the Need to Put Boots on the Ground." *Parameters* 30, no. 2 (2000).

Hellman, Christopher. "Cdi Fiscal Year 2004 Budget." Washington: CENTER FOR DEFENSE INFORMATION, 2004.

Higgins, Rosalyn. "The General International Law of Terrorism." In *Terrorism and International Law*, edited by Rosalyn Higgins and Maurice Flory, 28. London ; New York: Routledge : LSE, 1997.

Hillen, John. "American Military Intervention: A User's Guide." *The Heritage Foundation: The Backgrounder* (1996).

Hoffmann, Stanley. *The Ethics and Politics of Humanitarian Intervention.* Indiana: University of Notre Dame Press, 1996.

Holmes, Robert. *On War and Morality.* Princeton, New Jersey: Princeton University Press, 1989.

Holsti, Kalevi. *International Politics: A Framework for Analysis.* Englewood Cliffs: Prentice-Hall, 1988.

Honig, Jan, and Norbet Both. *Srebrenica: Record of a War Crime.* New York: Penguin Books, 1997.

Human Rights Watch. "Bosnia and Herzegovina. A Closed Dark Place. Past and Present Human Rights Abuses in Foca." *HRW Report* 10, no. 6d (1998).

Human Rights Watch. "Civilian Deaths in the Nato Air Campaign: Principle Findings." *HRW Report* 12, no. 1 (2000).

Igric, Gordana. "Kosovo Rape Victims Suffer Twice." Institute of War & Peace Reporting, 1999.

International Crises Group (ICG). "Crises Web News: War in the Balkans: Consequences of the Kosovo Conflict and Future Options for Kosovo and the Region." 1999.

International Crisis Group, (ICG). "Annual Report 2000: Review of 1999, Plans for 2000." 2000.

International Federation of Red Cross and Red Crescent Societies. "Can Military Intervention and Humanitarian Action Coexist? World Disasters Report 1997, Section 1, Chapter 2,." International Federation of Red Cross and Red Crescent Societies.

Janzekovic, John. "Responding to Terror: The War That Is Not a War." Paper presented at the Australasian Political Studies Association, DUNEDIN , New Zealand, 28-30 September 2005.

Jett, Dennis. *Why Peacekeeping Fails*. New York: St Martins Press, 1999.

Jones, P. "Human Rights, Group Rights, and Peoples' Rights." *Human Rights Quarterly* (1999).

Kagan, Shelly. *Normative Ethics*. Oxford: WestviewPress, 1998.

Kamm, F. "Responsibility and Collaboration." *Philosophy and Public Affairs* 28, no. 3 (1999).

Keeley, Laurence. *War before Civilisation:   The Myth of the Peaceful Savage*. Oxford: Oxford University Press, 1996.

Kenney, George. "Kosovo: On Ends and Means." *The Nation* 269, no. 22 (1999).

Kewley, Gretchen. *Humanitarian Law in Armed Conflicts*. Melbourne: VCTA Publishing, 1984.

Key Centre for Ethics, Law, Justice and Governance (KCELJAG). "Globalising the Rule of Law." Paper presented at the Griffith University's Vice Chancellor's Symposium, Parliament House, Brisbane Australia 2000.

"Kosovo Untamed." *The Economist*, 26 February 2000.

Lackey, Douglas. *The Ethics of War and Peace*. New Jersey: Prentice Hall, 1989.

Lahad, Mooli. "Darkness over the Abyss: Supervising Crisis Intervention Teams Following Disaster." *Traumatology* VI, no. 4 (2000).

Lizza, Ryan. "The Numbers Game." *The New Republic* 221, no. 3/4 (1999).

Lorenze, F.M. "Operation Restore Hope." *Parameters* (1996).

Lyman, Robert. *Possibilities for 'Humanitarian War' by the International Community in Bosnia-Herzegovina, 1992 - 1995*. London: The Strategic and Combat Studies Institute - British Army Review, 1997.

MacGregor, Douglas. *Breaking the Phalanx: A New Design for Landpower in the 21st Century*. Connecticut: Praeger, 1997.

Mackinnon, Barbara. *Ethics. Theory and Contemporary Issues*. New York: Wadsworth Publishing Company, 1995.

Mandelbaum, Michael. "Nato's War against Yugoslavia: A Perfect Failure." *Foreign Affairs* 78, no. 5 (1999).

Margaret, Macdonald. "Natural Rights." In *Human Rights*, edited by Abraham Melden, 41. California: Wadsworth Publishing Company, 1970.

"The Massacre at Mazar-I Sharif." *HRW Report* 10, no. 7c (1998).

Mays, Antje. "War and Peace: Of Law, Lawlessness, and Sovereignty." Paper presented at the Joint Chiefs of Staff Conference on Professional Ethics XIX, Washington, D.C., 30-31 January, 1997.

McCoubrey, Hilaire. *The Blue Helmets: Legal Regulations of United Nations Military Operations*. Vermont: Dartmouth Publishing Company, 1996.

McDonagh, M. "A Just War Also Has Its Dark Sides." *New Statesman* 12, no. 570 (1999).

McGrew, Anthony. "Conceptualising Global Politics." In *Global Politics : Globalization and the Nation-State*, edited by Anthony G. McGrew and Paul G Lewis, 3. Cambridge: Polity Press, 1992.

McNaughton, D. "Intuitionism." In *The Blackwell Guide to Ethical Theory*, edited by Hugh LaFollette, 268-71. Oxford: Blackwell Publishers, 2000.

Merriam, John. "Kosovo and the Law of Humanitarian Intervention." *Case Western Reserve Journal of International Law* 33, no. 1 (2001).

"Messy War, Messy Peace." *The Economist*, 12 June 1999.

Mills, Kurt. *Human Rights in the Emerging Global Order: A New Sovereignty?* New York: St Martins Press, 1998.

Minear, Larry. "The International Relief System: A Critical Review." Paper presented at the Parallel National Intelligence Estimate on Global Humanitarian Emergencies, Meridian International Center, Washington, D.C., September 22, 1994.

Moore, Patrick. "U.S. Generals Say Ground Forces Could Protect Kosovars." *The Balkan Report* 3 (1999).

"The Morality of Warfare: Is Closer Necessarily Worse." *The Economist*, 17 July 1999.

Morgenthau, Hans. *Politics among Nations*. 6th ed. Chicago: University of Chicago Press, 1984.

Nakarada, Radmila. "Critical Thought and the Lessons of War." In *The Collapse of Yugoslavia: Protraction or End of the Agony*, edited by D Kovacevic, 96. Belgrade: IES, 1991.

Narveson, Jan. "A Critique of Pacifism." In *Life and Death. A Reader in Moral Problems*, edited by Louise Pojman, 471. Singapore: Jones and Bartlett Publishers, 1993.

NATO. "Nato's Role in Relation to the Conflict in Kosovo." *NATO Handbook* (2004).

Nelan, B. "The Balkans: More Talking, More Bombing Despite Diplomatic Progress." *Time Magazine*, 18 September 1995.

Nicholson, Brendan. "Lib Slams Anti-Terror Law." *The Melbourne Age Newspaper*, 27 June 2004 2004.

Nickel, James. *Making Sense of Human Rights*. California: University of California Press, 1987.

Nozick, Robert. *Anarchy, State, and Utopia*. Oxford: Blackwell Publishers, 1974.

O'brien, William. *The Conduct of Just and Limited War*. New York: Praeger Publishers, 1981.

Orend, Brian. "Kant's Just War Theory." *Journal of the History of Philosophy* 37, no. 2 (1999).

Ottaway, David. "Boutros-Ghali Opposes Bosnia Air Strikes." *The International Herald Tribune*, 20 January 1994.

OXFAM Australia, Community Aid Abroad. "Desperate Times: War and Famine in Sudan." *Horizons* (1998).

"Peace at Last, at Least for Now." *The Economist*, 25 November 1995.

Phillips, Robert L. "Just-War Theory." In *Life and Death. A Reader in Moral Problems*, edited by Louise Pojman, 482-85. Singapore: Jones and Bartlett Publishers, 1993.

Plattner, Denise. "Assistance to the Civilian Population: The Development and Present State of International Humanitarian Law." *International Review of the Red Cross* (1992).

"Press Release, Arusha." International Criminal Tribunal for Rwanda, 1998.

Preston, Noel. *Understanding Ethics*. Sydney: The Federation Press, 1996.

Priest, Dana. "Kosovo Land Threat May Have Won War." *Washington Post*, 19 September 1999.

Railton, Peter. "Alienation, Consequentialism, and the Demands of Morality." In *Ethics: The Big Questions*, edited by James P Sterba, 164-67. Malden, Massachusetts: Blackwell Publishers Ltd, 1998.

Rainwater, Herbert. "Judgement at Fort Benning." *Newsweek* (1971).

Ramsbotham, Oliver, and Tom Woodhouse. *Humanitarian Intervention in Contemporary Conflict: A Reconceptualisation*. Cambridge: Polity Press, 1996.

Rawls, John. *A Theory of Justice*. Cambridge: The Belknap Press, 1971.

Rehn, Elisabeth. "Excessive Reliance on the Use of Force Does Not Stop Terrorism." Paper presented at the Human Rights: Terrorism, The Hague, 18 September 2003.

Rehn, Elisabeth. "Human Rights: Terrorism, Excessive Reliance on the Use of Force Does Not Stop Terrorism." Paper presented at the Organization for Security and Co-operation in Europe, Seminar in the Hall of Knights, The Hague, The Netherlands, 18 September 2003.

Report, Australian Broadcasting Commission News. "Albanian Kosovar Ethnic Cleansing." 1999.

Report, Australian Broadcasting Commission News. "Nato Will Not Use Ground Troops." 1999.

Roberts, Adam. "Nato's Humanitarian War over Kosovo." *Survival* 41, no. 3 (1999).

Robertson, Geoffry. *Crimes against Humanity. The Struggle for Global Justice*. London: The Penguin Press, 1999.

Rogerson, Kenneth. *Ethical Theory*. Orlando: The Dryden Press, 1991.

Rome Statute of the International Criminal Court. "Setting the Record Straight: The International Criminal Court." United Nations Department of Public Information, 2002.

Rosen, Fredrick. "Individual Sacrifice and the Greatest Happiness: Betham on Utility and Rights." *Utilitas* 10, no. 2 (1999).

Ross, Ralph. *Obligation. A Social Theory*. Michigan: University of Michigan Press, 1970.

Rossman, Douglass. *On Killing: The Psychological Cost of Learning to Kill in War and Society*. Boston: Little Brown and Company, Back Bay Books, 1996.

Sandoz, Yves, Director for Principles, Law and Relations of the ICRC,. "The Right to Intervene on Humanitarian Grounds: Limits and Conditions'." Paper presented at the Committee of Foreign Affairs and Security of the European Parliament, Brussels, 25 January 1994.

Scheffler, Samual. *Consequentialism and Its Critics*. Oxford: Oxford University Press, 1988.

Sharp, Jane. "Appeasement, Intervention and the Future of Europe." In *Military Intervention in European Conflicts*, edited by Lawrence Freedman, 43. Oxford: Blackwell Publishers, 1994.

Shaw, William. *Contemporary Ethics: Taking Account of Utilitarianism*. Oxford: Blackwell Publishers, 1999.

Shawcross, William. *Deliver Us from Evil: Peacekeepers, Warlords and a World of Endless Conflict*. New York: Simon and Schuster, 2000.

Sherman, Nancy. "Empathy, Respect, and Humanitarian Intervention." Paper presented at the Joint Services Conference on Professional Ethics, National Defence University, Washington D.C, 30-31 January 1997.

"Shift in Stance on 'Just War' Perceived in Recent Statements." *American Journal of Public Health* 180, no. 6 (1999).

"Sierra Leone: Sowing Terror. Atrocities against Civilians in Sierra Leone, Part 3." *HRW Report* 10, no. 3a (1998).

Silajdzic, H. "The Consequences of Interreligious Hatred: The Case of Bosnia and Its Lessons for World Peace." Paper presented at the Rabbi Marc H. Tanenbaum Memorial Lecture., TanenBaum Venter for Religious Understanding. New York, 14 May 1997 1997.

Simmons, John. "Justification and Legitimacy." *Ethics and International Affairs* 109, no. 4 (1999).

Singer, Peter. "Famine, Affluence and Morality." In *Philosophy, Politics and Society*, edited by Peter Laslett and James Fishkin, 33. Oxford: Basil Blackwell/New Haven Yale University Press, 1987.

Singer, Peter. *Practical Ethics*. 2 ed. Cambridge: University Press, 1993.

Sivard, Ruth. *World Military and Social Expenditures*. 16 ed. Washington: World Priorities, 1996.

Smith, Dan. *The State of War and Peace Atlas: International Peace Research Institute, Oslo*. 3 ed. London: Penguin Books Limited, 1997.

Smith, Michael. "The Blackwell Guide to Ethical Theory." In *Blackwell Philosophy Guides*, edited by Hugh LaFollette, 15. Oxford, UK ; Malden, Mass., USA: Blackwell, 2001.

Snow, Donald. "Peacekeeping, Peacemaking, and Peace-Enforcement: The Us Role in the New International Order." Paper presented at the US Army War College Fourth Annual Strategy Conference, 24-25 February, 1993.

Stacy Sullivan of the Institute for War and Peace Reporting. "Milosevic and Genocide: Has the Prosecution Made the Case?" *Guardian Unlimited*, 27 February 2004.

Starke, Joseph. *Introduction to International Law. 10th Edition.* 10th ed. London: Butterworths Publishing, 1989.

State, US Department of. " Us Department of State Dispatch: Fact Sheet." 1995.

Stojanovic, S. "A Serb's View of Nato's Bombs." *Free Inquiry* 9, no. 13 (1999).

Stremlau, John. "Ending Africa's Wars." *Foreign Affairs* 79, no. 4 (2000).

Svarm, Filip. "Bosnian Thunder: Refugee Days." *Vreme News Digest Agency*, no. 79 (1993).

Talbott, Strobe. "The Crisis in Africa: Local War and Regional Peace." *World Policy Journal* 17, no. 2 (2000).

Tan, Kok-Chor. "Military Intervention as a Moral Duty." *Public Affairs Quarterly* 9, no. 1 (1995).

Tanner, Michael. "Croats and Serbs Launch Joint Attack." *The Independent*, 28 June 1993.

Tanner, Michael. "Gorazade Begs for Help to End Bosnian Siege." *The Independent*, 15 June 1993.

"Terror in Timor." *The Economist*, 30 Oct 1999 - 5 Nov 1999.

The China Daily. "Leaders Put $4b to Work at Tsunami Summit." *The China Daily* 2005.

The Delaware Criminal Justice Council. *The Nature of Terrorism* [Internet]. 17 May 2005, 2005. Available from http://www.state.de.us/cjc/terrorism/nature.shtml.

The Joint United Nations Programme on HIV/AIDS. "Aids in Africa: Three Scenarios to 2025." United Nations, 2005.

Tim Lindsay interviewed By Mark Colvin ABC Radio. "Bali Bombers Could Evade Jail." Australia: Australian Broadcasting Corporation (ABC) Radio National and PM, 23 July , 2004.

"Un May Evacuate Bosnian Muslims Serb Forces Are Blocking Aid; `Safe Area' Is Too Dangerous." *St. Louis Post-Dispatch*, 3 July 1993.

UN Press Release. "Note to Correspondents: Rwanda Mission Provided Assistance Beyond Mandate." United Nations, 1996.

United Nations. "Document S/21541." 1990.

United Nations. "Document S/22627 Additional 1." 1991.

United Nations. "Human Development Report 1991." Oxford: Oxford University Press, 1991.

United Nations. "Security Council - 4 3989th Meeting (Am) Un Press Release Sc/6659." New York, 1999.

United Nations. "Un Security Council Resolution 693, 46 Unscor." 1994.

United Nations. "United Nations Security Council Document, 752/Res/(1992)."

United Nations. "United Nations Security Council Document, 786/Res/(1992)."

United Nations. "United Nations Security Council Document, S/Res/1199 (1998)." 1998.

United Nations. "United Nations Security Council Documents, 753/Res/(1992) and 754/Res/(1992)."

United Nations. "United Nations Security Council Documents, S/Res/1203 (1998)," 1998.

USA Today. "Rumsfeld: Guantanamo Bay Suspects Held Indefinitely." 9 November 2003 2003.

Vincent, R.J. *Human Rights and International Relations*. Cambridge: Cambridge University Press, 1986.

Vogler, John. "Regimes and the Global Commons: Space Atmosphere and Oceans." In *Global Politics: Globalization and the Nation-State*, edited by Anthony G. McGrew and Paul G. Lewis, 119-21. Cambridge: Polity Press, 1992.

Walzer, Michael. *Just and Unjust Wars : A Moral Argument with Historical Illustrations*. New York: Basic Books, 1992.

Walzer, Michael. "The Politics of Rescue." *Social Research* 62, no. 1 (1995).

Wasserstrom, Richard. *War and Morality*. California: Wadsworth, 1970.

Weller, Mark. "The International Response to the Dissolution of the Socialist Republic of Yugoslavia." *American Journal of International Law* 86, no. 3 (1992).

Williams, Bernard Arthur Owen. *Morality: An Introduction to Ethics, Harper Essays in Philosophy*. New York,: Harper & Row, 1972.

Williamson, Roger. *An Ethical Framework – or Just Intervention in Some Corner of a Foreign Field: Intervention and World Order*. New York: St. Martins Press, 1998.

Winkler, Alan. "Just Sanctions." *Human Rights Quarterly* (1999).

Wirawan Adnan interviewed by Eleanor Hall ABC Radio. "Lawyer Says Australia Should Stay out of Indonesia's Justice System." Australia: Australian Broadcasting Corporation (ABC) The World Today Program, 25 August , 2004.

Wolfers, Arnold. *Alliance Policy in the Cold War*. Baltimore: John Hopkins University Press, 1959.

"A World More Scared Than Scaring." *The Economist*, 17 April 1993.

Zagreb, Veliki geografski atlas Jugoslavije (Large Geographical Atlas of Yugoslavia). "Map Zagreb,1987 Census." 1987.

Zifcak, S. "International Human Rights and Humanitarian Law." Paper presented at the Vice Chancellor's Symposium, Griffith University Key Centre for Ethics, Law, Justice & Governance, Queensland Parliament House, Australia, 18 August 2000.

# Index

Note: bold page numbers indicate maps and diagrams. Numbers in brackets preceded by n refer to footnotes.

For Product Safety Concerns and Information please contact our EU
representative GPSR@taylorandfrancis.com
Taylor & Francis Verlag GmbH, Kaufingerstraße 24, 80331 München, Germany